9-22

DAWN OVER AMAZONIA

the story of Wycliffe Bible Translators in Peru

DAWN OVER AMAZONIA

James and Marti Hefley

WORD BOOKS, Publisher

Waco, Texas

*Dedicated
in appreciation
to our wonderful neighbors
who house-sit for us while we are on trips—
Mike and Louise Chamberlain,
Marty and Sharon Nowak, and
Dennis and Sue Wegl*

Contents

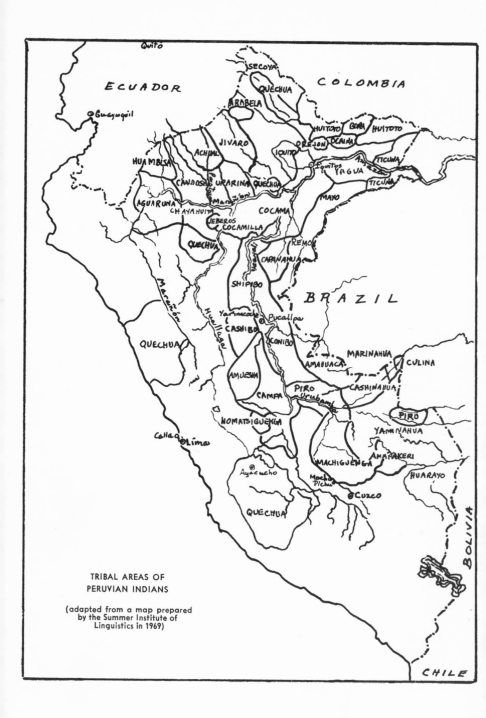

TRIBAL AREAS OF
PERUVIAN INDIANS

(adapted from a map prepared
by the Summer Institute of
Linguistics in 1969)

1.

"Half the Fun Is Getting There"

The stands were full but the horses weren't running that sultry August afternoon. Billy Graham was the feature attraction for the climax of a week-long evangelistic crusade at Arlington Park Race Track near Chicago.

The evangelist, his associates, the local crusade board, and a few honored guests sat on a small unshaded platform across the track and facing the audience.

The heat quickly became unbearable—at least for me, the board secretary. I sneaked off the platform during the singing and discovered somebody else had the same idea.

"I'm Cameron Townsend," the perspiring man whispered. "The heat was too much for the honor. I hope Billy will forgive us."

"You're a missionary, I believe."

"I'm with the Wycliffe Bible Translators. Did you know there are still over two thousand tribes without a single verse of Scripture in their language?"

Then I placed the name. He was the founder and general director of Wycliffe.

He looked at me with a peculiar gleam in his eye. "By the way, what's your line of work?"

"Free-lance writer," I answered.

"Marvelous. I've just been praying to find a writer. Have you heard of Chief Tariri from Peru?"

I hadn't.

"He's the converted headhunter we had at the World's Fair recently. We have a big mural there that describes his life. Thousands have seen it in our aboriginal hut."

I felt embarrassed to admit I had just been to the World's Fair on an assignment, had noticed the Wycliffe pavilion, but hadn't seen the mural.

"That doesn't matter," Townsend went on. "I can tell you about Tariri and a lot of other stories, too. Let's have lunch together tomorrow. I'll be at Wheaton College. We could meet at President Edman's office. Say about 11:45."

He didn't give me the opportunity to say no.

At lunch the next day he told me the dramatic story of Tariri's con-

9

version and about the chief's trip to California and New York. He gave me leads on a dozen other tribal stories from Peru.

Some of this stuff was hard to believe, yet I didn't think he was putting me on. "Why hasn't this been published?" I asked.

"Tariri's story is coming out in a book," he said. "But our folks have just been too busy to tell about all the miracles."

"Too busy making miracles, huh?"

He grinned. "You might put it that way. It's marvelous what happens when the Word of God is put in a tribal language. Why, they quit praying to snakes, stop killing one another, and become gentle and kind like Christians should be. The whole jungle in Peru is changing."

He swallowed a bite of cherry pie, then said, "You ought to visit our base in Peru. Stories—there are hundreds just waiting to be picked off. You could write about Lorrie Anderson fighting off a monstrous boa constrictor that attacked her in a canoe. Tell about other single girls fighting rapids and treacherous whirlpools. Daring pilots flying a million and a half air miles over the jungle without a single fatality."

He stopped and motioned for the waitress. "Could I have another piece of cherry pie, please? That's my favorite."

The girl brought more pie and we kept talking.

"Almost fifty years ago as a boy of nineteen I went to Guatemala to sell Bibles. I discovered 200,000 Cakchiquel Indians who couldn't read Spanish and didn't have a verse of Scripture in their own language. It took fourteen long years, but I finally finished translating the Cakchiquel New Testament. All the time I kept hearing about other Bibleless tribes from a preacher friend named Leonard Letgers who had visited Amazonia and seen wild Indians.

"Letgers and I realized we couldn't do the job alone. While I was recovering from a bout with TB, we started a linguistic school in an old Arkansas farmhouse. We figured it would be best to start field work in Mexico. The Mexican government had closed its borders to missionaries, but the president let us in when he saw that we wanted to help the Indians in practical ways. After we got going well in Mexico, my wife and I took a second group to pioneer in Peru on the headwater streams of the Amazon. The Peruvian government gave us land for a central base, put gas in our airplanes, and within a few years translators were in thirty tribes. The government continues to back us because we're helping the Indians become good citizens. Why, you ought to see the government's Indian school at the base. Where tribesmen used to kill one another, now they are studying together to be teachers, medicos, agriculturalists, merchants, carpenters, and mechanics. It's just amazing what the Lord has done."

Uncle Cam finally ran down and I thanked him for the interview. I returned home and told Marti, "We must go to Peru."

"I'm with you," she said. "But where do we get the money for the children? We can't pawn them off on relatives and go packing off into the jungle for the whole summer."

MARTI: I wanted to go as badly as Jim. To make matters worse for me, a new publisher, Word Books, sent him off to the Dominican Republic on a rush assignment. He had a ball down there; once was surrounded by hostile students who thought he was a CIA agent. I had to stay home and miss the excitement.

"Talk to Word about Peru," I urged. "Maybe they'll send us."

Jim wrote to Word and while we waited for an answer, Uncle Cam called from California.

Jim hung up the phone. "Find a babysitter for tomorrow afternoon. We're going to a motel near the airport to interview two Auca Indians who helped kill those five missionaries about ten years ago."

"Really? They've been converted, I hope."

"Sure," Jim said. "They're returning from the World Evangelism Congress with Rachel Saint."

The wheels were spinning. "I remember her. She went to translate the New Testament into Auca after the Indians killed her brother and four other missionaries."

So the next day we buzzed off to swanky O'Hare Inn, where the carpeting is the kind that you walk through instead of on. A short, blue-eyed lady with graying hair answered our knock on the door. "You must be the Hefleys whom Uncle Cam sent. Come in. I'm Rachel Saint. Meet Kimo and Komi."

The Indians, looking uncomfortable in suits and ties, smiled but were otherwise quite shy. We asked a few questions which Rachel translated along with their brief and quite unenthusiastic answers. Then Jim mentioned an article he had written about the Aucas from material sent by Uncle Cam. He just "happened" to have a copy with him.

What a reaction! The article was totally unintelligible to the Aucas, but the pictures needed no translation. Pictures of their homeland, and best of all, one of Dayuma, who is Kimo's wife. They chattered and giggled. Jim said they could have the article with pictures and they were obviously thrilled.

That really broke the ice. We were friends now. It was strange, but I realized for the first time how much can be communicated without words. Not just through smiles but through gestures and expressions we could sense a lot of what they were telling us even before Rachel translated. This was especially true as they told how Auca life had changed since they had come to know the living God through reading God's "carvings" (translated Scripture).

After·we had the information which Jim felt was needed to write the article, I asked Rachel some of my "curiosity" questions—as Jim calls them.

"What do they think of this fancy motel?"

"They call it a cave. They feel quite sorry for us because it is so cold in our land that we have to live in caves."

"Do the big airplanes impress them?"

"Not as much as you might think. They had seen planes before. We have a strip in the village. But the first time they saw "planes walking" (cars) they were terrified. I've told them how some people who live in America are afraid of the jungle. They can't understand how anyone who isn't afraid of the "planes walking" on our superhighways could possibly be scared of anything else."

I looked a little sheepish. "We're planning on going to Peru, and I am a little leery of taking our children there."

"How much do you know about jungle living and tribespeople?"

"I saw a lot of Tarzan movies when I was a kid."

Rachel gave a merry chuckle. "Just as I thought. You'll be quite surprised in many ways. The jungle isn't as dangerous as American think. And the Indians are not 'savages' just waiting to throw a spear at you.

"But you'll love Peru and the base at Yarinacocha. I do hope you can visit the Shapras. I started my Wycliffe service with them, you know."

Jim was all ears. "Do you know Chief Tariri?"

"Very well. He's a beautiful example of what the gospel can do for these so-called 'savages.' "

Rachel turned and spoke to the Aucas. Their faces brightened when they heard the name Tariri. "They know about the great chief of five rivers who lives not too far south of Auca land. Once they heard him talking over the radio. They always listen intently when I tell about his experience.

"But you need to remember," Rachel added, "that Tariri's tribe is only one of over thirty in Peru where our folks are working. You'll find enough information for ten books."

Back home we told our girls—Cyndi, 12; Celia, 8; and Cheri, 4—about the interview and Peru. "We'll all enjoy going there," I said. "And think of what you'll have to tell your friends."

Celia, the sly comedian and third grader, grinned. "We won't have anything to tell if we get eaten by a snake or a tiger."

Then a military junta took over the Peruvian government. Relations between the United States and Peru became strained over nationalization of an oil company. As the diplomatic sparks flew back and forth and Americans began leaving Peru, the prospects of our going dimmed more.

Jim went to Mexico on a weekend assignment. Without me. He stopped off in Texas on the way back and when I picked him up at the airport, he was grinning till it must have hurt! "Guess what, honey? Word is sending us all to Peru, but you're expected to help with the book to justify the added expense."

I clapped my hands in glee. "I'll work! I'll work!" I squealed. "I'll interview. Edit. Even write. Anything. Wait till we tell the kids." In my excitement I had forgotten all about the scare headlines in the newspapers.

We learned that Uncle Cam's oldest daughter, Grace, lived on Chicago's North Side, a half-hour's drive from our house.

"You won't really be roughing it as much as you think," the pretty young woman told us. "The base at Yarina is like a little town. They have electricity and indoor plumbing. You can drink water right from the tap."

"Yeah, civilization! I'll bet it wasn't like that when you first went there."

"I didn't go there. I was born there. Our first house was a scream. It was really just two little tents hooked together. Then we had a grass-roofed hut. But when we came back from a trip to the States, the jungle had reclaimed that. Some trees grew right through it. Finally we got a real home with a bathtub that may have been the first in that part of the jungle. Can you believe that one year my folks had over 450 over-night guests? Generals, ambassadors, scholars, and all kinds of people who wanted to learn about our work with the Indians."

"It must really be something," I ventured.

"It is," she sighed.

Jim had been busy talking to her husband, Tom, a young engineer. "What was it like being an American kid in the jungle?" he asked Grace.

Grace laughed. "Fun. Well, not everything exciting was funny. I remember that one time we found a dead monkey in our rain barrel."

"Yech!" I exclaimed. "Not your drinking water, I hope."

"It was. It had been tasting funny, and—oh, don't worry, Marti. They've got a water purification system now."

"We're taking our children," I said. "What can they do while we're working?"

"They can swim in the lake that borders the base. And there'll be a children's program for the kids. They'll find plenty to do."

"Great. But is the lake safe?"

"Perfectly safe. Alligators haven't come near the base in ten years. And it's been at least five years since they killed a boa constrictor at the swim ramp. The last one had swallowed a seven-foot alligator. Imagine! Oh, you're worried about the piranhas people talk so much about. They don't bother anyone who isn't bleeding."

"Grace, you're not exactly encouraging me. I'm not sure I want to expose my girls to all that."

"Don't worry. They'll love it. They'll have a lot of freedom on the base, since it's isolated, but at the same time they'll feel secure, since there are friends everywhere. There'll be plenty of playmates for them."

I wondered aloud if she happened to have any artifacts and curios. Did she ever! Out came boxes of jungle stuff—a museum buyer's bonanza: beetle-wing earrings, beaten bark cloth, monkey skull spoons, a deliciously soft alpaca rug from the mountains, a snakeskin that made Jim's eyes bulge. "It's from a small boa," she said. "About fifteen feet long."

I anticipated an interesting summer.

Peru required only smallpox shots for visas, but since we were going to the jungle, the doctor suggested we have the works: typhus, typhoid, paratyphoid, tetanus, and yellow fever, plus smallpox. The girls wailed in unison, "We don't want to go."

They got their shots anyway. Seventy dollars worth. After the first week, we got smart and had the doctors give them to us in the right arm one week and the left arm the next. That way you knew which side was sore and could avoid bumping the other fellow too much.

Our girls have been flying places all their lives, so they weren't particularly impressed with the all-night flight. They did seem intrigued with the European-type clock in the international terminal in Miami. According to that, we arrived there at 23 o'clock.

"Boy, we thertainly are thtaying up late tonight!" lisped Cheri.

They slept through our stop in Panama. Then moaned and groaned and crawled all over me during the rest of the flight.

We were all still half asleep, and rather bedraggled looking as we staggered through customs in Lima. Suddenly a Peruvian lady ran up and hugged me. She was talking so fast my Spanish couldn't keep up with her. I caught the word "Pablo" and realized she was the mother of a student friend in our church back in Chicago. We were friends of her son and were visiting his country. She and another son had come to make us welcome.

The understanding was rough, but the sentiment was great. She insisted on taking us to Lima House, Wycliffe's residence in the capital. Although Cal Hibbard, whom Jim had met in Mexico, and Kenny Gamon, the house host, were there to meet us, that mattered not at all. She must do us a favor!

So our first guide in Lima was a Peruvian.

2.

The "City of Kings"

MARTI: A half-hour ride through a middle-class residential section dotted with tropical palms and bursts of below-the-equator winter flowers brought us to Wycliffe's group house. A beaming, motherly woman rushed us into the comfortable parlor of the two-story Wycliffe house. "You're Jim and Marti. We've been expecting you. I'm Elizabeth Cudney, the Lima House manager."

We introduced Mrs. Cudney to Pablo's folks, the Alvas, and she insisted they must stay for coffee. She wanted to know how our trip was and would we be in Lima very long. Jim said a week to get some background knowledge before jumping off to the jungle.

Mrs. Cudney said she was from Chicago. "I came here after my businessman husband had a fatal heart attack seventeen years ago. Followed my daughter Harriet Kietzman down. She married one of our first translators in Peru. They're now in California where he's the extension director in our home office."

Our Peruvian friends left and Cal and Kenny said they would show us to our rooms. "You're worn out," Mrs. Cudney said solicitously. "Rest awhile before dinner."

The men carried our bags to two upstairs adjoining rooms. Modest but nice. "Enjoy the hot shower while you're here," Cal said. "You might not have it in the jungle."

I unpacked with Jim mostly getting in the way. The kids were too excited to sleep. "Okay, you may walk around," Jim said. "But don't leave the courtyard. And don't get in anybody's way."

I had just closed my eyes when the big kids came galloping back. "We found a game room," Celia, the eight-year-old, squealed.

"They even have some easy-readers for me!" said our precocious four-year-old, her eyes dancing.

That made my day. I knew the girls would be content as long as there were books to read. Now if they just didn't fight over the games.

Jim was snoring and I couldn't go to sleep. I would look around and let him sleep.

From the long second-floor balcony I could see that the cement block building was sort of F-shaped with a high stone fence all around. There were two patio areas, one paved, with basketball hoops and a gym set for kids.

15

Downstairs, I ran into a nice little lady who introduced herself as
Ginger Gammon, Kenny's wife. "We're here helping Mrs. Cudney for
the winter—oh, I forget it's summer where you came from," she said.
"Just too many people for her to handle."

"Who uses these facilities?" I asked.

"Mostly our members who are coming or going from the jungle, on
business or vacation. Missionaries who need somewhere to stay for a few
days. People like yourself who are visiting our work."

We walked around the building and peeked into the parlor. Two or
three men and several children were watching an old Tarzan movie
in Spanish on the television. Ginger laughed. "No matter how long
they've lived in the jungle, they still like Tarzan."

At the head of the stairs Ginger opened a door. "The radio communications room. We stay in touch with both our bases and the tribal
locations."

"Two bases?" I questioned.

"Oh, you didn't know. The big one is at Yarinacocha in the jungle.
The other is at Ayacucho in the mountains. I hope you'll go there, too."

The shrill ringing of a bell startled me. Ginger saw my puzzled look
and explained. "For dinner. It'll ring again in five minutes."

I was just going to wake Jim up when he appeared on the balcony.
He has a sixth sense when it comes to food. The children needed no
urging either.

Downstairs, there was a vacant chair at Cal Hibbard's table. "Leaving
me with the children," I protested.

"I need to talk with Cal about our schedule next week," Jim said.
"He's going to help us see some key people here in Lima. Be over in a few
minutes."

We found seats with a family with three boys.

"Welcome to Peru," said the tall, sandy-haired father. "I'm Harold
Shaver. This is my wife, Betty, and our sons David, Tim, and Beetle-O."

I introduced myself, and it seemed the kids already knew each other.
Someone rang a bell; then a dark, curly-haired man stood and prayed,
and the meal began.

"I'm at a disadvantage here," I said. "Everyone seems to know why
we're here, but we don't know why you are here. Tell me something
about yourselves."

"Well," said Harold, his eyes twinkling, "Betty is a nurse and I'm a
missionary reject. We're with the Nomatsiguenga tribe."

"You're a what?"

"It's a long story. I'd had TB and applied to six mission boards without success. Then a friend, Wayne Snell, told me Wycliffe's director,
Uncle Cam, was an ex-TB man himself. So here I am."

"Where did you two meet?" I asked, while buttering bread and cutting up food for my girls. "Celia, if you want seconds on soup, go help
yourself as Beetle-O is."

"At Moody Bible Institute in Chicago. You see . . . "

"Screeeeeeeeeeeech." Beetle-O evidently had been trying to help Celia and had spilled a whole bowlful of boiling hot soup on her arm. Before I could get to her, a strange blond was running her into the kitchen at top speed. I caught up with them at the sink where she was already lowering Celia's arm in cold water and was calling for ice cubes. "Quick!"

While I sympathized with my wailing child she explained, "I'm Phyllis Woodard, a nurse. We've found that the quicker you get a burn in cold water the better."

"Well, you certainly were fast!"

"I doubt that she'll even get a scar. She really did get a bad burn though."

Someone rigged up a pan with ice water so Celia could sit at the table with her arm soaking while everyone waited on her. She was quite the center of attraction and everyone, especially poor Beetle-O who looked very pained, sympathized with her.

"Where did your son get such an unusual name?" I asked the Shavers when we resumed eating.

They laughed and Betty explained, "It's just a nickname he picked up at the base. His real name is Dwight."

"That's reassuring. But now, please tell me, what is the biggest problem in your tribe?"

They looked at each other, and through ESP seemed to elect Harold to answer.

"That's quite a question—we have many," Harold said. "Sickness. Poor diet, mainly starches. Illiteracy. But I guess our biggest problem is civilization."

"Civilization! That's a problem?"

"Definitely," Betty assured me. "We're straight east and just over the Andes from Lima. Settlers are coming in on the new road and grabbing up the land. Our people have always been nomads and now they have to live in communities. There's very little game for them to hunt. They can't speak Spanish very well. They have no concept of economics and are easy prey for exploiters."

The translator sighed. "We're trying to help, but if we could only have gotten to them a generation ago to prepare them. The same thing is happening in most of the other tribes, although our situation may be the worst. That's why we feel such a sense of urgency."

"This is a new thought for me," I said. "Other than spreading new diseases, I'd never thought of civilization causing problems."

After more talk the Shavers excused themselves and left. Our gallant nurse stopped by with her husband, the man who had prayed.

"I want to thank you again, Phyliss, for coming to the rescue," I said. "Does Wycliffe always manage to have just the right people standing by in case of an emergency?"

"You'll have to ask my husband about that. This is George, uh, Woody, one of our pilots."

I smiled at him. "How about my question, Mr. Pilot?"

He grinned shyly. "Well, the Lord has put us in the right place many times. Right now it's siesta time. Maybe we can get together for some tall tales later."

I took the hint, gathered up my girls, and moved over to where Jim and Cal were lingering over coffee.

"What will we be doing next week?" I asked.

"Tomorrow we go to church," Cal said. "In the afternoon you can see the offices and the museum in the Ministry of Education building. Good view of the city from the roof. Maybe you can sightsee a little. Monday through Wednesday, we'll take you to see some Peruvians so you can get their view of the work. Maybe an interview with a newspaper editor and somebody at the U.S. AID (Agency for International Development) can be arranged. And anybody else you'd like before you go to the jungle."

The next afternoon Cal took us all sightseeing. We drove down to the ocean—only six blocks away—and listened to the waves rushing in on the rocky beach. We hiked through a park filled with gnarled olive trees brought over by the conquistadors in the 1500s. The winter flowers were beautiful. I especially liked the *lluvia de oro*, a climbing vine with blooms like golden raindrops.

Cyndi had a question. "Beetle-O said it never rains in Lima. Why, Uncle Cal?"

"There was a rain back in 1945. An inch or two," Cal said.

"But how can plants grow without rain?" our inquisitive daughter persisted.

"Well, we do have irrigation and an extremely heavy dew, which gives them a drink. But it's so damp here all the time that they don't get very thirsty. To be more precise, the Andes Mountains, which Lima is right up against, cuts off the west winds from the east and the cold Humboldt ocean current that runs near the shore keeps back rain from the other direction. Now don't ask me any more. I'm not a meteorologist."

We left the park and looked at houses. What contrasts! Magnificent colonial residences and tin and cardboard shanties. High-rise apartments and 300-year-old carved balconies on the historic cathedral. Inside the cathedral we saw Pizarro's body in a glass casket. The children showed no horror at seeing the shrunken skin of the man who had conquered the Incas with 27 horses and 180 men. Celia did remark disdainfully, "The meat's all gone."

JIM: Cal said our last stop would be for both business and pleasure. He took us to the 21-story Ministry of Education building which dominates the Lima skyline. Though the building was closed, a guard recognized Cal immediately and let us in. We zipped to the roof in a swift elevator, stepped out, and there the City of Kings lay at our feet. On this unusually clear day, we could see the ocean before us and behind us the bare foothills of the Andes where squatter *barrios* (slums) clung to the slope.

Cal pointed west. "Only a few miles out there is the Atacama Trench, one of the deepest sea canyons in the world. Behind us the mountains go up to 22,000 feet. Nowhere else in the world is the contrast between depth and height so great in such a short distance. And where else can you fly in a few hours from the desert to snow-capped mountains and on to a rain forest that rivals the Congo?"

Cal was obviously wrapped up in Peru. "Peruvians will also remind you of the contrasts in people."

"So different?" Marti asked.

"Yes. There are sophisticated, cultured people here in Lima who would feel right at home in the North Shore suburbs of Chicago. There are intellectuals who can match wits with scholars anywhere. There are Indians who never saw an automobile and are hardly aware that they live in a country named Peru. Well, let's go downstairs and see the museum and the offices."

Cal stopped the elevator at the fourteenth floor and led us down an empty corridor past the portraits of jungle Indians who stared back at us. He stopped and opened a door to the museum. When he switched on the light, we were in another world.

The displays were arranged by tribe. There were bows and arrows, spears, blow guns, stone axes, homespun clothing, skins of various animals, ceremonial artifacts, cooking utensils, even a hut built without hammer or nails. Inside the hut were two Indian mannequins in typical poses. Our kids were properly impressed.

We thumbed through illustrated books, health manuals, Scripture portions, primers, dictionaries, and other texts. Each page was bilingual, with the Indian language above and the Spanish below. A display of photographs hung on the walls showing contrasting scenes of tribal life between the old and the new. "We want to show how the Indians lived when we arrived and how they live now," Cal said.

"The bilingual method is the key to Indian education. Teachers from the various tribes are trained and sent back as government teachers to help students become literate first in their own languages and then in Spanish, the national language. The government has about 150 tribal schools manned by over 200 teachers in operation now."

He pointed to a large wall map of the jungle which bore the caption: THE COOPERATIVE WORK BETWEEN THE PERUVIAN GOVERNMENT AND THE SUMMER INSTITUTE OF LINGUISTICS. "Here, reaching almost up to Ecuador, is our northernmost tribe, the Arabelas. And here at the bottom is the southernmost, the Amarakeri. They're a thousand miles apart, yet they have a common need for education and spiritual enlightenment." Photographs around the map illustrated the work: a radio technician testing equipment, mechanics overhauling an aircraft engine, a doctor listening to the heartbeat of a puzzled Indian, the Peruvian Minister of Education visiting a tribal school. "We keep everything out in the open," Cal stressed. "We want everybody to know the way in which we are able to serve the government. But let's move on."

"We have offices in the suite to the left," he said with a sweep of his hand. "Gene Smith; myself; our office manager, Elsie May Hartog; and Mary Mollhagen, the secretary and publicist. Our Peruvian colleagues have their offices on the right."

"How much rent do you pay?" I asked innocently.

Cal's eyebrows lifted. "Rent! Why should we? These are offices of the Ministry of Education."

"You are really working for Peru, not for an organization back in the States," Marti said.

Cal burst into a broad grin. "Smart lady. We're here to do a specialized job for the Peruvian government in education, and for the Lord and for Bible translation. Our personal support as Wycliffe Bible Translators comes from individual Christians and churches at home who are interested as we are in Bible translation. The government pays the school teachers we train."

The children were getting restless and Marti suggested we start back. Going down in the elevator, Cal made a further point. "It's important you understand our organizational structure as it relates to the government. We're members of both the Wycliffe Bible Translators and the Summer Institute of Linguistics—*Instituto Linguistico de Verano* down here. SIL is the scientific and educational organization through which we contract with the government. Don't let it confuse you, but we'd prefer that you use SIL or just the 'Institute.' "

"I knew about your dual setup in Mexico. But I heard a pastor back in the States call this deception."

Cal frowned. "We are very careful to be open and above board with everybody. But to accomplish our main task of Bible translation, we must work in secular channels. A mission board couldn't sign a contract with a government. On the other hand we don't sneak in the Scripture. You saw the New Testaments on the table in the museum. You'll find that we do a lot of things which are essential sidelines to the main task of Bible translation: We operate a jungle airline and radio network. We train Indians in service occupations. We do a lot of things that some might call the social gospel. But it's all related to one goal—Bible translation. You'll understand after you've been in the jungle a few weeks."

After a marvelous night's rest and a hearty breakfast, we left the children at Lima House and went with Cal for an interview with a Peruvian whom Cal called an old friend. "After this one, I'll hand you over to Gene Smith. With a new government, it's essential that I stay in close touch with key people."

Marti looked at Cal as he guided the VW through morning traffic in the smart Miraflores section of Lima. "I know what you are now," she said smugly. "You're a diplomat."

"We all have to be," Cal said. "We're guests in a foreign country. Now, the man we're going to see was Minister of Education when the bilingual school program began. He's always been a hearty supporter."

General Mendoza, nattily dressed and graying at the temples, welcomed us into his home. He easily warmed to the subject. "To understand Peru, you must know that half of our country is Indian. For many years we took only a paternalistic attitude toward them. We sent out teachers who spoke only Spanish. I recognized the problem when I was in the army in the highlands. My officers had to have Indian interpreters to communicate with soldiers who spoke only Quechua. So when the Institute's Mr. Cameron Townsend came to me and asked to serve Peru by helping the Indians first become educated in their own language and then in Spanish, I immediately saw a way out of this dilemma.

"Townsend understood my point of view very well. He saw that we must begin with the language of the soul. He also saw that we must give something to the Indians besides the gospel. So the president of Peru and I pledged our cooperation and I signed the document allowing the Institute to begin work. Each of my successors has continued to back the program."

He looked at Cal with obvious approval, then back at me. "These linguists you will visit in the jungle are like their founder. He has a heart for humanity. We do not think of him as a Peruvian or an American, but as a man sent from God."

Tuesday, Gene Smith escorted us to our next interview: Dr. Martha Hilderbrand, whom Cal had said was the outstanding linguist of Peru.

Dr. Hilderbrand turned out to be a vivacious lady in a stunning black dress. While admitting German descent, she termed herself a Peruvian in the "fullest sense," adding, "We are all *mestizos,* if not in blood, at least in soul."

Over coffee she told us, "I've known the Institute people for twenty years, since I was a student at San Marcos. Uncle Cam—we Peruvians call him that too—arranged for me to attend their linguistics school at the University of Oklahoma. Later I began teaching linguistics at the University of San Marcos."

"What do you think of the Institute's work with the Indians?" I asked.

"I'm fully convinced that our way is the right way. The Indians must first become literate in their own language; then Spanish. Of course, many say the Indians should start with Spanish. But they wouldn't want their children to begin school in a foreign language."

Marti smiled. "I notice you used the plural possessive. Are you a member of the Institute?"

The linguist tossed her shoulders. "Officially, no. In my heart, yes."

Gene raised his hand. "We consider you one of the family. You helped set up the first bilingual program under General Mendoza and have been a good friend ever since."

"You lived at the jungle base?" Marti asked.

"Yes, indeed. It was quite primitive back then. I stayed with the

Townsends and it was so sticky I took three baths the first day there. They finally had to tell me they were running out of drinking water. I felt so ashamed."

Our hostess laughed. "One day when I was talking to my mother the radio burned up. They took it apart to see what was wrong and there was a big green snake—all toasted. Oh, and once in the middle of the night I began screaming, 'Uncle Cam! Uncle Cam! There's a tiger in my room.' He came and found a monkey chasing bats under the thatched roof."

On the seventh floor of the imposing AID building we ran into the special projects officer. Mike Roha, an ex-Peace Corpsman with long reddish sideburns and a Nixon nose, brightened at mention of the Institute. "I've worked with them in Viet Nam, Bolivia, and now Peru," he said. "We just put in a sawmill out on the Amazon for the Ticuna tribe. Lambert Anderson's the linguist out there. He has a real gift for identifying with the people."

"How do you assess their work?" I asked.

He looked away for a few seconds. "They try to improve the whole man rather than just part of him as so many missionaries do. They are like this priest down in Bolivia who told me, 'You can't preach to empty stomachs.' I'm Catholic, by the way."

Before we left, Mike said, "I wish you could talk to Don Lindholm who just left for the States. He just resigned as AID's program director in Peru and is coming back as a member of the Institute. I know he took a huge cut in pay, but apparently he feels their work is more important than ours."

Back at the Lima House the kids were itching to leave for the jungle. "Day after tomorrow," I promised them. "There's a missionary I want to see tomorrow."

"But why do you have to see so many people?" Marti asked. "I'm sick of the kids complaining of not being able to go anywhere."

"We need to get different viewpoints," I insisted. "I'll ask Mrs. Cudney to tell them on the radio tomorrow that we'll be coming Thursday."

The following morning J. Bryan "Breezy" Brasington, the senior Southern Baptist missionary, gave us the glad hand in his office above the Baptist Book Store in Lima. "I ought to know about Wycliffe," he said. "My son has a girl friend out at the base.

"We just don't have the personnel to work with the jungle Indians," he said. "With only six couples, we can't cover all the cities. But the Wycliffe linguists do wonderful work. I just wish we could help develop the churches that arise from Bible translation."

Back at Lima House, Mrs. Cudney said, "They're expecting you. They have a house all ready. It belongs to some folks who are leaving for their tribe."

Celia and Cheri danced around,.shouting, "Goody! We're going to the jungle."

3.

Yarinacocha

MARTI: Mrs. Cudney saw that we left for the airport on time. How could anyone help but love this smiling woman, so busy and efficient, yet always willing to show sympathetic interest in someone else's problems.

"She'd be too old for a regular mission board," I said to Cal as we sped along the boulevard.

"I suppose so. But we don't worry about age, so long as people are willing and able to serve. You'll meet some more senior citizens out at the base."

"I hope they're as cheerful as Mrs. Cudney."

"They are. Oh, did you know that a blind man is joining us here in Peru?"

"Really? You'd accept most anyone then?"

"Uncle Cam says, 'We'll consider anyone except the bartender and we'll take a second look at him after he's converted.' But I should add that the senior citizens, except for Mrs. Cudney and a few others, are short-term assistants—STAs, we call them. They sign up for six months, a year, two years. But they feel very much a part of the team."

Jim and Cal checked our bags plus two more suitcases for a pilot's wife returning from burying her husband in the States. She would be bringing her children back to the base in a couple of days. The plane was an hour late so the girls and I window-shopped along the stalls that sold souvenirs. I carried a mail pouch that Mrs. Cudney had asked us to deliver, a standard chore for people flying back and forth.

The girls were "freezing" despite warm heavy sweaters. "Don't worry," I told them, "you'll be wishing for this cool weather when we get to the hot jungle."

"Humph," Cheri grumbled. "I don't think it's hot any place in the whole world."

We finally boarded the plane. Jim looked like the abominable *turista* with camera, tape recorder, and briefcases. He insists that one should never trust anything but clothes to airline baggage.

The plane climbed through the thick layer of fog and finally nosed into the sunshine. There were the mountains sticking up like hooded falcons above the clouds. The plane banked northeast and soon we were scooting along over the top of the second highest mountain range in the

23

world. The snow-covered peaks to the north were impressive even to our children.

We passed over a glacier and a pristine lake that sparkled in a shallow mountain bowl. Then a picture card little Andean valley with pill-sized houses perched along both sides of a blue stream. And more and more gorgeous scenery. Jim went wild taking pictures.

Then the terrain became flat and tree-covered—quite boring—so the girls all found someone to talk to. They've been traveling all their lives and just never meet "strangers." They think everyone in the world is a friend.

After an hour-and-a-half's flight we began descending to Pucallpa, the big river town that squats on the banks of the Ucayali River about seventy-five miles from the Brazilian border. "From here," my encyclopedic husband said, "ocean vessels sail downstream to the Amazon and on across Brazil to the Atlantic."

The girls didn't complain about the cold when the stewardess opened the door. Heat! I mean hot. The sweat was rolling off our faces before we got into the small yellow terminal building. The light from the sun was blinding, even with sunglasses.

Our girls found two barefooted American boys, each with a snake around his neck. They were properly intrigued. The boys were part of the James Gang. Ted and Pat James welcomed us to the jungle, then Jim and Ted grabbed our bags and helped the touring quartet of ladies find their bags. Pat and I got acquainted on the way to the bus. Ted, she said, was from Maryland, a teacher by profession and now the guidance counselor for the Yarinacocha School. She was a secretary. "Everybody in your group works," I commented.

We piled into their Bluebird bus. The little breeze brought in by the movement of the bus did little to cool me off. Neither did being squished into a springless seat with two excited kids and all the sweaters on top of me. I realized the folly of wearing a wig in the jungle. I might be vain, but not enough to wear it again in the daytime.

We turned off a narrow strip of pavement and onto the dustiest, bumpiest road imaginable. Ted and Pat played tour guides. "Some of these little houses we are passing belong to the Shipibo Indians," Ted noted.

"Indians? Where?" Cyndi asked quickly.

The people we saw looked like the Peruvians we had seen in poorer sections of Lima, except maybe a little darker. "They're becoming acculturated," Ted said. "By that I mean they're moving into the Spanish culture. They speak the Spanish language and wear the white man's clothes. If you were to ask them if they were Indians, they would probably deny it. They're ashamed of their heritage."

Celia had her mind on something else. "Are there dangerous animals at the base?"

Pat smiled at this. "Not really. There are a few iguana lizards that look scary. Oh, you do need to watch out for the izula ants, though. They're an inch long and when they bite, you know it."

The bus lurched, almost bouncing us into the ceiling. "This road is really in good condition now," Ted said in mocking humor. "You should see it during rainy season!"

"What's the difference between the rainy season and the dry season?" I asked, between bumps.

"During the rainy season it pours; during the dry season it just rains."

Soon we were driving between screen-walled houses that looked as if they belonged to a summer resort. The yards were lovely and came with gorgeous shrubs and flowers, many in full bloom. As our bus pulled to a stop I saw a cloud of dust around a corner and then a minibus appeared. After it stopped beside us, a blond woman jumped out. "Hi, everybody. I'm the temporary base hostess. My name is Lolly Sawyer. It's easy to remember my name because I'm shaped like a lollipop."

Lolly, the base comedienne (that's what she was before joining Wycliffe), seemed to have everything under control. After Ted dropped the tour ladies off at the guest house, Lolly helped us transfer to the base minibus. "Since you're going to stay awhile, we've assigned you to the Schmidt's house. They've gone to a tribe."

Lolly bubbled on. "It's the newest house and sort of off by itself. We thought writers would like peace and quiet." I started to tell her that we had only come to dig up information and would do the writing back home, but I didn't.

Lolly drove across an old landing strip that the jungle was trying to reclaim. She turned sharply to the right through some high grass and stopped in the newly cleared yard of a frame and screen house. While Jim was pulling the bags out of the minibus, she handed me a map of the base and a one-page telephone directory. "My number is underlined. If you have any problems or need anything just call."

"Can we call long distance?" Jim asked.

"You will have to use the ham radio in the radio shack for long distance," Lolly said. "The telephones are strictly closed circuit for the base. You can't even call Pucallpa from them."

"Who installed them?"

"A supervisor for Bell Telephone in California, Jack Kendall, came here and got the idea. He located the equipment and had it installed. He did most of our electrical work, too. I don't know what we would have done without him."

A man roared up on a Honda. "That's my husband, Buzz," Lolly said. "He's a mechanic for JAARS. Buzz, meet the writing Hefleys."

Buzz grabbed a couple of our suitcases and let us in the door. Then the Sawyers left.

The kids and I ran around inspecting the two-bedroom house. I noticed blankets on the beds and wondered what on earth they needed them for. There was a bathroom with shower and a new kitchen—luxurious for the jungle. There was a note propped against a platter of freshly baked rolls.

Dear Hefleys: Have an enjoyable stay in our house. We'll be back in August. Use the bananas, potatoes, and grapefruit in the kitchen. If you'd

Air view of the base at Yarinacocha. Lake is in foreground
with Indian School and experimental farm on left
and JAARS air strip on right.

like a maid, ask Lolly to call our Balbena. We pay her 30 soles (75¢)
per day.

Love,
LaMont and Shirley Schmidt

Then the phone rang. Jim answered.

"Hello." Pause. Big smile on his face. "Sure would." Pause. "I'm sure
she'd like to go, but I doubt if she'd want to leave the girls right away."
Longer pause. "Oh, if you're sure they wouldn't be a problem." Pause.
"Wonderful. Then we'll see you after siesta."

Jim said, "That was Bob Mickelson. He's the base director and he will
take us on a tour of the base after siesta. His wife, Jan, will take the girls
swimming in the lake. That's if they want to go."

"Yeah! Yeah!" They were all yelling at once. "Dig out our suits,
Mommy."

So after nap time (siesta to my husband—he doesn't like people to
know he takes naps) Bob Mickelson stopped by in the International bus
Lolly had been driving. Bob, by vocation a city planner from Anaheim,
California, and his wife had come for a year as STAs and were thinking
about staying for two.

A cool breeze was blowing. Jim remarked that it didn't seem so hot
now. "No, it isn't," Bob said. "You arrived at the hottest time of the day.
That's why we have siestas. Mornings and evenings aren't so bad."

Bob drove through the weeds and onto a dirt road. As he threaded through the winding streets I remarked that a city planner might be needed. At least to name the streets. Our blond-headed guide laughed, "I admit it's a little confusing at first. Especially since the footpaths aren't shown on the map. But you'll learn your way around in no time."

He crossed a small wooden bridge and turned right. "That long building on the hill is the clinic. Our base doctors take care of us and the Indian teachers. And one of our nurse members trains Indian medical workers. They go back to their tribes and furnish competition to the witch doctors."

He turned a corner on the dusty road. "Indian teachers live in those little houses on the left while they're taking courses at the base. Indians who once warred against one another go to school together now. It's wonderful what happens when they discover God's love in the Scriptures.

"Now on your right is the agricultural department and the farm. We bring Indians in to learn modern agriculture and how to raise cattle, chickens, ducks, and so on. We figure people who are starving to death aren't going to care about Scripture.

"Back on your left is the dining hall for the Indian teachers and just ahead are the classroom buildings. Up ahead is the bazaar or trading post. The Indians can sell their hides and other products here and buy whatever they need at a decent price."

Bob stopped near a high bank that overlooked the lake. "We're at the upper end of the base. The JAARS hangar and airstrip is at the other end. JAARS stands for Jungle Aviation And Radio Service. I'm sorry to run you through so fast. I know you have questions."

He drove back into the residential area of the base. The spacious lawns with fruit trees and flowers looked gorgeous. We saw a beautiful jungle bird on a tree limb. "Toucan," Bob said, "and they don't leave here. This is a paradise for kids to have pets: toucans, parrots, ocelots, monkeys, snakes, wild hogs, you name it—we have it here."

"Do you ever have problems—I mean, do people ever complain about the animals? Not everybody likes to have a zoo next door."

"Now, why did you have to break up my nice little public relations talk," Bob pretended consternation. "The minutes of old base meetings are full of discussions over pets. They finally decided that a pet was okay if it didn't offend people by sight, smell, or sound. One family had a donkey here years ago. I still hear about that."

"Then you don't have heaven here yet?" Jim said.

"Nope. But we're pretty good neighbors. Now up ahead are various offices: finance, technical library, administrative offices, publications, and the dining room."

Bob waved a hand toward the lake. "Over there is the radio tower—Control Central for the jungle. Our people are scattered up and down the jungle for a thousand miles. Every station has a sending and receiving set.

Bob stopped the minibus at a fork in the road. "Uncle Cam and his family lived in that big house. It sort of grew like Topsy. The Oiens bought it after the Townsends went to pioneer again in Colombia."

He started the bus up again and took the right hand turn in the fork, keeping the minibus in a low gear. I heard some familiar voices over the sound of water splashing. "Don't let them see us right now," I begged.

"I understand," Bob said. "My little fuzzies are down there too. Here at the bottom of the hill is JAARS and behind that yellow plane is the radio shack."

"What is that monster?" I asked, pointing to a large two-story airplane that resembled a floppy dog.

"That monster," Bob said, "is the best ship we have. It's a Catalina. The government and citizens of Mexico presented it to the government of Peru for the linguistic and bilingual school program. Can you believe it!"

A slim lady on a Honda drew up beside us then. "Hi, Millie. What's up?" Bob asked.

"I've been trying to catch up with the Hefleys. The Cat's taking a group to Machiguenga land tomorrow morning and we've saved two places for them."

"Tomorrow," I moaned. "We just got here."

"Oh, that's all right," Millie said brightly. "I have a list of what you'll need to take, and Bob will help you get anything you need to borrow. Won't you, Bob? And somebody will keep your children for you."

Our genial guide nodded.

"I'm coming along," Millie said, "so I'll get to know you then." And off she zoomed on her Honda.

Bob laughed. "That's Millie Lyons. Always in a hurry. She's the secretary for the radio department. Her husband, Floyd, is the flight controller."

Bob took us by the school and finished the tour with a few more spots. Jim and I finally ended up at Bob's house where our kids were waiting. "This is a fun place," Cyndi said. "We want to go swimming every day."

Jan, Bob's tall blond wife who looks more like a model than a missionary, volunteered some of her camping equipment for our trip in the morning. "I just returned from two weeks with Millie Larsen in Aguaruna land. Everything is right here. Your girls can stay with us."

I looked at my daughters questioningly. "Go do your work, Mommy," Cyndi said as she piled into a hammock. "We'll be okay."

"You're sure you don't mind, Jan?"

She replied with a smile, "I'm sure."

"Well, you are the bravest people. When I get back, I want to hear about your trip to the Aguarunas. Jim has them on the list as the tribe he'd most like to visit."

"We've heard a lot about them," Jim said. "How they were once head-hunters and defied any whites to come near them. Is it true that thousands of Aguarunas have become Christians and they have the most advanced school system in the jungle?"

"Some remarkable things have happened out there," Jan agreed. "I hope you can go to Aguaruna land and have Millie tell you all about them."

We then started walking toward the dining hall and arrived just as the sun was sinking in a golden halo. As we entered, Jim almost tripped over three little puppies playing around the step. Celia, our animal lover, grabbed for one, but Jim shooed her inside.

We joined a short line and picked up our food cafeteria-style from Peruvian waitresses. The girls quickly discovered that the aluminum pitcher of lemonade was refillable at the ringing of a bell. They drank and drank and drank. "I've never had all the lemonade I want," Celia said.

A boy at the next table scowled at her words. "You will if you stay around here awhile."

We met more new friends while we ate. Bob Nelson, an airplane mechanic who said he was temporarily managing the commissary, explained that most people ate at their own homes. "Guests, short-term workers, and regular people when their schedule's tight eat here."

We had finished and were talking when I suddenly realized Celia was missing. "Maybe she went to play with the Mickelson kids," Jim suggested.

We walked out on the porch to check on Celia and there she was playing with one of the puppies; an adorable little black and white mutt that looked part beagle and part shepherd. Jim had to pull her away to get her started home.

I stepped from the light of the porch into the dark night. "How did it get dark so fast?" I asked.

Some teens who were lounging on the porch overheard me and one said, "You've never lived in the jungle, have you?"

"Obviously," I responded.

The boy went on to explain. "We're just a little south of the equator. When the sun shines around here, it shines. When it sets, it sets. Days and nights are almost the same the year round. Can you find your way back to your house?"

"Sure," my confident husband said. "We've got street lights."

"All the modern conveniences," the boy said. "And people back home think we live in grass huts all the time."

Two blocks or so away Cheri begged, "Daddy, carry me." A little further down the road, Celia wanted to be carried.

We passed the last street light and then remembered that the "newest house on the base" was so new that it had no road to it. "I think I goofed," Jim conceded. "I should have at least borrowed a flashlight."

"We didn't even leave the light on," I lamented.

We waded through the thick weeds and finally found the steps. Once inside, I moved Cheri toward the shower. She screamed when I turned the water on. It was ice cold and there wasn't even a handle for hot water.

I finally got the girls scrubbed down and tucked in bed. Jim told them a story and prayed with them while I got ready.

Did that bed feel delicious! Jim switched on a table lamp and handed me a bulging folder. "Here's the Machiguenga file. You can start reading it while I take my shower," he said.

"Read all of this now? You've got to be kidding."

"If we're going out there tomorrow, we should learn enough to ask some intelligent questions."

"I can always ask questions."

"I said, 'intelligent questions,' " he snorted.

Dutifully I started reading. Jim came back in the room a few minutes later. "What time is it?" I asked.

"Ten after nine."

"Just listen to those crickets and frogs. Hear the bird squawking out there?"

"The noises aren't bothering the girls. I looked and they were asleep."

"We can't finish all this tonight," I protested.

"Okay." He turned off the light and snuggled down beside me. "Now I know why we have these blankets," he said.

"Me, too. But that bird is so loud I'm never going to be able to sssssszzzzzzzz."

JIM: On the way to breakfast we stopped at Mickelsons and picked up the duffel bag containing our sleeping gear for the Machiguenga trip. Marti would bring the children back after breakfast while I got our baggage to the plane before eight o'clock.

Breakfast over, I kissed the girls goodbye and strolled around the dining hall to the lane that ran along the high lake bank. According to the base map, I was halfway between the Indian School and the hangar that marked the north and south boundaries of the base.

The gunny sack containing our gear wasn't heavy. The morning dew still sparkled in the high grass. I walked along entranced by the sights and sounds. The sawmill growled from a block behind me. The smooth lake wore a glossy sheen, ruffled only by an Indian paddle near the shore in a dugout canoe.

Suddenly I caught sight of a strange form wrapped around the base of a tree. The dark green iguana lizard, about four feet long, blended with the grass. I snapped some pictures, poked it with a stick, and the big reptile scrambled down the lake bank into a mass of vines.

A woman's voice from above caught my ear. "Yarina calling Culina. Over." And then a crackling noise and another woman's voice. "Culina here. I've got an order for you. Three pounds of rice. Two hundred aspirin. Smith-Corona typewriter ribbon. Please read back. Over."

I looked up to the radio tower, remembered that Culina was the name

4.

Machiguenga Land

JIM: A long dugout canoe powered by a small motor came putt-putting across the river. A man wearing a panama straw hat splashed to the water's edge and greeted Ron and Terry.

Wayne Snell, pioneer translator to the Machiguengas, hurried half of us into the long canoe, and the Indian pilot took us across the swift muddy Urubamba and into the calmer mouth of the green Camisea River. We stepped out and sunk above our ankles in gooey mud. While the Indian took the dugout back for the others we struggled up a steep bank, through head-high grass, and along a trail that led to a hut.

"Home sweet home!" cried Ron, who had come along with us on the first trip. "Well, it's one of our homes," he added. "We have eight strung along these rivers." The hut was built native fashion using vines instead of nails. The floors and walls were *pona* which is made by slitting open pona palm trees and rolling or splitting the bark.

"We've never tried to headquarter in one place or build a compound," Wayne said. "We don't want the Indians to become dependent upon us, but rather to build their own spiritual foundations upon the Scriptures."

Across the high grass, I could see a long open space. "Landing strip?" I wondered out loud.

"Yes," the translator replied. "Three of our seven single-engine planes are landlubbers. The Cat is amphibian but this strip is too short for it. Those of us who work in tribes always live close to a suitable landing place. Usually that's a river."

Marti kicked at an odd-looking piece of equipment in the weeds. "What's that contraption?" my forever curious wife asked.

Wayne laughed. "The mower. The blade is from an old truck spring. Two men can cut the air strip in half a day. Using machetes, it takes the whole village five days.

"But where's the motor?"

"On the canoe. It's a little 9-horse Briggs & Stratton. The Indians call it a 'pecky-pecky' because of the sound. It's the workhorse of the jungle. The Indians use it to haul their beans, coffee, and other cash items to market. You might have noticed the long propeller slanting out behind. That makes it possible to run a canoe through shallow water close to the banks and away from fast current. On land, the 'pecky-pecky' also runs the village sawmill and light plant."

"Who repairs them?" I asked.

"Indian mechanics we train at the base."

By this time the second load had arrived. Wayne stood up and gave a short speech:

"We found these Indians twenty years ago scattered in small family groups over four hundred square miles of jungle territory. They existed by hunting, fishing, and slash-and-burn agriculture. The only whites they had ever known were river traders who kept them in virtual economic slavery. So many people were dying from disease and revenge killings that, when we told them we were going to the base for a few weeks, they would invariably say, 'I won't be here then. I'll be dead.' They thought the Milky Way was a river where a fortunate few might bathe after death and receive an immortal skin. Most people thought the soul of the dead entered a red deer, a tiger, or a buzzard. A dead person was thrown in the river by the nearest relative without ceremony.

"That's enough history for now. Plenty of questions will come up as we move around. We'll go first to the village of Camisea, which incidentally was founded by a Christian Machi who wanted to improve the spiritual and economic welfare of his people. I think you are mature enough to act as Christians should. Just remember, these are raw unsophisticated Indian believers. Please don't give the Indians anything. You may buy whatever you wish that they want to sell for a reasonable price. If you want to know what's reasonable, ask me. Oh—leave your gear here. The Machis haven't acquired the white man's habit of stealing yet."

Marti and I agreed that I would have first shot at Wayne and she would stick around with the Snell boys and the other teenagers. So I fell in step beside the translator as he led the way to the village.

Wayne led us past the landing strip and back toward the large river. We emerged into a long clearing which held a scraggle of ten huts set on freshly swept bare ground overlooking the Urubamba. Chickens and ducks fluttered around a few naked toddlers that gazed at us with wonder.

While the women in long sacklike dresses held back, a man greeted Wayne warmly.

"This is Navidad—Spanish for Christmas," Wayne said. "He's one of the church deacons."

Lean and brown, Navidad barely reached my shoulders. He wore a brilliantly dyed robe with vertical stripes and shiny black artificial bangs.

"The garb is a *cushma*, the traditional dress of this tribe and a few others," Wayne explained. "When we came, some of them wore only beaten bark. No trouble to tell the sexes apart. The males always wear vertical stripes; the females horizontal stripes."

A mat covered with brown beans lay in front of Navidad's hut. "Coffee beans," Wayne said. "He's getting them ready for market. They also take cocoa and regular beans down river. It used to take them seventeen days by pole and paddle. Now they make it in one day with the pecky-pecky."

The smell of fresh meat spiked the air. "Navidad has been dressing a wild boar and a deer," Wayne noted. "The other men haven't got their game yet. We'll be going upriver to spend the night at another village and we'll come back here tomorrow for dinner."

Wayne pointed out a manually operated sugar cane press. "We haven't figured out how to use the pecky-pecky to manufacture sugar yet. But give us time."

"Are the ducks and chickens native to Peru?" Bobby Harrell, one of the Carolina boys, asked.

"No. We imported them. All of these ducks came from a drake and two ducks that I brought out years ago."

The teenagers had been buying artifacts right and left. Larry McDaniel, an art student from California, was trying to buy Navidad's *cushma*. But the Machi wasn't selling at any price. "If he had another fancy one, he'd sell it," Wayne said. "It takes a year for his wife to spin the cotton for one."

I followed Wayne into Navidad's smoke-filled hut. "Notice there are two fires. This means there are either two families living here or one man has two wives. Where there are two wives, the women take turns cooking over their own fires. In this case, there are two families. The total population of Camisea is only about sixty. You rarely see an Indian village over one hundred.

About a hundred yards back from the village was the school, a small, one-room frame building with a tin roof. Twenty-three children of assorted ages sat behind rough wooden desks. "From the sawmill powered by the pecky-pecky," Wayne whispered about the desks. "These are all the children in Camisea. No, there's one more, who's retarded."

We stood outside the rustic schoolroom and watched the eager-eyed children through the screen walls. Andres, the Yarina-trained professor, wrote a math problem on his chalkboard and the kids dutifully copied it down, then held up their hands as they computed the answers. "When we came here the people couldn't even count," Wayne said grinning proudly.

At Wayne's suggestion, the maestro had a small black-eyed girl about the size of our Celia stand up and read in Spanish. Wayne told us, "Andres just happened to pick out his own daughter to show off."

"They start with a controlled vocabulary in a Machiguenga primer," Wayne explained. "The stories are folk tales which have been told around their fires for centuries. During the first three years they study Spanish as a foreign language, then progressively they go into Spanish books. Their language has very long words and seems complicated to an outsider, but it's easy to them.

"You might be interested in the schedule. They arrive at seven, line up in formation, salute the Peruvian flag, and sing the national anthem. Then they march inside and the teacher leads them in fifteen minutes of Bible study from Scripture in their own language. They have a couple of recesses and close class at one."

"But it's almost three now," I said.

"Today, they came back for us. They're proud of their chance to get an education.

"The law of Peru specifies that the Christian religion be taught every day in the public schools," Wayne said after we took pictures and waved goodbye. "In the Spanish schools, this means the Catholic religion. For the bilingual Indian schools, our teachers have a special decree allowing them to teach Scripture in the native language. We provide the Scripture. The Indian teachers always do the teaching."

We walked through the jungle toward the Snell hut. "In the old days," Wayne said, "most Machis didn't even know they lived in a country named Peru. Only four years ago a chief's wife saw a teacher raise a flag at a new bilingual school and asked, 'What is he doing to that cloth? Does he need to dry it out?' "

I asked how many Machi bi-li schools there were.

"We just opened the ninth. There are also six Machi pastors. You'll hear one speak tonight. And we have literacy and community development programs going in various villages. Of course, Betty and I can't keep up with all this. Our colleagues, Harold and Pat Davis, move from village to village. They supervise the schools, hold adult literacy classes, and keep agricultural and vocational projects humming. This frees us to push ahead with Bible translation.

"You can find evangelical people," Wayne continued, "who say we limit ourselves by working under the government and that we compromise by signing contracts. It's true that we ourselves don't preach or conduct religious services. But we translate the Scripture and train Indians to teach that Scripture in their own language. And the schools keep turning out thousands of new readers. This results in truly indigenous churches."

We reached the airstrip and the hut was in sight. Wayne kept talking. "I found the Lord through the Navigators when I was a gunner's mate in the Pacific during World War II. You know how the Navs emphasize Scripture courses and memory work. Well, Daws Trotman, the Nav's founder, told me about Wycliffe. He was on their board. Knowing how the Bible changed me and other sailors, I felt that Bible translation was what primitive people needed most. After almost twenty years with these people, I still feel the same."

We reached the Snell's hut and found all our sleeping gear right where we had left it. Not a flashlight was missing. "We'll have to make two trips to the upriver village," Wayne said. "Half of you will have to wait for about an hour."

Marti and I volunteered to stay behind with some of the kids. Millie Lyons and Aileen Petty, the South Carolina sponsor, and Terry Snell went on ahead with the others. The two pilots said they would stick around until the boat returned for us, then would spend the night in the plane.

Bart—the kids called him "Black Bart"—was in fine fettle. It took little urging to get the tall flight engineer going on JAARS stories.

"A couple of years ago Dr. Criswell from that big Baptist meeting house in Texas was flying with Millie Lyons' husband, Floyd. The Lyonses are now members of Dr. Criswell's church. They were zipping along when a bolt cracked and the engine went out. Fortunately, the Lord had a little creek waiting. Floyd swooped down between two trees and put her down in the shallow water. The Lord even provided a little village and an airstrip close by. The people filled up the pig holes and by noon the next day we had a plane out there to bring Floyd and the preacher in to the base. The preacher wasn't hurt; just scared.

"I came out on the pickup plane and stayed to babysit the damaged bird which had to have a new engine. So I set to work clearing away brush and trees so the plane could take off when we got the engine in. But there was one tree the natives refused to let me cut. 'It's our village tree,' they said.

"I finally persuaded them to let me cut off one large branch. The men stood around and watched as I climbed up to the fork. My first whack on the branch brought bees from a nest the size of five basketballs screaming after me. I slid down that tree like greased lightning and drenched myself with gasoline. The villagers laughed, but I got rid of the bees and cut that limb.

"I had the old engine out when the guys flew in a new one. But then when we got everything hooked up, the water was too low for takeoff. We prayed. Two days later the Lord sent rain and Floyd flew her out of there."

Bart was still spinning yarns when the boat came back. We piled in for the trip up the small river. At one point we had to get out and walk around some small rapids which Ron Snell insisted were nothing compared to the fast water upstream where there were undertows. "If you go under in one," he said, "just hold your breath and an undercurrent will shoot you to the top—eventually."

The second village, Shivankoreni, was high on a bluff overlooking a cool swimming hole. While the kids splashed and cavorted in the water, Wayne gave us a tour of the village. He stopped at a vacant hut which he explained had been the community store. "The storekeeper had salt, fish hooks, needles, flashlights, batteries, shotgun shells, and a certificate from the Yarinacocha School of Merchandising. I'm not kidding. We do teach merchandising. Graduates come back and compete with river traders who have cheated the Indians for centuries. One trader gave an Indian a shotgun shell for a jaguar skin that was worth over $100. When the Indian protested, the trader replied, 'That's all it cost you!'"

Eyeing the empty shelves, Marti inquired, "What made this branch of Marshall Field's go bankrupt?"

Wayne grinned. "I wish I could show you a successful store upstream. In this situation, the villagers had no money. The storekeeper was ahead of the times."

With the shadows falling fast, the kids came groaning up the bluff. "Food, Aunt Millie. Where's the food?" the vanguard gasped.

After Millie distributed the grubstake, I asked her how she happened to be "aunt" so many times. "That's tradition with us," she said. "Kids at Yarina call all adults aunt or uncle. It's a compromise between Mr. or Mrs. and using the first name."

"Just so they don't call me Miss Marti," my wife commented. "It always comes out sounding like Miss Smarti."

Wayne then began assigning the houses. Marti and I would chaperone the girls. We could throw our sleeping bags on two cane pole cots in the back room of another Snell hut and the gals would sleep on the *pona* floor in front and above us in an attic. The boys would bed down in a hut next door.

Suddenly the sky was full of bright stars. Looking up, I had the eerie feeling we were in another world. The constellations in the southern sky were different from home. The familiar North Star and Big Dipper had disappeared.

The church services were by candlelight. The men sat on the right facing the pulpit; the women on the left on backless cedar benches, the lumber for which was produced by pecky-pecky power. Among the Indians, only the preacher wore shoes.

Behind the pulpit was a chalkboard on which was printed in block letters: *BIENVENIDO HERMANOS* (Spanish for "Welcome Brothers").

José, the preacher, Wayne told me later, was also the village school teacher and a brother of Andrés, the teacher at Camisea. José greeted us with Wayne standing beside him to do the interpreting. Then everybody prayed in unison.

Afterward the Machis sang one of their repetitive hymns, something of a paraphrase of John 14:1:

Where my Father lives, there are very, very many houses.
Where my Father lives, there are very, very many houses.
If there weren't any, I would have told you.
I would then have said to you, "Up high there are no homes."
CHORUS: I'll return, I'll return.
               I'll come back and get you all.
               Wherever I am, truly you will be, all of you.
Now because I'm going, I'll prepare, I'll prepare for you,
Houses up high, so that you won't so that you won't suffer.
The Lord Jesus said, "I am the trail,
If you all will follow me, you'll live up high with God.

"It's their favorite hymn," Wayne said afterward. "You'd understand why if you'd witnessed as much death among your relatives as they have seen among theirs. There's hardly a family that hasn't lost two or three children."

The South Carolina kids came to the front with guitars and sang a hymn for the Machis. Then Pastor José gave a simple exhortation for Christian living, with Wayne continuing to interpret for us.

The constant wheezing and coughing in the audience gave the feeling that we were in a tubercular ward. Across the dirt aisle, I saw Marti looking around and scribbling in her notebook. She would be after Wayne with curiosity questions in the morning.

The services ended and the Camisea people started down the steep trail to their canoes. The kids messed around for a few minutes until Wayne suggested they go to bed and let our hosts get some sleep. Before leaving, young Bill Goodman asked Wayne if bugs would be a problem. "No, there are no mosquitoes in this village. The only things you have to worry about are big enough to shoot," he replied cryptically.

Ron overheard. "Hey, Dad, didn't you wound a jaguar up here a couple of nights ago?"

"Sure did. If you hear any strange noises, stay in your beds. You'll know he's back."

All of us were properly impressed.

We had to walk across the girls snug in their sleeping bags to reach our bunks which were end on end, running the length of the narrow room. I dozed off right away, only to be awakened by a crashing sound from the attic, followed by a shower of dirt and leaves. The intruder was Betsy Funk, fiancée of the oldest Snell boy. The love birds had been out for a stroll.

MARTI: It was barely dawn when Jim shook me. "Rise and shine. The Indians have been out swimming already."

I moaned. "Why do you have to wake up so bright-eyed and bushy-tailed?"

I dragged out of bed and went to help Millie make sandwiches for breakfast. I was too sleepy to realize that most of the kids had gone, along with Jim. Suddenly there were yells and dogs barking down below. Boom! went a shotgun. I followed some of the Indian women to the top of the bluff and saw the boys chasing a funny-looking wounded animal along the river bank. It had a hog's body and an elephant's nose. The gringo kids were throwing rocks and chunks of wood at the defenseless animal. But no one seemed to be hitting the mark. I expected it to drop dead from sheer fright any moment.

The Indians raced on ahead of the boys and kept it from getting away. One Machi in a canoe aimed an arrow. The creature keeled over in the water as Chuck McKeown beaned it with a pole. Big game hunters! Ugh!

By the time I got down the steep trail, Jim was already taking pictures. "What is it?" I asked.

"A tapir," Wayne replied. "Must weigh four hundred pounds. Another big one got away."

Bobby Harrell came splashing through the water. "Man, I thought they were coming after me," he said. Then he sheepishly admitted he had climbed a tree.

I bent down to look at the strange animal. "Is a tapir good to eat?" I asked Wayne.

"They make delicious steaks. After the Indians dress it, I'm going to buy a side to take back to the base."

"Won't they give you some?"

"If I asked. But we figure it's better to pay for everything we get from them and sell them things of ours they want."

"Even Scriptures?"

"Yes. Their Scripture portions are quite cheap because they're subsidized—they pay less than a fifth of the actual cost. But they always pay something. This makes what they buy seem more valuable to them. And it helps the purchaser keep a sense of dignity to pay his own way in life."

"Hmmmmm, that's a good philosophy."

"I guess so. Say, you two really know how to pick a fellow's brain. Jim has been following me around all morning with his recorder, and now you're starting on me."

"Well, I do have a few questions. Like, why did that young girl in church last night have a cloth tied around her head?"

"Oh, that has to do with their puberty rites. When a girl first menstruates she must go live in a hut apart from the village for three or four months. During that time, she sees only her mother, who teaches her to cook, sew, and spin. When she learns all she needs to know to be a good wife they give her a drink that makes her vomit. Next, they cut off all her hair and she wears the scarf until the hair grows back. She is then considered marriageable."

"Does a girl usually marry soon after this?"

"Yes."

"Pays to advertise, I guess."

"This custom may seem strange to you, but it's really more practical than having your daughter 'come out' at a debutante cotillion. Isn't that announcing to the world that your daughter is ready for marriage, too?"

"Score one for you, Wayne. I noticed that the preacher used Spanish numbers in his sermon. Why didn't he use their own?"

"They don't have any."

"There are no numbers in the Machi language?"

"No. They only count one, two, and many. So when we teach them to count, we use the Spanish names instead of making up Machi names. This way they can't be cheated by traders."

"Another question. Why do the Machis all have Spanish names?"

"A new baby usually isn't given a name. Perhaps because only three out of ten children live. Machis usually call each other by their relationships. Sister, brother, father. For that reason I'm 'related' to everyone. One man in a village will start calling me 'brother' or 'father' and the rest of his relatives then call me by the appropriate title."

"Doesn't this get confusing?"

"It sure does," he chuckled. "Sometimes I wind up being my own grandpa. Next question?"

"What's the stuff the men use to make their facial markings? Will it come off? Do the different markings have special meanings?"

"The black lines are rubber smoke tattoos and they never come off. The red markings are *achiote* and they eventually wear off. There are about ten different designs, some for special purposes, such as for scaring away dead spirits, but most are for beauty."

"Pardon my ignorance, but what is *a-chi-o-te*?"

"It grows around the base, too, so I'd better show you. If your kids get into it they can really make a mess out of themselves. See this pod?" He pulled one loose from a large bush. "You pop it open like this and all that soft red stuff in there makes a great dye. It is used in food coloring. It used to be put in little packets and sold with uncolored margarine in the States."

"Very interesting. What about the little headbands they wear over their foreheads?"

"Those are made from toucan feathers. Instead of cutting their hair to make bangs, as some other tribes do, the Machis just wear these bands. Their own hair is so black that you have to look closely to realize they are feathers and not hair. By the way, your husband already bought one. He also bought a monkey skull spoon, some beads, a necklace made of jaguar teeth, a reed flute, and a clay pipe."

"It sounds as if he found some real gems. Especially that spoon made from a monkey's skull. We'll get a lot of use out of that!"

"It makes a good conversation piece," Wayne offered.

"I noticed that the women carry their babies in a sling thing in front instead of like papooses on their backs. What are those?"

"I'd better spell the name for you—*sagompuirontsi*. And sometimes they do carry the babies on their backs, whichever way seems to be most convenient."

"Oh, and I noticed a man last night at the services sitting in the back. He had a mustache! I thought Indians had very little facial hair. But his mustache was really thick, and shaped like a gondolier's."

"I know who you mean. He's from an upriver village where all the men have beards. This goes back to a visit by a group of Italian anthropologists about twenty years ago."

"Oh. And what about . . ."

"What about let's go help load up for our trip back to Camisea? You can ask more questions later, okay?" he asked while edging away.

He didn't leave me much choice so I helped get things together. Since it took so much time for the canoe to make two trips, Wayne decided some of the kids could float down on a raft. I would have loved to go with them, but my kill-joy husband wouldn't allow me.

So the rest of us climbed into the canoe with the gear. It's amazing how much faster one goes *with* the current instead of against it. The raft-trip gang arrived long before us, soaking wet, but proud of their great adventure.

Wayne broke us up into groups of three and four and assigned us to eat with different Indian families. "Marti, you and Ellen follow Navidad to his home, and I'll join you there later. Jim, you go with Bart and Larry to the teacher's home."

Ellen McClesky, one of the South Carolina kids, and I huffed and puffed after Navidad. Indians can really move! Thirty seconds into the jungle we lost sight of the others, so we didn't dare let the Machi out of our sight. We entered the clearing near his house and he led us to the front porch of another hut. He evidently wanted us to wait here while he went over to the fire and talked with his wife.

"These Machis speak so seldom and so softly, I don't see how the Snells ever learned their language," I said.

"Maybe they use ESP," Ellen said regarding the Indians.

"How have you been enjoying your summer, Ellen?"

"Oh, it's the greatest. Really the most. I thought before I left that I was really sacrificing to give up my whole summer to help down here. But now I wouldn't trade the experience for anything. It's really been great. And this trip to the tribe is the best of all. Just being with these people for a couple of days helps you understand why the translators are willing to spend their lives helping them. They're a real challenge."

Wayne joined us about this time. He called greetings to our hosts and sat down on the *pona* floor with us. "Now I expect you two to eat whatever is offered you," he said with a twinkle in his eye. "These people have been working hard preparing this meal, and I wouldn't want you to insult them."

Ellen and I looked at each other, and gulped squeamishly. "Okay, we'll eat it. Just *please* don't tell us what it is until afterward."

Our host came carrying a pot of food. He had changed into his new cushma we had all admired the day before. A young girl brought tin bowls and spoons. The spoons were stainless steel, not the monkey-skull type.

"Where did they get these dishes?" I asked.

"Probably from traders, I imagine. And we sell things sometimes. They don't really like to use monkey skulls. As a matter of fact, they can't imagine why gringos would buy their old ones. They think you are a little crazy if you want a monkey skull when they know you have the other kind available."

Our hostess joined us—a tiny little lady. She was very shy and kept her eyes down. Wayne helped with the serving and she giggled a little.

"You see," Wayne explained, "in this culture the women never eat with the men. She feels a little out of place here, but since the two of you are here they decided she should be here, too. She seems quite thrilled about it. This is a big occasion for her."

Wayne handed me a flat bowl with some kind of stew. It did smell good! There were pieces of meat and some kind of white stuff swimming around in a thick yellow gravy. There were also some fried bananas, which I could identify, so I started eating that. Then I swallowed, took

a deep breath, and tasted the stew stuff. It was good! I mean delicious!
I was relieved.

"Mmmmmm," I said. "Out of this world. Really great. I don't care
what it is, it is delicious. I've never had anything better. What is it
anyway?"

"Wild boar stew," Wayne replied. "I knew it would be good. Why do
you think I assigned myself here?"

"Tell them we really like it," said Ellen.

He did, even though it was evident by their satisfied looks that they
knew we approved already.

"I can't get over how delicious it is," I said again. "The gravy reminds
me of my chicken and dumplings. My husband thinks I make that the
best in the world. I've never told him my secret—I put yellow food coloring in it, and because it looks more appetizing, he thinks it's great.
What's the white stuff?"

"That's yuca. Manioc is the English name, I believe. It's a root. A
member of the potato family. It looks more like a sweet potato, but it's
white and a little more stringy."

"What makes the gravy yellow—the meat?"

"No, I'm sure the meat wouldn't do it. I don't really know."

"Ask our hostess."

"Oh, just eat, it isn't important."

"But I'm curious," I insisted.

"You certainly are!" he agreed. He asked her for me, so I would stop
pestering him, I presume. Then he threw back his head and really haw-
hawed. He said something to the Machis that made them laugh. The
three of them enjoyed the joke while Ellen and I sat looking at each
other blankly.

"What's so funny?" we asked in unison.

"She said she puts achiote in the stew for coloring. Food coloring!
She uses the same trick you use."

We laughed too. "The world is a pretty small place after all," I had to
admit. For the first time Navidad's wife looked me in the eye and we
enjoyed the coincidence together.

All the Machis from the village gathered around to bid us farewell.
Millie and Aileen had things they had brought to give them. We hadn't
thought to bring anything, but gave them some canned meat, sugar, and
other foodstuffs we hadn't used. They seemed pleased.

"It's okay to give them these things, isn't it?" I asked one of the Snell
boys.

"Sure. In a way you are paying for your dinner. They won't consider
it charity."

We made the canoe trip back to the plane. Our baggage was all mixed
up, but nobody seemed to mind.

Everyone was laughing and joking over the roar of the engines. The
noise level must have been above 100 decibels. It didn't bother Wayne.

He sat on a large can and "turned off" distractions while reading the latest issue of *Time* which his boys had brought. He didn't even look up when Jim snapped his picture. I don't know if living so many years in Indian villages has compelled him to acquire this deep concentration, or if it was his four kids. If the girls were anything like the boys . . .

We landed in the lake at Yarina, then lumbered up the cement ramp like some prehistoric monster. Kids were gathered all around the field. We strained to find our girls. "There's Celia," Jim called. "She's with one of those tow-headed Mickelson boys."

"And there's Cyndi," I said. "Good grief, she has a snake wrapped around her neck! It sure didn't take our gals long to adjust!"

We climbed out of the plane, hot, tired and exhausted. I was feeling the lack of sleep and was looking forward to even a *cold* shower.

"Hi, dolls," I said, wrapping an arm around each of my girls. "Have you had a good time while we were gone?"

"Yeah! We went swimming. And we had a slumber party with the Mickelson kids. And how do you like the boa constrictor?" They both jabbered away at once.

I acted properly horrified about the snake although I was really too tired to be frightened. "Where's Cheri?" I asked.

"Oh, she was with Aunt Jan at the soccer game last time I saw her," Celia said.

"No, I think she was playing with Brucie Nelson after that," contradicted Cyndi.

"But they both went up to the playing field together," Celia countered. "*I* saw them!"

"Well, let's go look for her," I interrupted. "Jim, if you'll stay and get our gear, we'll go look for Little Bit."

With his consent, we began hiking toward the soccer field. I was really dry, and hot. How anyone could play soccer in weather like this was beyond me, and right in the heat of the day.

"Now, let's find your sister, girls," I said. "I'm getting anxious to see her."

"Aw, we want to go play with our friends," Celia protested. "And I have to return this boa; he's very valuable, you know," Cyndi declared.

"Well, all right, but you'll have to come home in one hour. We're going to a pizza party at the Snells."

"Yea! We love pizza," Cyndi squealed with joy.

They went their own way and I trudged on alone. "Boy, they really missed us," I thought. "It's nice that they're getting independent, but they don't have to be *that* independent."

I finally made it to the field. Cheri wasn't there, but there were two ladies serving lemonade to the soccer players: Jan Mickelson and Corny Hibbard, Cal's wife. I never have figured out why they shortened Cornelia to Corny instead of Cory.

"Hi," smiled Corny. "You look beat. Just get back from your trip?"

"Yes, and I'm so thirsty I'm about to perish," I hinted.

"Well, I guess we could donate one glass of lemonade to insure a good press," Corny said, as she handed me a big frosty glass of the delightful stuff.

I nodded my thanks.

"Jan, my big girls met the plane, but where's Cheri?" I was still worried.

"Oh, she's riding around on the Honda with Bob."

"No wonder she didn't come to meet us. How can a mere mother compete with a motorcycle?"

"I'll have him bring her to your house when I see him," she said.

I dragged myself back to the house. Jim was already there. "You know what I've decided," I told him. "We're the only ones out here living in the jungle! The Wycliffe people are all together over there in civilization!"

Our family eventually all got together. We showered and got ready for the pizza party. My hair was an absolute mess, so since the sun was down and it was cooler, I wore my wig.

By the time we'd hiked to the Snells, who had a big house on the far side of the base facing the lake, we were ready for pizza. We came in the back door, since it was closer, and we were greeted there by an older girl. "Hi. I'm Betty Snell," she said cheerily. "I hope you didn't get lost."

The party was going slam-bang. All the teen summer workers were talking at once. Everything was delicious. In the confusion, I never did meet Wayne's wife.

Though tired and full of pizza, I did perk up when the Snell boys held up a long strip of paper on which was printed the longest word I ever saw.

Wayne Snell demonstrates the longest Machiguenga word found so far to Peruvian military students visiting the base.

Irapusatinkaatsempokitasanoigavetapaakemparorokarityo.
Betty stood up and said, "This is the longest word we've found. Even
some of the Machis don't understand what it means."
"I can see why," I heard Jim mutter.
"I'll give you a breakdown of the parts," Betty continued. "The first
letter, *i*, is third person masculine subjunctive 'he' or 'they'; *r* is future;
apusatinka is a verb root meaning 'head over heels' or 'end for end'; *a* is
a 'liquid'; *tsempoki* indicates the form of legs up in the air; *ta* is a
verbal; *sano* is an intensifier; *iga* is a plural, referring back to the subject; *ve* is a frustrated action; *ta* is a verbal; *paa* indicates that the
action takes place on the subjects' arrival; *k* means it's nonrepetitive;
empa is a reflexive; *rorokari* expresses probability; *tyo* means it's
emphatic.
"The total meaning is, 'They will probably really go head over heels
into the water upon their arrival, but they won't stay that way.' "
All I could say was, "Good grief!"

5.

Faith That Dares

MARTI: Sunday morning arrived too soon. "I really slept well last night," I told Jim when he brought me a cup of wake-up instant coffee. "Must be the fresh-air walls. What time are worship services?"

"The information booklet says Sunday school starts at nine."

"What an awful hour. Why so early?"

"Probably to beat the heat."

"That's reasonable. Okay, I'm coming alive now. I'll get the girls ready and you can take them to Sunday school. I'll get ready and meet you as soon as I can. We've been so busy since we got here, I haven't even unpacked."

When the family finally trooped out, I pulled the least wrinkled thing I had out of a suitcase. I still hadn't had time to fix my hair, so I stuck it all on top of my head with bobby pins and put a fancy wiglet on top. It looked a little too dressy for the jungle, but it was cooler.

The auditorium was only halfway to the dining hall, so the hike was quite pleasant along the dirt trails, with the towering trees providing a nice shade. Sunday school hadn't dismissed yet so I had time to look around. The building seated about three hundred and had the usual aluminum roof and screen walls. The wide overhang made it shady and inside it was quite pleasant with overhead fans. The long wooden benches weren't fancy, but at least they had backs.

People started coming in. It made me feel at home to realize I knew quite a few of them. The Mickelsons waved, while keeping their three youngsters in tow. Betty Snell entered and sat at the back with Wayne. Ron followed carrying a girl with her legs in casts. I presumed this was the other sister. Ron had told us she had had surgery on her feet. She was about thirteen or fourteen and looked like quite a load. It didn't seem to bother "Jungle Boy," though. I noticed Millie and Floyd Lyons with three stair-steps, all boys.

The leader for the day strode to the platform. It was our silver-haired pilot, Ralph Borthwick. After a couple of songs, and prayer, he called for announcements.

A man behind us stood up and said, "Some of you may have noticed Ted Long, Harriet, and Hattie flying over the base practicing parachute basket drops last week. Well, they are now out in Mayoruna land and are planning on making a drop tomorrow. The guys at the radio lab worked

47

hard on perfecting the transmitters hidden in the baskets. Let's pray that
the Mayorunas will talk near enough to the basket so their voices can be
captured on tape. Harriet and Hattie feel that contact can't be too far
away. So please keep praying for the Mayoruna Advance."

Everyone listened intently to this announcement. I got the impression
that this "Mayoruna Advance" was a big deal.

Another man stood up. "We just got word from John Tuggy that one
of the Shapra school teachers died suddenly about a week ago, leaving a
widow and four young children. Remember the relatives who are sad-
dened. And remember the Tuggys, for this man's death could present a
real problem. It's Shapra custom for the paternal uncle to get the children when a brother dies. And the uncle in this case is an unbeliever."

Jim nudged me. "Remember Chief Tariri whom Uncle Cam told us
about? He's a Shapra."

Ralph then introduced the visitors in a casual folksy way. When we
stood up, he said, "The Hefleys are nosing around asking questions but
they're not with the CIA. They are here to write a book about our work
in Peru.

"We have some new members who just arrived," Ralph continued.
"Stuart and Mary Shepherd from Great Britain. Will you stand up with
your children?"

The Shepherds were just in front of us. Stuart was tall and slim. Mary
had beautiful black curly hair—just the thing for jungle living, I
thought. They had two little girls about the right ages to play with our
girls. And a mischievous-looking red-headed son, not yet two, I guessed.

"And we're especially glad to have Marge Bondurant, and Doug,
Marcia, and Carol back. Welcome home, Marge."

When Rol Rich, the speaker, walked onto the platform, Jim whispered,
"He's the director. I'll be seeing him tomorrow."

All I remember about Rol's sermon is his advice to the parents:
"You'd better go home and pull page 26 from the latest issue of *Time*
magazine. We have to protect the morals of our young people." I could
just imagine the stampede of teens after church all racing to see what it
was they shouldn't see. Rol looked funny after he said that. He must have
realized his goof.

When Rol closed his message, he announced an emergency meeting
for the adults. This was the first we had heard of the rash of robberies
at the base. Several motorcycles had been stolen and a couple of empty
houses (the owners were in tribes) had been broken into. A vigilante
committee was formed to stand watch and catch the thieves. The alarm
could be sounded by dialing a certain number.

"They've got everything around here," I whispered to Jim.

We stayed to talk for awhile, mostly about the robberies. That's when
I learned that Betty Snell was Wayne's wife, not his daughter! I was too
embarrassed to admit my goof.

Then it was time for Sunday dinner. That cute little black and white dog came bouncing up to Celia as we neared the dining hall. Smitten with puppy love, she was thrilled that he was getting to know her.

We got our food and sat down opposite a lady with twin girls about Cheri's age. "Hi. We're the snooping Hefleys," my gregarious husband said.

She smiled and said, "I'm Lillice Long and these are my daughters, Merrilyn and Merrily. And my big son, Paul, is at the table behind us."

"Long. Long. Is that your husband who was mentioned in one of the announcement-prayer requests?" I asked uncertainly.

"Yes," she smiled.

"What's it like being a pilot's wife, staying here while he goes off on these dangerous missions?"

"Well, you learn to pray a lot and keep as busy as possible."

"What's your job, Lillice?" Jim asked.

"I'm chairman of the publicity committee. Vera Borthwick, another pilot's wife, works with me. You'll probably be looking for us since we have all the historical files. We're along the lake, second house beyond the Snells. The office is on our second floor. Come over whenever you wish."

"Thanks," Jim said. "We'll be there."

"Everyone around here seems to have a job," I noted as I poured Cheri a second glass of lemonade.

"We do. Literally. All wives are expected to put in at least three hours a day. We have a nursery for our little ones and a children's program while school is out to give the mothers free time. My work in publicity keeps me involved in what's going on."

"Anything beats ironing," I joked.

"Well, with maid service so cheap, we really don't have to worry about that either. We feel our time is more valuable than the 10 cents an hour it costs for domestic help; we are here for a purpose. Then, too, the people need the money so badly, and it gives us an opportunity to get to know some of the local people, and witness to them. At the same time we get to practice our Spanish."

"That sounds logical. Is your husband gone a lot?"

"Yes, but not usually for long periods of time. This situation with the Mayorunas is rather unusual."

"Are they really all that fierce?"

"Oh, yes. Worse than the Aucas, they say. That's why it's gone so slow. We don't want to go ahead of the Lord. He has put these people on the girls' hearts, but we don't want a tragedy."

"How long have they been trying to get into this tribe?"

"The first presents were dropped back in 1964. I don't know how much of this you know."

"Very little; fill us in, please," Jim said, turning on his tape recorder.

"I'll go back a way. The Mayorunas were treated like slaves by rubber hunters around the turn of the century. They were cruelly punished for the slightest infraction. An arm or a leg might be cut off for not meeting a quota, and other atrocities like that. When the rubber hunters got through with them, they shot some down like animals. Other tribes were treated this way, too. Unlike some of the others, the Mayorunas retreated into the jungle and began raiding white settlements in the area south of Iquitos. They would make a surprise appearance, kill the men, and capture the women and small children. The Peruvian army has tried to pacify them for years. I've heard that the army has a list of over 1,000 people the Mayorunas have killed or captured."

"They do sound fierce," I said. "The way they were mistreated by the rubber hunters helps explain why they act the way they do. But why do they steal the women?"

"This has to do with their marriage customs. A girl baby who isn't spoken for by a man at birth is strangled. Captured wives make up for the shortage. One of these, a woman named Sofia, escaped—so far as we know, the first woman ever to do so—and moved to Iquitos. About six years ago she came to the base and helped Harriet Fields with language study. Harriet, a new translator from Indiana, was interested in the Mayorunas.

"A couple of years later the Peruvian army picked up a young Mayoruna man on a river and brought him here. No one knew why he had left the tribe. Harriet put a cot in her living room and tried to befriend him. For a while he seemed to be in shock, but little by little, Joe—as we called him—opened up and helped Harriet learn his language.

"That was in 1965. In October of that year the army gave permission for us to try and contact the Mayorunas. We have to get their permission to enter certain areas. But there was some fighting between the Mayorunas and soldiers, so our flight couldn't go in until early in '66. Ted took Harriet, Betty McIntyre, Joe, and a little dog given to Joe here at the base. Betty was the first of several temporary partners for Harriet. They camped on a river bank and waited for Mayorunas to visit them."

"But wasn't this dangerous?" I asked.

"Yes, but the Lord has always taken care of our people. I remember the reports radioed back here to the base. They heard bird calls, monkey noises, things that made them sure the Indians were all around. But no one ever came.

"Then in August Ted took Harriet and Priscilla Bartram, one of our base teachers, and Joe back out and left them for a few weeks. This time Joe left and they've never seen him again.

"Ted went out a third time in 1967 and took Harriet Fields and her permanent partner, Hattie Kneeland, and left them in an isolated spot on the Yaquerana River."

I gasped. "Ted left those two females there with the bugs and the wild Indians and the wild animals!"

Lillice took a bite of her food. "Uh-huh. They stayed a couple of months. He and the plane were needed elsewhere. Besides, the Mayorunas kill the men but just take the women as captives."

"Just!" I echoed. "And they stayed two whole months?"

"They would have stayed longer except for some flooding. They had a radio and a plane could get there in a couple of hours."

"That must have been reassuring," I said sarcastically.

"But that was over two years ago," I said. "You mean they still haven't made contact?"

"No, and they've been out there camping for months at a time, first in one location, then another hoping for Joe or some of the Mayorunas to come out."

"But couldn't Ted or another of the pilots locate the Indians from the air?" Jim asked.

"Once they located some people—they thought Joe was among them— and made gift drops. The girls camped only four flying minutes away. But when they flew back over the area, all the houses had been burned. However, a few weeks ago, Jerri Cobb, the lady pilot who wanted to become an astronaut, flew her plane down here and offered to help search for the Mayorunas. She found three long houses, all inhabited, about fifteen miles from the Yaquerana River. Now the girls are out there with Ted. They're camped on the Yaquerana and will start making gift drops tomorrow. The boys in the radio lab have rigged up a wing speaker so Harriet Fields can invite the Indians to the river camp."

"What perseverance!" I exclaimed. "Now that you've told us all this, we'll really be praying for them. Will Ted be staying out long this time?"

"Just a few days. He'll be back in for our vacation which is due soon."

We got the girls started home. Celia had to be pulled away from the puppy again. With the sun beating down on us, I really dreaded the long walk back to our house. Then I thought of those gals out on that river bank waiting for the fierce Mayorunas to come.

Jim was strangely silent. "Why so quiet?" I asked.

"I was thinking about the Auca incident when those five missionaries were killed back in 1956," he replied solemnly.

The girls griped, groaned, and grumbled about the long hot walk, and finally Jim had to carry Cheri. We were passing near the last house before the open field when a friendly voice called, "Say, Hefleys! Would you like to stop for a cold drink?"

"Would we? Wow!" The door swung open and tall, dark-haired Linda Smith stuck her head out. "Come on in. I don't know if you remember us, but we met in Lima House last week." She looked familiar. I didn't remember Glenn, her husband, but our three C's remembered their three: Cindy, Cathy, and Chrissie.

The girls went off together to the living room. Our three wiggled into the principal piece of furniture—a large, wide, white hammock. Jim and I followed Linda to the kitchen for that cool drink. It hit the spot.

We were introduced to Frank and Carol Duda, who were also visiting. Jim and Glenn started swapping stories about Youth for Christ. (Glenn had been involved as a youth, and Jim had written a book about YFC.)

"What tribes are you with?" I asked Linda and the Dudas.

"Oh, we're support personnel," Linda replied. "Glenn's in radio, and I'm a secretary."

"And we're just STAs—short time assistants," said Frank. "I teach basic engineering at Allegheny Community College in Pittsburgh. We've just been telling the Smiths some of our experiences with Dr. Olive Shell among the Cashibos."

"Oh, that sounds interesting. Is she a medical doctor?" I asked.

"Ph.D. from the University of Pennsylvania. One of the first translators in Peru. A Canadian. She's been working with the Cashibos for over twenty years. Dr. Shell really impressed us. But she won't brag about herself or her work for anything. She just says, 'We haven't had any mass conversions; the work has progressed slowly, but steadily,' " explained Frank.

"But she is really something," said Carol enthusiastically. "She ran us ragged! And she must be in her sixties. What energy!"

Frank agreed. "She was always the first out of the canoe if we were stuck or anything."

"And one time," his wife interrupted, "we were climbing into a plane to take off from a river and the Indian who was supposed to push us off kept turning us in the wrong direction. He just couldn't understand why it made any difference to the plane, so she jumped out, pushed it herself, then leaped back on the pontoons, climbed back in and calmly sat down, not even winded!"

"Sounds like quite a gal," I laughed.

"She certainly is," said Frank emphatically. "One time we were in a canoe that got caught in some rapids—the canoe got twisted sideways. Were we scared! We finally got out, but when we spotted some more rapids ahead she asked if we could swim. We said yes, so she turned to the man who was poling the canoe and asked, 'Would you mind looking after me if we should tip over? I can't swim.' "

"You mean she's been traveling up and down those rivers by canoe all these years and she can't swim?" Linda was appalled.

"She just isn't afraid of anything," Frank answered.

"It sounds as if you've had quite a summer," I said. "I can't help thinking that teaching school back in the States will be awfully blah after this."

Frank and Carol looked at each other and smiled. After a pause, Frank said, "We've been thinking the same thing. If the Lord opens the doors, we just might wind up here permanently."

"Well, Marti," Linda smiled, "you've just discovered one of the purposes in having STAs. People come for a 'short time' and get involved for life."

JIM: While Marti had the Dudas in a corner, I was talking to Glenn. Thin and dark-haired, the 31-year-old radio engineer sketched what had happened since he left YFC. "We've been at the base a year now, and it's still hard to believe how well the Lord prepared me for my job in the radio lab here. I was repairing and testing radio equipment for the planes of Mohawk Airlines when we discovered the challenge in the tribes. I resigned. We sold our house, raised support, and here we are."

"Is your work here much different?" I asked.

Glenn took his seven-year-old Chrissie on his knee. "Not really, except we don't have fancy equipment and we encounter problems peculiar to the jungle. For example, the high humidity is hard on transformers and capacitors. And there are no navigation stations to speak of across the jungle.

"We've installed automatic direction finders in all our planes. If a pilot gets weathered in and has to set down on a jungle river, we can find him fast. We're working on ADFs for radios which our tribal people can carry along the trail. If they need help and are unable to transmit, we can home in on their location."

"The Mayoruna girls would like something like that," I commented.

"I suppose so. We've all been praying hard for them and doing everything we can to insure their safety. That's the story of this outfit from the beginning: Trust the Lord and prepare for any contingency. But we're much better prepared now than 20 years ago. The old-timers can tell you some hair-raising experiences."

"We're invited over to Al and Janny Townsend's tonight after church for doughnuts and coffee," Marti interjected. "I hear they've been here awhile."

"Ask Janny Townsend to tell you about the 99 letters that got lost and Al's proposal," Linda offered.

I scribbled a note and yawned. Marti frowned at me. "My husband must have his siesta. Thanks a lot for the refreshments—I don't think we could have made it home without them. We'd better be going."

After church services that evening, Marti and I walked home with Janny and Al Townsend (no relation to the founder of Wycliffe). Cyndi had volunteered to babysit Cheri and the middle one would "sit" herself.

"I'm chief of maintenance and carpentry here at the base," Al said. "When someone wants to build a new house they come and see me."

"Do individual families build their own houses?" I asked.

"Yes. And two singles who are partners in a tribe usually build their house together."

"What does a house cost to build?"

"Depends on what you want. Three to five thousand will put up a good four bedroom house around here. That may not sound high to you, but remember most of our folks have to raise the funds by faith."

We passed Al's carpenter shop. From behind it the big diesel engines were throbbing. Al chuckled. "Back in the old days we ran the base with a 2000-watt generator. When lights would start flickering in the evening, Les Bancroft, a mechanic, would hear the engine coughing and run out and work on it. It was an old U.S. Army surplus job, belt driven. Often he had trouble getting a spark from the coil. The lights would go out and we'd have to use candles until Les got the thing going."

Left: Amahuacas reading primers prepared by translators Delores and Bob Russell.
Below: "Uncle Cam" and Elaine Townsend chat with high Peruvian army officer at twentieth anniversary celebration of Wycliffe service in Peru.

Al added, "You should go by and look over the new equipment. See Art Jackson or Lee Gray. Lee's new with us. He helped build the moon landing ship. Gave up a high-paying engineering job and brought his big family down here to help us get the job done with the tribes."

Al and Janny's house was situated next door to the JAARS hangar. Two other couples arrived soon after we did—the Haltermans, Vic and his wife, Helena, who was expecting, and Jim and Anita Price, the house parents for the children's home, *Niño Tambo.*

When Vic identified himself as the "county agent," big Al guffawed. "His territory is the whole jungle," Al said. "How about that?"

"More accurately," Vic explained, "I work under Herb Fuqua and handle community development. We have a unique opportunity here. The schools have drawn the nomadic Indians into villages. Scripture in their own language has changed them from the heart out. This makes them want to help one another. The medical work is giving them energy resources. Now we must help them build their communities."

"In what ways?" I asked.

"Municipal government. Agriculture. Vocational trades. Sanitation. Anything that will help build a stronger community. This involves instruction of community leaders here at the base, visiting and encouraging tribal communities, supplying seed projects to get them started. Come out to the farm and I'll fill you in on the details."

"I will," I promised.

Marti, who had been all ears, asked, "When's the baby due?"

"*He* should be saying howdy about the first of September," Vic said with a broad grin.

Everybody laughed and we turned to get acquainted with the Prices.

"Get Jim going and he can tell you some stories about the old days," Al said. "Jim and Anita have been two of our indispensables. He's been a pilot and a mechanic. The kids of tribal workers live with them at the children's home during the school term. Jim also teaches math and arts and crafts in our base school."

Jim looked a little embarrassed, but Al kept going. "The kids love this barefoot character. He can get anything out of them. You oughta go by and look at the catamaran he's building for his furlough trip back to the States."

While we had our coffee and doughnuts Janny Townsend opened a photo album. "Would you like to see some pictures of the good old days?"

We would, indeed, and for the next hour saw old photos of the base as it had been twenty years before.

"Yarina was just a few thatched houses and an airstrip back then," Marti commented.

"Yes," Janny said, "and the town of Pucallpa where you landed in the commercial plane was just a frontier rivertown."

"Tell us how Wycliffe got started in Peru," I asked.

Jan put down the album and sighed. "Okay, but please check my statistics."

I promised we would.

"Uncle Cam came down from Mexico in '45. He convinced the government that we could really help with education. The government arranged for him to fly all over the jungle and make spot surveys. He came away convinced that the Indians couldn't be reached without airplanes.

"He went back to Lima and signed a contract with the government that permitted us to live in Indian tribes, study their languages, and translate Scripture. Then he went home and brought back twenty-four pioneers who scattered over the jungle and began groundwork in seven tribes. They were so eager to get started that they didn't even wait for radios and planes.

"A few churches and individuals back in the States gave them enough to live on for the first three months. After that they lived by faith. And we still do today. Of course, Uncle Cam gave the Peruvian Air Force the *honor* of putting gas in the planes. And the government helps in other ways."

Janny noticed that Al was laughing and stopped talking. "What's so funny?"

"Tell them about starvation at the old base."

"Oh, we didn't really starve. Wait, I forgot to tell you that it was Uncle Cam's idea to have a central base in the jungle. The group was loaned an old hotel at Aguaytía, about halfway between here and the Andes. The food supply got so low there that sometimes we had to count the peas when we divided them into portions.

"After a year or so, the group located this place where we are now. It was just a patch of thick jungle then that overlooked Lake Yarina-cocha. The lake had been formed from an old river bed of the Ucayali.

This was centrally located between the tribes in the far north and those in the far south. Planes could land and take off on the lake. And it was near Pucallpa, the second largest town in the jungle. Iquitos is the largest.

"The building that is now the dining hall was built first. We put up curtains to divide the living quarters. We slept, ate, worked, and had the clinic in there. We used lights at night only in case of emergency. One night someone warmed a flashlight instead of a baby bottle.

"We had a precious fellowship back then," Janny continued. "And still do. There were fewer of us and we were closer together. We had some wonderful leaders. Uncle Cam was gone a lot to the States, for he continued as general director. Bob Schneider was our director for several years. Then Ken Watters."

Al was laughing again. "Tell them about getting your ring.

Jan smiled. "Let's see. I was with Ellen Ross doing tribal work out in Machiguenga country. Our old Duck plane flew over our village about every three months to drop mail and see if we were all right. On the flight in September, 1949, the plane dropped a mail package containing 99 letters that we never found."

"Half of those letters were from me," Al said.

"We got the other package which the plane dropped. In it was a note telling us where to meet the plane in about two weeks for a trip back to the base. We took a three-day canoe trip downriver to a spot where the water was deep enough for a landing. Through rapids, whirlpools, and rainstorms. It was rough going.

"The plane came in about an hour after we arrived and taxied close to the beach. What a thrill to see Al jump out and come running to me."

Vic Halterman laughed. "How romantic."

"I thought it was. Then while we were flying back over the jungle, he gave me the ring. When we finally reached Yarina, he showed me the little thatched roof house he had built—the first residence on the base."

Al smiled. "I wasn't in the Army Engineers for nothing."

"And you were married and lived happily ever after," Marti said.

"Not exactly. We flew to Lima and had a simple but beautiful wedding in a home. Larry Montgomery, our first pilot, was Al's best man."

Janny burst into a peel of laughter. "We planned on honeymooning in a little mountain town near Lima, but I came down with appendicitis."

Vic Halterman stood up and helped his wife to her feet. "Sorry, folks, to be a party pooper. But I've got to get my wife and *son* home."

Helena looked at her confident husband. "Pride comes before a fall."

Vic replied, "After two girls, we can't miss this time."

At that moment a redheaded teenager rushed in. Jan said, "That's Barbara, the third of our four kids. Did you have a good time, dear?"

"Marvelous. Did you hear about the excitement?"

We looked at her blankly.

"I wasn't there. But Uncle Herb says Ron Snell scared the wits out of the summer girls."

6.

"Your Servants for Jesus' Sake"

MARTI: Monday morning the big girls got ready for Children's Program while I dressed Cheri for nursery school. Jim had volunteered to drop them off on his way to the post office.

I was watching the four of them marching down the trail when the phone rang. "Good morning," I answered cheerfully. (This is an act I put on to make people think I'm good-natured early in the morning.)

"Morning, Marti, Bob Mickelson here. Lolly and I were talking, and thought maybe you'd rather stay in a house nearer the center of things."

"Would we! You've made my day. Is there one available?"

"Yes. The Shanks. It's a block or so from the dining room, on the second street from the lake. How fast can you pack?"

"Pack! I've never had a chance to get unpacked. It'll take me maybe five minutes to pick up pajamas and toothbrushes and I'll be ready."

"Fine. Lolly will bring the truck over and you can move this morning."

The jovial base-hostess was soon Lolly-on-the-spot to help me carry things to the truck. "The blankets, sheets, pillows, towels, go with you. They belong to the base. Don't worry about cleaning this house," Lolly assured me. "We have the maids do it and add the cost to your bill. That way everyone knows they will have a clean house to return to, no matter who uses it."

"Then lending houses is the norm around here?"

"Sure," she laughed. "People don't like leaving their houses empty. Bugs, mold, mildew, and sometimes the jungle itself will take over if you leave things alone. Works out fine because so many are in and out of the tribes or on furlough. Those who don't own homes can rent a place to live.

"The Shankses, whose house you will be staying in, are on furlough now. He's one of our first radio men."

We pulled up in front of a fence covered with blooming bougainvillea. "What gorgeous flowers," I said.

"Yes. Ann Shanks is quite a gardener."

The three bedroom house was shaped like an H with the living room in the middle. We soon had all the stuff inside—work goes fast when you're with Lolly.

While we were catching our breath, I remarked about her good humor. "The kids at school wouldn't always agree," she said.

"At school? What do you do there?"

"I'm the art teacher."

"Oh, really? I love art. But what is it the kids don't like?"

"My rule about their snakes. I insist that they keep them in their desks while I'm teaching. If there's one thing I can't stand, it's a boa sticking its tongue out at me. Well, gotta go now. Come visit me when you get a chance," she called as she went out the door.

"I'll do that," I replied.

I looked at the row of suitcases. "Oh, phoo. I can do that this afternoon when the girls are home. I'll go visit Betty Snell while I have the opportunity to talk to her without interruption."

I got my sunglasses, notebook, pencil, and tape recorder and started down the dusty road. The Snells' two-story house faced the lake, just a couple of houses down and across the road from our new abode.

"Knock, knock," I called through the screen door. A small dog began barking furiously.

"Calm down, Chico! Calm down. He's the barkingest dog on the base. Come on in, Marti. He won't bite."

"Meet your new neighbor. We just moved into the Shankses'."

"Great. Welcome to civilization. You were rather far removed out there.

"Have you met my daughter, Mel?" she asked.

"No, I haven't. How are you, Mel," I smiled to the pigtailed girl sitting in her wheel-chair.

"Okay," she replied, petting the white kitten curled in her lap.

"Right now Mel is rather bored. It's hard for her to be inactive, but she has only a few more weeks until the casts come off," Betty explained cheerfully. She was obviously trying to help Melody be optimistic.

"Mother, I'm thirsty," she complained.

"I'll make us some lemonade. Marti, would you like some? Or would you prefer coffee?"

"Lemonade! It's too hot for coffee. Do you have time to talk? I've got a barrel of questions to ask you."

"If you don't mind my working while we talk," she replied, going to the refrigerator. She took out the biggest lemon I'd ever seen.

"Is that a lemon or a grapefruit?"

She laughed. "Oh, this is a lazy lemon. We call it that because you only have to squeeze one to get half a cup of juice. The only disadvantage is the lemonade doesn't keep. You have to drink it all in one day. But with the boys home from school in the States this summer, that's no problem."

While she was fixing the drink, I plugged the mike into my recorder. "This is Marti talking to Betty Snell," I said into the mike for the benefit of our typist. "Betty is Wayne Snell's wife. Their children are Ronny, Terry, and Melody."

"And Sandy!" she exclaimed rather indignantly.

"Well, I thought there was another sister," I explained, pushing the OFF button on the mike. I told how I had gotten confused because I thought she was one of the girls. She and Mel seemed to enjoy my embarrassment.

"In that case, you're forgiven," she replied jokingly. "I'll have to admit you really had everyone impressed with your fancy hairdos—until one of the summer girls figured out you must have brought some wigs. They're new to us jungle folks. Well, what would you like to know?"

"We'll be getting all kinds of stories about the difficulties of being a translator. I'd like a few tales about raising children in the jungle. There had to be some unusual problems," I said, pushing the ON button discreetly.

"We've had a few," she admitted. "We first came to Peru when Terry was five months old, then Ronny was born in Lima ten months later. So my first trip to our tribe was with two bouncing baby boys to keep me company. It was nine months before I left our jungle home in that little clearing."

"What was the one thing you missed most?"

Without hesitation she exclaimed, "Mail! There was one three-month period, including Christmas, when the plane was broken down, and we received no mail or fresh supplies. Letters from home can mean so much in a situation like that."

"How did you survive?" I gasped.

She chuckled at my naïveté. "The Indians have been living like that for centuries, you know. The diet gets rather monotonous, but you really learn to identify with the Indians after an experience like that. People don't have to be left for such long periods now that we have more planes and pilots."

"I understand why your boys acted so much at home in the jungle. It really was home to them."

"Yes, and the girls love it just as much. In the early years the children were quite a help to us. They learned the language at play while we were struggling over it. They learned how to fish, hunt, and swim along with the Indian children.

"We had so very much to learn. The people were cold and distrustful for a long time. Language barriers can be very frustrating. And Indians can be most uncooperative at times. I remember once when Sandy was a baby and the boys were three and four, we had to move into a roofless house during a premature rainy season. We were five cold, wet gringos," she sighed. "But that was long ago. And it was more than worth it. The Lord has blessed us in so many ways. By the spring of 1955 we had the first draft of four chapters of Mark, and we had the joy of seeing two Machiguengas come to know the Lord."

"Great. Did your children go to the Indian School?"

"No. We didn't have a school at that time. We had to teach them ourselves."

She added, "We now have an excellent school for all our children here at the base. Ron and Terry were two of the first three graduates. We really are thankful for the school. It means we can keep our children near us through high school, instead of sending them to the States."

"But if they are here and you're in the tribe you still have to be separated a lot, don't you?"

"Yes, more than we'd like, of course. They stay at the children's home while we're away, but we try to be together as much as possible. We get into the base for annual conference and the children come out for Christmas and vacations. We have weekly radio skeds with each of them. That helps a lot, along with the knowledge that in case of emergency a plane would come to bring us in. Knowing we're in the Lord's will and that he's watching over them and caring for them helps most. I believe you pray more for your children when you are separated. In a way, the separations have made us a closer family. We appreciate each other more when we are together."

"What about Mel's illness?" I asked glancing at her. She was drawing a horse, using pastels, and seemed to be paying no attention to what we were saying.

"She first became sick when she was only twenty-one months old. At first our doctor thought she had tubercular meningitis, but the final diagnosis was polio. She's had several operations, wore braces and spent a year in the Crippled Children's Hospital in Massachusetts, while Wayne was getting his master's in anthropology and I was studying Greek. But this time, Lord willing, she's going to be better."

"Have you had other sicknesses?"

"We've all had hepatitis at one time or another. And malaria. About the worst thing we've been involved in was a measles epidemic in the tribe. About 25 died in Camisea and many, many more were disfigured for life. The Machis have had famines and floods, so many more problems than our family. Don't believe the Eden stories some anthropologists try to push. The jungle Indians are *not* living in paradise!"

About that time Ron entered, barefoot as usual, wearing cutoff jeans with his T-shirt hanging out. The broad-shouldered youth towered above his girlish looking mother. He sliced off a hunk of cake and proceeded to wolf it down. I glanced at my watch. Nearly 11:00.

Betty laughed. "If you're thinking he'll spoil his appetite, you're just dreaming. Nothing has ever spoiled it yet."

I was rather embarrassed at being so transparent. "Say, Ron, what's this we heard about you scaring the summer worker girls last night?"

He cackled, then stuffed in the last bite of cake and washed it down with lemonade. "They started it all," he began, enjoying the opportunity to retell his latest escapade. "One of them stole the key to my Honda. They wouldn't return it and I needed it. It got late and they went in the girls' dorm. I stood out there a while pounding on the door, threatening to break in, but they just yelled, 'You can't come in, we're not decent!'

"So I got some of the guys in a huddle, and we decided that we'd take the five-foot iguana we'd caught that afternoon and throw him in the dorm.

"We did, and man, you never heard such screaming and yelling in your life. They were really climbing the walls." He laughed out loud just thinking about it. "Boy, were they scared! They were all yelling, 'Ronny, come get this thing; take this monster out' and stuff like that, but I just answered, 'I can't, you're not decent!' Hoo, man, was that ever neat!"

"But that was dangerous, wasn't it?" I asked.

He answered rather condescendingly, "An iguana is ugly but won't usually attack. If you ever go after one, watch out for his tail. They use them like bullwhips. That poor thing we threw at the girls was probably more scared of all the commotion than they were of him."

Betty, Mel, and I were still laughing as he departed with a satisfied grin on his face. "And that's the student from Moody Bible Institute?" I asked.

"Yes," Betty sighed. "And Terry is attending LeTourneau College. He wants to be a missionary pilot."

"What does Ron want to be?"

"A professional missionary kid," quipped Mel.

We all laughed again and I commented, "At least your family has a good sense of humor."

"That's practically a prerequisite to being a translator," she replied, jokingly. Then she looked rather thoughtful and said, "Anyway, it certainly does help."

JIM: Cyndi and Celia ran ahead and I hoofed along beside Cheri. When we reached the school where the summer workers were conducting the children's program, I noticed a bungalow across from the auditorium and checked my map. The base library.

I took Cheri to her class. The teacher had a pet monkey she brought to class, so "Little Bit" never even noticed when I left. I stopped back by the library. A trim young woman was sitting at a desk patching the binding of a book. "You have to do lots of things for yourself when repair services aren't near," Ruth Campbell, the librarian, said.

"Our downstairs books are for school and general reading around the base," she explained, as she showed me around. "Books from the travel library upstairs can be taken out to a tribe. People come by and pick up several just before leaving, or they'll radio in and ask for certain books, or for so many books, to interest certain ages."

"What reading material is most popular?" I asked.

"The *Reader's Digest Condensed Book* series for adults. And *Dr. Seuss* for the kids, I guess."

"Your encyclopedias look well used."

"They are, and the nature books, too. People come in here to get ideas for bird and animal illustrations in their tribal dictionaries."

"Our children will be thrilled with this," I said. "All three are book-worms."

Ruth laughed. "That's the kind we like. We have pattern books, too. *Simplicity*. *McCall's*. The teenage girls use them a lot."

"Did you train for this job?" I asked.

"I have a master's in library science from the University of Michigan. But they didn't teach some of the things I must do."

"Such as?"

"Oh, making puzzles to send out to the translators' kids. I've got to do that this afternoon. But I'm not complaining. I really enjoy keeping our people mentally alert."

"Thanks, Ruth. I'm glad I stopped by. My girls will probably be around to see you this afternoon."

She smiled. "I'll be looking for them."

I found the post office conveniently located just in front of the dining hall. The postmistress was Corny Hibbard. She assigned us a box for receiving mail. "You'll get everything our members receive while you're here," she said. "Reports, the base weekly newspaper, all the inside gossip—er, information—about what goes on around here."

She continued, "The base bulletin board is over there. Lost and found. Announcements. Daily news from the world and from the tribes."

My research antenna shot up. "Do they keep files of all these reports in the publicity office?"

"They keep files on everything."

Corny continued showing me around. "The drop boxes by the door are for outgoing mail. It goes out whenever someone from the base goes to Lima. We also have the photo files back here. We've got, I guess, thousands of pictures going back for twenty years. All filed and catalogued. Come in when you get time and look at them."

I walked over to peek in our mail box. The door swung open easily and I fished out a mimeographed sheet.

The "Yarinacocha Weekly News Bulletin" contained a potpourri of happenings. It was a company newsletter and a community newspaper rolled into one. The speaker for the next Sunday's church services was posted, along with the purpose of the offering, and an announcement of the upcoming monthly day of prayer.

There followed a page of comings and goings; to and from Lima, to and from the States (furloughs), to and from various tribal locations, and a guest list that included the sons of two high Peruvian officials.

Corny interrupted my reading. "The bulletin will be more interesting after you've been here awhile and get to know the folks."

I thanked her and asked about the commissary. "Just behind the post office," she said.

Bob Nelson, an aviation mechanic, was running the store, "because no one else is available for the job," he said.

"Where do you get the supplies for the commissary?" I inquired.

"We have a man who goes into Pucallpa six days a week and buys right from the market. More stuff comes from Harold Beatty, our buyer in Lima. He sends it over the Andes by truck, which adds to the cost."

The finance office just down the road was my next stop. Treasurer Doyle Nystrom, a slender, dignified man, greeted me. "We have two sets of books. One is for our people, numbering about two hundred now. The other is for the Indian teachers. Financial support for us comes from churches and individuals. The Peruvian government pays the salaries of the Indian teachers.

"We've already set up an account for your family. Anything you deposit will be credited toward what you buy through us. Your house, laundry, food, meals, tribal flights, even offerings in church can be charged. You'll get a statement in your post office box at the end of the month."

"Almost the cashless society," I commented, handing him a deposit check on our home bank.

The treasurer grinned.

Looking around, I saw a half dozen workers busy with adding machines and typewriters. "Did you have special training for this job?" I asked on impulse.

Doyle smiled. "I attended a little business school, but I came down as a translator. Betty and I started among the Nomatsiguengas. The group needed somebody to keep books when Ken Watters, our first treasurer, went to the home office. They asked me to help out temporarily. I'm still here."

I looked at the treasurer, whose hair had turned gray. "Have you regretted not being able to translate?"

"There are moments," he admitted. "But then I stop and realize that the translators can't get the job done without backup people at the base and in Lima. And without the Christian folks back home who contribute to our support. It takes a team effort and not everyone can be on the front line."

"I'm beginning to realize that myself," I said.

Doyle looked at a dark-haired girl at an adding machine. "There's proof that people are happy down here. Joyce, come and meet Jim Hefley. Joyce Powlison, Jim. She was raised in the Yagua tribe, went home and got her degree, and is back helping us. Her family is on furlough while her father is getting his doctorate."

Doyle returned to a ledger while Joyce and I chatted. "Dad's writing his thesis at Indiana U. on Yagua folklore," Joyce said. "He hopes to help other linguists to use folklore in preparing to translate."

"Why is folklore so important?" I asked.

"It's mixed in with their religion. The Yaguas, for example, call the moon 'Our Father' and say that the sun is the moon's son. You must be very careful that a biblical word or name doesn't carry the wrong connotation."

"Did you find life interesting while living with the Yaguas, Joyce?"

"Life wasn't dull, that's for sure. We lived about forty feet from the witch doctor's house which had no walls. From our kitchen table we could hear his smoke-blowing, throat-clearing, sucking routines. My dad says his treatment of sucking on a patient's mouth to cure a disease sounded like an old car's starter grinding away on a cold morning. This witch doctor threatened to kill through witchcraft any Yagua who dared help us learn the language. When our language helper did die, the witch doctor rejoiced and took the credit.

"My folks are the adventuresome sort," Joyce continued. "Once for a vacation we carried our back packs across the Andes to Lima—all five of us. We hiked; we rode trucks, buses, and trains. The highlight was a 90-mile hike through the first range of mountains. We slept wherever night found us. You don't forget things like that."

I knew they had work to do so I turned to leave. Doyle called me over. "Here in 2 Corinthians 4:5 is one of Uncle Cam's mottos. It expresses our philosophy of service."

I read the phrase, ". . . ourselves your servants for Jesus' sake."

"That says a lot," I had to agree.

I walked a few steps toward the lake to the administrative offices. The director, Rol Rich, was on the phone. While waiting for my appointment, I got acquainted with Loys Munday, his secretary, who had worked as a medical secretary before coming to Peru. "I found the Lord in Billy Graham's Madison Square Garden campaign," she said. "Since that my life has never been the same. Some friends told me about Wycliffe and I came down here as an STA. After a year, I applied for permanent membership."

The director opened the door of his small office. He looked casual in an open short-sleeved shirt, and with a pencil behind one ear. He insisted I call him Rol. "I'm a misplaced translator right now," he said. "The members elected me director three years ago and I've been trying to break loose and get back to my tribe ever since. My wife's out there now with a temporary partner."

I instantly liked this man from Portland, Oregon, who looked me straight in the eye.

"Saw you and Marti in church services yesterday," he said, "but you got away before I could speak to you."

He stood up and pointed out his tribe's location on a wall map. "The Arabelas are way up here just below the border of Ecuador. Our northernmost group. About four hundred miles from the base. We found them pitifully impoverished, enslaved to witchcraft and exploited by traders and big land owners. They're still our smallest tribe in Peru, and their population has been decreasing for the usual causes."

"What are they?"

"Oh, diseases they catch from outsiders coming in. Measles epidemics, for example. Just plain oppression. Greedy whites have a pretty sordid record back in these jungles. But things are getting better. The Peruvian government is trying to bring law and justice into these isolated places. They want to raise the Indians to full citizenship. What they're doing out here in Indian education and the backing they give our work is pretty good evidence of that."

"What does your contract with the government specify that you will do?"

Rol fished a document from his desk. "Here's a list of our commitments. You can see they're divided into two divisions: language investigation and practical projects."

I read the document.

LANGUAGE WORK:

1) Produce an intensive study of each language.
2) Provide a comprehensive collection of each language's vocabulary.
3) Classify Peru's Indian languages in relation to other world languages.
4) Preserve on recordings the living voice of each tribe for posterity.
5) Collect anthropological data and an archive of photographs that show the people and how they live.
6) Collect data in respect to medicinal herbs and dyes.
7) Study the legends, songs, and other folklore.
8) Cooperate with all organizations interested in scientific investigation of other aspects of the Indian tribes.

PRACTICAL PROJECTS:

1) Provide interpreters for educational, health, and other government agencies that visit the region.
2) Organize linguistic courses for groups of school teachers who teach in Indian centers and do not know the languages.
3) Prepare primers in the Indian languages for literacy.
4) Prepare bilingual primers for the purpose of teaching the official language.
5) Translate into the Indian languages articles of law, sanitation procedures, farm manuals, skin curing instructions, and other articles and books of high patriotic and moral value.
6) Promote athletics, patriotism, and group cooperation.
7) Provide a program to eradicate vices by all possible means.

When I finished, Rol said, "When we reach those goals, we will donate this base and all other property to the Peruvian Ministry of Education."

"Have you completed work in any tribes?"

"We've phased out work with the Iquitos and the Jeberos. They've moved far enough into Spanish culture, so that more translation doesn't seem to be justified. Another tribe, the Cocama, is close to this stage. But we've still got lots of work to do."

"What type of personnel do you need?"

"We need at least thirteen translators, plus many more support people. We need people in literacy, education, agriculture, medicine, aviation, publications—well, we can use almost anybody who can qualify and is willing to serve."

"Give me some specifics," I requested.

"A pharmacist to manage the ordering, storing, and dispensing of all drug and first aid supplies through the clinic. A lab technologist. A pedagogical technician to serve as a consultant to the bilingual school system. We have a number of partnerships that need completing in the tribes. For example, Thelma Schoolland is doing literacy with the Capanahuas. She needs a partner interested in the same work."

"How many tribes are there left to enter?"

"Well, there are only two or three jungle tribes left, plus some dialects within tribes where we are already working. I'm being a little vague because there are isolated groups of wild Indians that we know little about.

"But, now, the Quechuas are an entirely different ball of wax. These mountain people make up almost half of Peru's population. I hope you can visit our base in the mountains before you leave."

"We plan to go there before we leave Peru," I told him. "Rol, let's go back to your commitments to the government. Where is Bible translation in that list?"

The director laughed at this. "Didn't you see it? It's included in number five of practical projects under 'books of high moral value.' Is there anything better than the Bible?"

"But what about churches? I mean, isn't this what missionaries are expected to do—establish churches?"

"We're not ecclesiastical workers, and we don't baptize, marry, or perform religious ceremonies. We do translate the Bible. People read the Scriptures, believe, and organize their own churches that best fit with each tribal culture." His dark eyes twinkled. "You're really an inquisitor, aren't you?"

"My wife is worse. Now could you tell me how you folks in Peru fit into the total picture of Wycliffe?"

"Sure. We're a peculiar outfit. Worldwide we accept a common doctrinal statement and certain broad policies. But each of our branches is autonomous and pretty independent. We have five branches in Latin America alone—Mexico, Central America, Ecuador, Brazil, and Bolivia along with Peru. Then there are other branches in Asia, Australia, and Africa. Peru is third in membership behind New Guinea and Mexico."

"How about what businessmen call a flow chart on your operations here?"

Rol pulled the pencil from behind his ear. "To begin with, we're the Summer Institute of Linguistics, not Wycliffe. Has anyone explained to you that we're members of dual organizations?"

"Cal Hibbard has urged me to include this in the book."

"I agree," Rol said. "We don't want to tell you what to write, but we do want the facts straight. SIL is the scientific and educational side of the coin through which we contract with the government.

"Now, the Peru Branch of SIL has its own constitution and Peruvian corporation papers. A director and an executive committee are elected by members voting in conference each year. The director chooses four department heads with the approval of the executive committee: the

Yarina base director, the Lima director, the JAARS director, and the tribal affairs director. Obviously, tribal affairs has the most subdepartments: Indian education, publications, agriculture and community development, translation, and linguistics. Jerry Elder is our tribal affairs director. Wish you could talk to him, but he's out of the country now."

"We're trying to give everything the once over. But I can see this won't be easy. Tell me, Rol, did Uncle Cam have all this in mind—a blueprint, when he brought the first workers into this jungle?"

Rol stretched his long arms. "Uncle Cam had the basic ideas. He saw the need of a well-rounded program in addition to Bible translation that would serve the people in practical ways. Some of us didn't see it all at first, especially agriculture and community development. But Uncle Cam kept telling us about how his practical projects in Mexico helped win the support of the president. We actually got tired of hearing about Uncle Cam's 'cabbage patch' until we finally realized that if we didn't serve the Indians in practical ways, we'd have to leave verses like 1 John 4:17 and James 2:15-17 out of our translations."

The ding-a-ling of the dinner bell broke into the conversation. "Let's go eat," Rol said.

We walked outside.

A bearded stranger and several young men were clustered around Dan Velie, the public relations director.

"Who are the young men he's talking with?" I asked.

"The man with the beard is a professor of anthropology from California. The young guys are probably his students. We get all kinds of visitors here. A Swiss TV group is around now, and the Chilean ambassador to Peru is coming next week."

"I can understand why," I replied.

When we reached the dining hall, I saw Marti and the girls already at a table. Rol took the arm of a white-haired woman standing in line. "Jim Hefley, meet my mother. 'Gran-gran,' everybody calls her."

"Came down to check on Rol, huh?" I asked.

Her eyes twinkled. "Not really. I'm an STA. They have me working in publicity."

Rol was grinning. "My sister and her husband have joined the team, too. It's getting to be a real family affair for us."

7.

San Francisco

MARTI: Jim came home one evening and announced, "Cal is in from Lima. We're invited over to the Hibbards' this evening for root beer floats. It seems to be a tradition with them."

"Fine," I responded. "I haven't had much chance to get to know Corny."

So after tucking our little gals in, we made sure Puppy hadn't "followed" them home again. Leaving Cyndi to babysit, we got our flashlight and started down the road to the Hibbards'.

"We certainly are close to everything now," I said as we entered their backyard. We walked along a path lined with orange, lemon, and grapefruit trees, toward Cal's house, which faced the lake.

"What are all these Hondas and bikes doing out here?" Jim mumbled as he stumbled.

"There you are," called a voice. "Are the Hefleys ever on time for anything? I was just coming to see if you'd gotten lost."

"Oh, Cal, you know we always show up eventually," I responded. "What's with the bike shop out here?"

"Our son, Jonathan, is the base fix-it man. Has his own business."

By this time we had walked around to the front of the house, and entered the door.

"We have some guests we thought you would enjoy meeting," said Cal. "Lucille Eakin and Norma Faust. They've just returned from a trip down the Ucayali, working with the Shipibos. Girls, meet Jim and Marti Hefley."

We all said the appropriate things, and I went into the kitchen to help Corny. We served the floats and sat down in the paneled living room.

"You don't know what a treat it still is for us to have root beer floats," said our hostess. "We used to dream of them, and could hardly wait for furlough to get some ice cream. It still seems odd that we have it available now here on the base."

"Are you translators?" Jim asked.

"No," replied brown-eyed Norma. "We're school supervisors. We go from school to school, testing children, observing the teachers, and helping with special problems. The principal translators for the Shipibos are Jim and Hettie Loriot. They're in the States on indefinite leave because of illness, but are sending back manuscripts for checking. The LeClairs are also assigned to the Shipibos, but they're doing community development."

"What's unique about your work?" I asked.

The girls looked at each other and laughed, "Perhaps our mobile home," answered Lucy. "Instead of flying, we have a 26-foot houseboat that takes us to villages along the Ucayali River. It has its disadvantages, but it does save a lot of packing."

I was intrigued. "What's the boat like?"

"It's small. It has two beds that become benches in the daytime, a two-burner butane stove, a roof, and a radio for contact with the base," she answered.

"And a bucket," added Norma.

"A bucket?" we all inquired, puzzled.

The girls laughed and Norma explained. "Our launch has a habit of leaking a bit. It's in Pucallpa right now. We hope to get it fixed some before we take off again."

"How many schools and teachers do you supervise?" Jim asked.

"At present we have twenty schools and thirty teachers, with plans for more," answered Norma.

"And how much of the New Testament has been completed?"

"Luke, John, and Acts are in the hands of the Shipibos now," she answered. "A good deal more is in various stages of completion."

"Is this the tribe I read about where the men beat the women?" I wondered.

"Oh, no!" came a chorus from both the girls and the Hibbards.

"You must have them confused with the Culinas," said Cal. "That's Arlene Agnew and Patsy Adams's tribe. As a matter of fact, the Shipibos are a matriarchal society."

"Yes," agreed Norma. "If anything, the women beat their husbands. Why, just the other day we heard about a woman who hit her husband over the head with a two-by-four! Split his head open!"

"This is unusual, though, isn't it?" I persisted.

"Yes, in most tribes the man is very much the master of his own household," said Cal. "All the stories of a super-female tribe in the Amazon are pure Hollywood."

"What else is unusual about your tribe?" I asked.

"Their custom of flattening their infants' foreheads is unique," Lucy stated. "But we only see children with flat foreheads occasionally now. The adults still bear the disfigurement, though."

"How do they do this?"

"They shape the infants' heads with special boards strapped tightly to the forehead which are later removed. After they're grown, there is nothing that can be done. Some of the men are ashamed now and try to hide it under caps."

"But why would they do this?"

"So they won't look like monkeys," came the amusing but sad reply.

"If you'd like to visit a Shipibo village, there's one just forty-five minutes by pecky-pecky."

"Could we take our girls?" I asked. "They've heard so much about going out to the tribes from their friends that they are really curious."

"Certainly," Cal said. "Tell Bob Mickelson when you want to go and he'll arrange for an Indian to come for you in a boat. It would be a good experience for your girls, and the Shipibos always like prospective customers. They're famous for their beads and pottery. The village is named San Francisco. Your kids will get a better idea of what jungle living is really like than they get from the base."

"What else is unique about the Shipibos?" Jim asked.

"They have an extensive folklore," Lucy said. "Jim Loriot translated the miracle of Jesus casting the demons from a man and sending them into a herd of hogs that ran into the Sea of Galilee and drowned. When the Shipibos heard this they said, 'Now we know where dolphins come from.' They believe the dolphins in Lake Yarinacocha are water demons."

My husband yawned inadvertently. "Thanks, Lucy and Norma," he said. "But it must be getting late."

"He means it's near his bedtime," I said.

"Mine too," agreed Cal. "And I know these gals have had a long day."

At only ten p.m. I was just coming awake. But since everyone stood up to go, I followed suit.

When we reached home we checked the children. "Puppy" was in bed with Celia. Jim wanted to put the animal out, but I said, "Oh, what's the use? He'll just stay outside and whine as he did last night. Why fight it? Let him stay."

The cold shower didn't make me any sleepier. I climbed into bed, put my cold feet on Jim, and said, "I wish we could stay longer. How are we going to see everybody we need to see in the next six weeks? Besides, I'd like to hang around and see how this Mayoruna thing comes out."

"We'll just pray that they make the big contact before we leave. Then we can get it into the book."

"Dear, the Lord doesn't run his time clock by our travel deadlines," I said sarcastically, snuggling up closer.

JIM: I had to agree with Marti. We had been in Peru only two weeks and were already staggered at the wealth of story possibilities. How does a person write about a quarter century of service in an area larger than Texas? "It isn't just the geography," I told her. "They're working in over thirty tribes and each is a story in itself. And look at the facets of ministry besides Bible translation in which they're involved: schools, medicine, agriculture, community development. Why, the Wycliffe people are doing here all that evangelicals in the States are criticized for not doing. They emphasize the vertical, man's relationship to God in Bible translation. And also the horizontal, man's relationship to man, in the various social ministries."

Marti nodded. "I've been thinking. We can't tell the whole story in every detail. Perhaps we can zero in on two or three tribes, then look for what's unique in the others."

"That might work," I agreed. "We've covered the Machiguengas pretty well. And we'll be flying out to the Aguarunas. I checked with Floyd Lyons and he promised a plane for early next month. I wish we could visit the Shapras, Chief Tariri's tribe. From the news coming into the base, they're having some real problems out there."

"Who are the workers?" Marti asked.

"I've been checking the files in the publicity office. Doris Cox and Lorrie Anderson started. They won Chief Tariri to the Lord. Doris is home on sick leave. Lorrie will be coming to the base next week. Beth Hinson, a nurse, will be back from furlough soon. John and Sheila Tuggy are out in the tribe and planning to stay awhile. I wish we could get a flight out there, but Floyd says that isn't likely. He'll accommodate us as much as he can, but with so much work over so wide an area, the planes stay tied up."

"I don't think we should criticize them for not dropping everything and flying us all over the jungle," Marti said.

"Certainly not," I replied. "In fact, I rather like the idea of being treated like their own. I'm skeptical of groups who try to put on a big show for journalists. I haven't felt anyone was trying to do that here."

"No. But everybody seems willing to cooperate."

"That's all we could ask."

"Who do you have on your list to see?" Marti asked.

"Translators—let's see. Lorrie Anderson when she comes in. Phyllis Manus this afternoon. Dan Velie, the public relations man, who is assigned to the Orejones. The Kindbergs, who work with the Campas, live just behind us. Others will be coming in."

Marti's eyes twinkled. "Have you been next door? Arlene Agnew is our neighbor. She works with Patsy Adams among the Culinas—the singing tribe that people have been telling us about."

"Okay, there's another one. Now have you thought of getting some sleep?"

I called Dan Velie the next morning. "Come over now," he said. "The Chilean ambassador is here with a group. Cal brought them over from Lima. I'll need to be with them this afternoon."

"What kinds of visitors do you have?" I asked.

"All kinds," he said. "You never know. A few undesirables, but mostly otherwise. University tour groups. TV crews. Archaeologists. Anthropologists. Just sent a couple of them down the lake to a Shipibo village. Tourists from the States, Europe, and other Latin American countries. Evangelical missionaries and church leaders from the States. Priests and nuns. Peruvian and foreign government officials."

"How do they hear about Yarina?"

"Our best booster in Lima is a lady named Rosa Corpancho. She knows everybody who is anybody and really talks up our work. Everybody likes Rosa. She's about the best friend we have in Peru. She not only urges important people to come visit us, but she also offers to escort them. She came with the Chilean ambassador's party.

"Then various embassies in Lima send people out. And some drive over the Andes and keep coming until they reach the end of the road. That's almost us. Tournavista is about forty miles further south."

"That's the operation of R. G. LeTourneau, the big machine builder?"

"Yes. He worked out a deal with the Peruvian government to clear and develop several thousand acres of land. Uncle Cam, I think, had something to do with it.

"We keep the red carpet out for Peruvian officials. President Belaunde was here while he was in office. Our kids sang the Peruvian anthem for him. Senators Birch Bayh and Fred Harris were here from the States. The Cat took them and their wives out to Shapra land. Bill Nyman had my job then."

"Our biggest weekend for visitors is at graduation time for the Indian School. You should have been here for the last one. The Minister of Education, a member of the new ruling military junta, came and spoke."

"What'd he say that was significant?"

"He tore up the speech he had planned to give and said he wanted to speak to us from his heart. He really gave the work a boost. Then, he mentioned the troubles between the United States and Peru. But he said, 'Please don't think of leaving. You're just the kind of North Americans we want to work with us.' "

"That's tremendous! What are the visitors most interested in?"

"The teacher training program. The occupational courses. Then we tell them the work isn't complete from our viewpoint unless spiritual needs are met."

"You talk about Bible translation to government officials?"

"Certainly. And to anyone else. We tell them how the Bible helps the Indians. Chief Tariri's testimony is always of interest. When he goes to Lima, he's quite a celebrity."

"What type of response do you get in a spiritual discussion?"

"This varies. A priest who was here recently said his opinion of us and his whole outlook on life had changed. The ambassador from Chile asked if we tried to push our belief on the Indians. I said we just shared what Scripture said about Creation, God's Love, life after death, etc. He seemed to appreciate that. He said he was going to talk to his president about inviting us down to make a survey of a couple of tribes in Chile. That's how God opens doors."

"We want to be hospitable," Dan continued, "and that's why I'm here. We want everybody to know what we're doing, especially government officials. It wouldn't pay to try to do things underhandedly, even if it's related to spiritual work. That's one reason why every government in Peru for the past twenty-three years has backed us. They know what we're doing all the time."

"Tell me about your tribe, the Orejones."

"I can tell you that Virginia and I need to be out there right now. But somebody has to do this job. Know a public relations man who'd like to come to Peru?"

I shook my head. "When did you and Virginia go to the Orejones?"

"In 1958. Bob and Ruth Sandberg worked with them for five years. Bob got sick and couldn't stay. We took their place. The word Orejone means 'big ears.' They've long been famous for the big disc ear plugs up to four inches in diameter the men wore. I've never found out why they wore them, except they call the full moon, 'God's earplug.' You seldom see anyone wearing the plugs now."

Dan walked over and stood by a wall map. "The Orejones are up in the northeast on the Napo River, just a few miles off the Amazon. When the Sandbergs moved into the area, only about 175–250 remained. The rubber hunters had done a lot of damage. Spread disease. Took the men off to work camps. In one section of the tribe today there are several defective children from close intermarriages.

"The Sandbergs first made friends with the Orejones by trading fish hooks. But they had trouble getting a language helper. A landowner in the area had control of them and wouldn't let the Indians help. They finally got a couple to come out to the base with them. The Orejone language is very difficult. We found two contrasting levels of tone. For instance, *ma* with a high tone means parrot, while *ma* with a low tone means trail.

"When we brought a language helper into the base, rumors were spread up and down the river that the American linguists were stealing and killing Indians and rendering up their fat to make oil for airplanes. They said this had happened to my informant, Daniel, when I brought him to the base. The superstitious Orejones believed this and even mourned for him. They were some surprised people when they saw the 'dead' man sitting with us in a boat as it came around a bend in the river.

"Later when we were leaving for our first furlough, Daniel said, 'I'll be dead when you return next year.' I didn't think anything of this. Indian societies are full of superstition and fears of death. I tried to encourage him. 'You're young and healthy,' I said, 'and even if you do die we can meet again in that wonderful place where Jesus is.'

"But when we returned he was dead. He had been bitten by a poisonous snake and lived four days. If I had been there, I might have saved him. If I had only been there."

"How did things go after that?" I asked.

"We got a couple of new language helpers. The landowner was still applying pressures, but he knew better than to harm us. The word gets around that we're in with the federal government. One of the two new men, Romero, became the first definite believer and also the first bilingual school teacher.

"Oh, and another of our young men has attended the Swiss Bible School to become a pastor. You been there yet? No? Well, you should."

Dan continued on that train of thought. "I'll tell you a little about it. In our contract with the government we have declared ourselves to be non-sectarian and non-ecclesiastic. We can translate the Bible, practice our own faith as individuals, and encourage the believers. But training pastors would be beyond our scope of work. So a Swiss group has started a Bible school close by. They train Indian pastors. Wonderful folks, those European missionaries. They send couples out to work in the tribal languages."

"We'll have to visit them," I said. "How are you coming with Bible translation?"

"We have Mark and are working on Acts."

"Could you give me an illustration of a cultural problem you encountered in translating for the Orejones?"

"There are lots of interesting words. A courageous or valiant man has a 'solid' heart. A kind and thoughtful man has a 'soft' heart. The heart is the center of emotion for the Orejones, whereas for other tribes it may be the liver or stomach. Our word for Lord and Lordship is 'the one who owns us.' This, of course, comes from their experience of being owned—that is, being kept in perpetual debt—by traders and big landowners."

I thanked Dan and stood up to leave. He pushed a piece of paper toward me. "Read this prayer which Josias, one of my informants, wrote:

Lord, you see us and know our work. You have given us this work to do for you. Help us in it. Give us more faith to do good works for you. Before, I didn't know your Word. Now recently I have heard and received it. Daniel [the translator] is teaching me your Word. Help us to have better memories and learn it rapidly and do this work rapidly, so that our fellow countrymen, our own people will hear and know. Thank you, Lord, because we now know.

"Beautiful," I said. Then I left to see Phyllis Manus.

"I know my house is a mess," the attractive mother of three said, as she stuffed pajamas into a suitcase. "We're trying to be ready for a flight in the morning."

Phyllis explained that her husband, Ron, had already left for the Urarina tribe about three hundred miles due north of the base. "We're both Inter-Varsity kids," she said. "We were at the Urbana Missionary Conference in 1951 and attended linguistic sessions. We came to Peru in 1959."

When I asked about the history of the Urarinas, she said, "I'll have to talk as I pack. Seems as if we do everything on the run. About our people. They were first called Shimacus by outsiders, a name that meant lazy, uncivilized robbers. Some missionary priests came through about 1700 and began calling them Urarinas, after the name of a plant that was the mainstay of their diet. Like most other jungle tribes, they have suffered from white traders and landowners. The worst came about twelve years ago when an epidemic of measles and flu cut the population from 5,000 to 1,000."

"Repeat those figures, please," I asked.

"You heard me right. About four out of five died. They're back up to 1,500 now."

"How did you find them?"

"Discouraged, demoralized. Maybe disintegrated is the best word. Debt slaves to the white landowners who told them what work to do and where to live. The whites had told them they couldn't have chiefs any more. They put the last Urarina chief in jail where he died from the flu. They didn't give us much of a welcome. They were hostile, but not outwardly aggressive. Just sort of withdrawn. Help me move this box, would you please?"

We moved the crate and I waited for Phyllis to continue.

"When we got there, the patrons were paying one shotgun shell, worth about ten cents, for a day's work. Ron had to pay up the family debt of our first language helper."

"How about their religion?"

"Their traditions were about gone. Except they did drink *ayahuasca*, a kind of hallucinatory drug made from an herb. It's something like LSD. It gives them visions which they believe help them make contact with God. They had a few witch doctors. Ron helped a sick one get well. He then began calling Ron 'younger brother' which helped gain their trust.

"They live in big houses, typically thirty or forty people in extended family groups. The land is very swampy with only bits of high ground near the rivers to cultivate. It's the malarial center of Peru."

"Has any of your family had malaria?"

She shrugged. "We've all had it except the baby."

"Is the language difficult?"

"Yes. One reason is that we've been unable to place it in a language group with any other language in South America. It's a different sort of tone language in that the tone runs over a whole phrase. For example, 'Look at the cat' and 'Look at the bananas' is spelled orthographically the same way and the tone is on the verb. But with 'Look at the cat' the tone stress is on the first syllable, while 'Look at the bananas' has the stress on the second syllable. Depending on what noun you use, the tone placement on the verb changes."

"How are you doing with translation?"

"Ron just got his grammar analysis approved. He's done a little bit of translation here and there. But we're ready now to move ahead. We've been trying to get a bilingual school going, too. But the landowners don't want it. We've received some threats."

"Really?"

"Oh, yes. They know that if the Urarinas get educated and become economically self-sufficient, they'll be out from under their thumbs. When we left for our last furlough, they told the Indians we wouldn't be back."

"Are you and Ron trying to help them become self-sufficient?"

"We do what we can. Ron is trying to help them get land titles. A

Christian man in Ohio gave us money to buy four cows and a bull. Ron has taken out some Japanese farm machinery to use in their rice fields. But it's very slow. After the way they've been mistreated, so many have just lost the desire to work.

"But we're not giving up. A few have learned to read and write. A few have become believers. We expect to have a school soon and more Scripture translated."

"They must learn pride and dignity," I volunteered.

The young mother stuffed a child's doll and a flashlight into a duffel bag. "Exactly. Before they can take their place in society, they've got to become a people."

Marti wasn't home so I strayed across to the Snells. Wayne and Victorino, his Machiguenga language helper, were busy at a work table piled with books and manuscripts.

"We're about to stop for a break," Wayne said. "Stay for some coffee."

Betty brought us steaming mugs. "What are you doing now?" I asked.

"I'm on the third recheck of Acts. Betty reads it and underlines what she doesn't understand or what she thinks can be said better."

"Any special problems?"

"The geography and all the proper names cause difficulty. There's no specific Machiguenga word for city. A 'place' can be a city, a river, or a country."

"How do you handle, say, Corinth?"

"We name the place and say it's where a lot of houses are grouped together. We call the temple God's house. The synagogue is the place where the Jews gather together repeatedly."

I ventured a sip of the coffee. "Well, obviously you don't translate literally word for word. How do you define inspiration, then?"

Wayne tapped the table with his pencil. "I'm a strong believer in verbal inspiration of the Scriptures. I define this as God inspiring the original, not the translations which we have today. That which God verbally inspired was for given cultures at given times. He communicated to the writers what he wanted them to say. Now it's my job to take and put that same sense into the Machiguenga language and culture."

"Will other people besides Betty and your Indian language helpers check your material before publication?"

"We have a translation checking committee. Betty and I give it back to them in English and they question particular words or phrases. Then we translators check one another's work. We all appreciate one another's help. We're in this together to get the best translations to the tribes as soon as possible."

MARTI: The following Saturday morning dawned bright and shiny. Our girls were all excited because this was the day we were to visit the Shipibo Indian village, San Francisco.

Their friend Rachel del Aguila came over early; she was to accompany us.

"What do you think of my beads?" I asked Rachel, referring to the triple strand of red, white and blue plastic beads I had roped around my neck. "Will the Shipibos like them?"

"Oh, they really will," she gushed, her brown eyes rounding in wonder. "I'll bet they'll want to trade."

"That was my thought, too. Maybe I can make a good deal for them." She smiled indulgently and the four girls started out the door.

Jim and I caught up with them in a minute.

"What's this excursion costing us, anyway?" I asked him.

"We get the use of the boatman and boat for the whole morning for the grand total of $2.75," he answered.

As we were passing the administrative office, Bob Mickelson stuck his head out and called, "Hey, Hefleys, your man is going to be a little late. About half an hour."

"Okay," Jim said. "We'll stop by the post office and read the news bulletins, and see who's around," I said.

"Good," said Celia. "I'll get to see my Puppy."

"He's *not your* Puppy," snapped Cyndi. "We love him, too."

They raced on ahead to maul poor Puppy, who seemed to love the attention. The Spanish-speaking maids had named him "Puppy" much as we might name a dog *"Perrito."*

Jim checked our mail box while I read the bulletins posted near the door.

The Mayoruna Advance is moving right along now. Last Sunday afternoon five men were spotted. Then another day, eleven men, and on Thursday, fifteen were counted, and one woman and a dog. The basket drops have been made and were well received, but so far the Indians have not talked back to them. They all seem friendly, and do not seem to be afraid. Ted Long is returning to base next week.

Sheila Tuggy came back from the Shapras last Friday with Junie, who had broken her arm. The only float plane available was all apart for inspection, but ready to be put back together again. All hands rallied to the job and by ten o'clock Tom Brewington flew off to bring them in.

Then Sheila had some more excitement on the base. While she and Junie were sleeping some men broke into the house and stole their record player. They also took their scooter, but it was ditched near the farm. They evidently thought the house was empty.

Jim Hefley, the author, will be our speaker in the Sunday morning services.

"Hey, I didn't know you were on tomorrow," I said indignantly. "Why didn't you tell me?"

"Oh, didn't I?" he mumbled while looking over my head at the news sheet. "I'm sorry," he said, insincerely.

We strolled on down to the swimming ramp where our guide was to meet us. Pretty soon we heard the pecky-pecky sound of his motor.

The Hefley girls visit a Shipibo village. (*l to r:* Marti, Cheri, Cyndi, Celia. Behind Cheri is friend Rachel del Aguila, whose father is a Peruvian member of Wycliffe.)

We climbed into the small launch; it wasn't the world's cleanest, and it leaked enough to make me glad we would be following the shoreline and not crossing the lake.

We could see an occasional thatched roof house along the lakeshore. The kids played their traveling game—counting the different animals they saw. There were three or four cows, lots and lots of ducks, etc. I just kept hoping we wouldn't see anything too exciting like alligators. But dolphins would be okay.

Our boatman finally pulled up on a low flat spot and we clambered out. We followed single-file behind Rachel, who had been there many times, along the narrow Indian path through a meadow. Jim brought up the rear with his camera and tape recorder.

After about a half a mile, we had to climb a steep embankment. At the top we saw the two rows of houses.

"But, Mommy," Cheri exclaimed, "these aren't real houses at all, only tops."

"Well, you see Cheri, it's so warm here they don't need walls to keep out the cold winds," I explained.

"Yeah, but what keeps out the wild animals?" our little philosopher wanted to know.

I grasped for some kind of satisfactory answer. "The dogs," I said. "The dogs scare away most of the wild creatures, and at least warn the Indians if something is coming."

She looked around at the mangy-looking dogs. I guess she decided they looked bad enough to scare most anything away.

"Mommy, Daddy," the older ones were calling. "Look! They have some things they want to sell. Let's buy something."

If there's anything my kids like to do, it's buy. Anything!

Then two Indian ladies noticed my long rope of beads. They fingered them yearningly, chattering the whole time. Other women came over to see what was going on. They kept coming and coming; I was surprised there were that many women in the small village.

"They want to trade," smiled Rachel. "I told you they would."

"Obviously," I answered.

One woman held up three of her necklaces and made gestures which meant, "I'll give you three of mine for your one."

I shook my head and said, "No."

Then they all started offering me more and more things and arguing among themselves. I decided it would be best if I didn't trade—I didn't want to start a tribal war.

They got the idea. One older woman stayed, though, and looked and looked at them. Touched them. Counted them. She said something to me in Shipibo. I can't explain how, but I knew she meant that the beads were long enough to double them around my neck if I wanted to and they would still fit fine. Mental telepathy? I don't know, but I've had this experience several times with different Indians. Perhaps it is just their expressiveness.

We scuffed along through the little village. Jim took pictures of everything that moved, and some things that didn't. The Shipibo children followed along behind us, and the dogs and a few scrawny chickens.

"Oh, Mother, look!" squealed sharp-eyed Celia. She was pointing inside a hut. There, hanging from a rafter, were three tooth brushes. Did they ever look out of place!

"Something tells me Wycliffe people have been here," I commented.

"Yes," Rachel said, knowingly. "Whenever we have a dentist on the base they work on the Indians' teeth, too. They probably gave them the brushes."

As we neared the end of the village and turned to retrace our steps, I asked the girls, "How would you like to stay and eat with the Indians?"

"But we didn't bring a lunch," Cyndi answered.

"Oh, I mean eat with them, what they eat, and with whatever dishes they have. And how about staying the night, sleeping on the ground?"

They looked quite thoughtful and a little squeamish. Finally Cheri answered. "Mommy, it's all right if you and Daddy go visit tribes without us. We'll stay at the base with our friends and eat in the dining hall."

The others agreed.

Our trip had served a purpose. The idea of visiting primitive places and living in the jungle under the conditions of the Indians had been robbed of its glamor.

We saw a man carving arrows, so we moved over to watch. He looked up and smiled. I noticed that he had his cap pulled down to his eyebrows, and remembered what Lucy and Norma had told us about their flattened foreheads.

He wanted to sell some of his things, so we bought a few bows and arrows. When we pulled out our money, the women reappeared and we bought some bracelets, necklaces, and feather flowers from them. Rachel knew how much we should pay and the Indians seemed glad that we had boosted the economy of their village.

"Let's go down to the other end of the village and see their church and school building," I suggested.

"Aw, Mom, we've seen enough," Cyndi said. "Anyway, it's getting hot."

"Yeah," chorused the other two. It's Saturday and they're having hamburgers!"

"And the soccer games will be starting," added Rachel.

We started down the trail, this time in Indian fashion, with the man going first. Cheri was slow so Jim beat us to the boat by a couple of minutes. When we got there, a tall, bearded young man who looked like an overgrown Eagle Scout was speaking to Jim in halting Spanish. Jim kept saying, "*Qué?*" (What?) Rachel and I looked at each other and laughed. Jim and the bearded man evidently each thought the other spoke only Spanish, but obviously knew very little themselves.

"Try English," I called to the stranger.

We were having a good laugh together when his friend came out of the bush.

"We're down here studying anthropology," explained Pete, the first young man. "We need a ride to the next village, but the boatman says he's not for hire."

"We've hired him for the morning," Jim said, "but you're welcome to ride back with us to Yarinacocha."

"Great!" they exclaimed. "We were beginning to think we'd never get there."

The personable Americans were graduate students and had some very definite ideas about missionaries who come to ruin the "paradise" of the Indians. Jim told them some of the cruel customs, terrible living conditions, superstitions and fears these Indians had in their paradise.

"We don't know about all missionaries," he continued, "but we've been around these linguists long enough to know that they are bringing hope, health, education, and a sense of personal worth to Indians who have been exploited by the white man for generations."

"But they're changing their customs," responded our nameless friend.

"They're preparing them for advancing civilization," Jim countered, "and helping them become worthwhile, contributing citizens of their country."

Before the discussion could get any more heated, I started teasing them. "The trouble with you guys is that you're just afraid there won't be anyone left for you to study."

They chuckled and agreed. "I guess we do have a rather romantic notion about Indian life," Pete confessed.

"The difference between you anthropologists and these linguists is that you just come to study primitive peoples, but they are here to help them," I pointed out.

We had arrived at our destination and the youths offered to pay us for their ride. Jim said, "No, indeed. It didn't cost us any more."

When they started to insist, I suggested, "If you'd like, you could tip the guide."

The Indian seemed to understand what we were discussing, and grinned as Pete walked toward him.

"It's been stimulating talking with you," Jim said as we started off in different directions. "If you get a chance, stop by the base and see just what is being done for these Indians. It might give you something different to say in your theses."

8.

Uncle Cam's "Bears"

JIM: It was Sunday morning. The red bougainvillea, fresh from another midnight thunderstorm, fairly sparkled in the sunshine. On my way to speak for the morning worship service, I caught up with Stu Shepherd, our new neighbor, lately arrived from Great Britain with his family. His wife was staying home with a sick child.

I wondered what Stu's impressions of the work were as a newly-arrived JAARS mechanic.

"Uncle Cam had some great ideas, didn't he? The blokes at the hangar credit him with every big advance that's been made. Operating a jungle airline. Training school teachers at government expense. Building strong Indian communities."

"But he didn't do all this himself. He got other people started."

"Righto, that's his secret."

I snapped my fingers. "Stu, I've got a joke with a point for this morning."

Stu looked puzzled but didn't ask me to explain. They were singing as we entered. I left Stu and walked to the front bench.

After I was introduced, I voiced our thanks for the hospitality and help we were receiving. "We're amazed at the scope of ideas Uncle Cam planted and you are harvesting," I added. "Which reminds me of a story:

"A Texan went to Alaska for some bear hunting. His Alaskan partners wondered why he had no rifle. 'I get 'em with my bare hands,' he said.

"His friends took a gun along for him anyway, but they had hardly put down their gear in a wilderness cabin when Tex bolted out the door. 'Come back, Tex! A grizzly will get you,' they pleaded to no avail.

"Nothing was heard from Tex until about an hour later. Then they heard a cry from the woods. 'Open the door, boys! Open the door!' Two steps behind Tex was a huge grizzly.

"The Alaskans threw the cabin door wide open and held their breath. But just as Tex reached the door, he stepped aside. The panting bear rushed inside. Tex whirled around and yelled, 'You skin that 'un. I'm goin' back after another.' "

When the people stopped laughing, I said, "Tex reminds me of Uncle Cam and all the bears he left for you to skin."

The crowd exploded.

At the end of the service, several men crowded around me, not to

82

comment about my message from Colossians 3, but to talk about bears. "You hit the nail on the head," a small intense man said. "I'm John Mishler, superintendent of JAARS." Cal Hibbard was also among the group. "That's Uncle Cam. He's tremendous at dreaming up plans for other people to carry through." And Walter del Aguila, the Peruvian who served in Indian education, said, "The Indian School is one of those bears that we're still trying to skin."

Sunday evening there was special prayer for the Mayoruna girls. Ted Long had flown over again and dropped another basket with a transmitter under the false bottom and gifts. The men on the ground waved the gifts from the last drop; one had made himself a pair of shorts from the parachute. Harriet Fields was shouting in Mayoruna through the wing speaker, "We're friends. Bring skins to the big river and trade."

"But the Indians haven't shown," Rol told the congregation. "It's frustrating for the girls to wait out there knowing the Indians are only about fifteen miles away. So maybe you can understand this request. They'd like some male volunteers to come and cut a trail to a small stream about halfway to the village. If anyone is interested, see me."

After the prayer, Marti whispered, "Where's the grand rush?"

Rol ended with a little speech about patriotism. "Tomorrow's the Peruvian Independence Day. Be sure to congratulate your Peruvian friends and fly the Peruvian flag. And don't miss the lantern parade and the fireworks at the lake tomorrow night."

"We don't have a flag," I whispered to Marti.

"Oh, yes, we have," she replied. "I bought one at the commissary yesterday."

So we flew the Peruvian flag on their Independence Day.

Over at the soccer field the students from the Indian School enjoyed a grand program of games. Besides soccer, there were centipede races, three-legged races, sack races, and frog hops. The gringo spectators laughed until tears came in some eyes. Once Cal Hibbard pointed to two Indians hopping side by side and said, "That's the new generation of jungle Indians. The men in their tribes used to raid back and forth. Today they'll play and eat together and tonight they'll sleep in the same dormitory."

After the games, we went to the Borthwicks' for a feast with the summer kids. The Borthwicks' two older sons were there, home from Florida State and talking in a buttery drawl that made them sound not at all like their Canadian parents. Heather and Brent, their "second family," and Celia and Cheri formed a friendly foursome. Vera outdid herself; the table reminded me of homecoming at a country church in Arkansas.

Ralph, usually quiet, was in a talkative mood. The kids sat around goggle-eyed while he shared some of his experiences.

"There was this rainstorm that I couldn't avoid. Right in the middle of it, my engine quit. I couldn't see anything; was losing altitude at a thousand feet a minute. Rol Rich, beside me, was pale and praying. I was praying, 'Lord, if you've got something else for me to do, please show me how to get the engine started.' Just then we broke through the clouds about a thousand feet above some little six- to seven-hundred-foot hills. The thought came, 'Turn on the carburetor heat.' I didn't think it would work, but I tried it anyway and the engine sprang to beautiful life. Just as I pulled up we saw a magnificent rainbow."

Ralph had also helped establish contact with tribes in Colombia and Bolivia. "Some of those tribes were pretty savage. You never knew whether they would be friend or foe. Once in Colombia I circled about a hundred and fifty feet over a village. The Indians were stark naked. That didn't bother me; we're used to naked Indians. Suddenly they began shooting arrows. We dropped some gifts anyway."

He started talking about boas. "Bolivia has some big ones. One time I almost hit one, maybe twenty feet long, with a float. And a ten-foot alligator received a very sore back from one of my landings."

"How big do the boas get, Uncle Ralph?" one of the boys asked.

"Some Indians in Bolivia gave me a skin twenty-eight feet long— without a head—and four and a half feet wide. Sorry we don't have it here, but downstairs there's a little skin about fourteen feet long which we can show you."

Vera broke in. "We used the big skin for missionary conferences back home. Spread it over the pews."

At seven o'clock we were all over at the swimming ramp: gringos, neighboring Peruvians, and the Indian students. Three gringos carried a supply of skyrockets (paid for from the public relations fund) in a canoe to the diving raft about 100 yards out in the lake.

A gorgeous full moon dispelled the gloom of a thin fog over the lake. The crowd, gringos included, sang the Peruvian national anthem and shouted, "Viva Perú! Viva Perú!"

After the remains of the last rocket fizzled into the lake, we ran with the crowd to the soccer field. In a few minutes we heard the drums and the marching feet. It was the traditional Parade of Lanterns put on by the villagers from neighboring Puerto Callao. Young and old with candles bobbing within large gaily colored crepe paper fish, birds, animals, stars, planes, and other objects, they marched round and round the soccer field.

After six or eight trips around, the marchers trooped away after their lead drummer in a circular route that took them through the base. Tradition called for marchers to give their lanterns to children and friends when the parade was over. Cyndi got a paper star, Cheri a jet plane and Celia a house. That night they went to bed deeply impressed with Peruvian generosity and patriotism.

Wednesday morning we hurried over to the Indian School's administration building to watch the students salute the flag. Walt del Aguila already had about sixty young Indians running through exercise drills beside the flagpole. About one-third were barefoot wives, holding babies. Most of the Indian men wore sandals.

Several men slouched when he called them to attention for the flag raising. "Don't stand like bandits," he shouted in Spanish. "Stand like this"—and he squared himself away—"like a Peruvian citizen." When the shoulders were straight he led out in the national anthem and the flag began rising.

"Keep in mind," he said, as he walked with us to his office, "that five years ago most of these fellows hardly knew they lived in a country named Peru. The formation and flag-raising comes first thing in the morning at every bilingual school. And after that, Bible study."

"Another reason the Peruvian government backs this work," Marti volunteered. "You're teaching patriotism and citizenship."

"We try. The goal is to help each Indian become a full participant in Peruvian society."

"We hear you were born and raised in the jungle," Marti said.

"I grew up in a little river town just south of Aguaruna country. My family was influenced by evangelical missionaries who encouraged me to become a teacher. I walked ten days through the mountains to catch a truck for the five-day trip to Lima. Then I got my bachelor's and master's degrees in the States. I met Beverly, my wife, at the Summer Institute of Linguistics in Norman, Oklahoma."

"Are you the only Peruvian member of Wycliffe?" I asked.

"Gerhard Fast was the first, and Esther Morales, one of our Peruvian employees at the base, wants to study linguistics and become a member.

"I think my Peruvian citizenship helps the program. The director and the faculty of the Indian School are employees of the Ministry of Education and are Peruvians. I can be one with them, while also identifying with my gringo colleagues whom I represent. I can be a bridge and help each group understand the other. Have you met Professor Tapia, the school's director? He eats in the dining hall every day."

"I was introduced to him," I remembered.

"Well, you'll see him again," Walt assured us. "Now what questions do you have for me?"

"Give us a rundown on the courses," I requested.

"The big one is the teacher training that runs from January 15 through March—ten weeks. The Cat flies most of the teachers and their families in. Population around here increases by more than 250 when they come."

"What do they study?"

"Basically, primary education, plus Spanish, and teaching methods. The teachers, themselves, get the grade school education they will pass on to their pupils out in the villages the following year. They come back every year until they complete what is equivalent to eight grades in the States. We started in 1953 with sixteen candidates, none of whom had any previous schooling. Now we are accepting only about twenty new candidates each year and they come to us with two or three years of education."

"From the bilingual schools in their villages?"

"Yes. You probably want some totals. Last term there were 256 Indian teachers working in 154 schools. About 100 are from the large Aguaruna tribe where we've had the greatest success. About half of the 256 have completed primary education, grade school. Most of these are going to high school. Three have graduated and one has almost finished university."

"Where is the high school?"

"In Pucallpa. It's only summer school. The students receive their regular teachers' pay while attending, then return to their tribes and teach the rest of the year. This shows the importance which the government places on the program.

"Look, let me give you three big contributions Indian bilingual education is making. (1) It gives tribal people identity as members of society. (2) Government recognition gives prestige to use of the native language and encourages people not to discard it. (3) It provides readers for Scripture and other valuable materials such as health books in the Indian language."

Walt glanced at his watch. "Perhaps I should tell you about our other two courses. From June 15 to October 15, we have the occupational course. You saw these students at the flag raising this morning. Here's what we have now: agriculture, 12; commercial—that's the merchandising course—9; mechanics, 6; carpentry, 9; home education, 17. Fifty-three in all. The last group, home education, includes the wives. They learn sewing, cooking, child care. If you have time, we'll look in on some of the men students.

"We have one other course: extension. For a couple of months each year we take our whole occupational staff and move into a tribal location. We don't teach the entire community, but a few who are interested from several surrounding communities. For each specialty, we concentrate on a specific project. Vic Halterman and the community development department get in on this."

Marti requested a "for instance."

"Last year our Aguaruna students built a carpentry shop, a small saw-mill, and started a cattle project. When you go to the farm, ask Vic and Herb to tell you about the cattle.

Walt checked the time. "Let's go see what the students are doing now."

We followed him along a path to the mechanic shop where three students were taking apart small motors. One saw us and grinned—Eduardo the Machiguenga, our friend from the Cat trip, I remembered.

"These are all pecky-peckys," Walt pointed out. "They take them apart, then put them back together and try them out in the lake. Sometimes we set up problems, such as throwing the carburetor out of adjustment."

I looked at the tools. "They could work faster with power tools."

Walt shook his head. "It's better for them to use only basic hand tools that they can have back in the tribes."

We moved on to the carpenter shop where an Aguaruna and a Huambisa were making a wooden locker. "Their tribes are supposed to be blood enemies," Walt said. "But you'd never know it by watching them work. The gospel brings people together."

"Does the Ministry of Education pay for the tools they take back?" Marti asked.

"No. World Neighbors has provided us with a revolving loan fund. A man borrows about $100, the cost of a basic kit, and pays it back as he earns from his trade. They have a very good payback record."

Walt showed us a display chart of sixteen types of jungle wood, including mahogany, cedar, and an extremely hard wood called *pumaquiro* which he insisted was too tough for termites. "We try to help the Indians find and use wisely the resources of the jungle," Walt said. "With game decreasing and colonists moving in this direction, we have no time to lose."

"You haven't said anything about the training of health workers," Marti observed.

"That's the clinic's department. See Dr. Swanson and Joan Lemke."

"Just now we have a date with the boys at the farm," I said. "We'll get the medics later. Thanks for your help, Walt."

Herb Fuqua waved howdy as we approached along the road that leads to the farm's saddle-shaped warehouse and office building. We had met Herb at church so we weren't strangers. Herb was eager to show us around. He pointed out a Peruvian agriculture teacher huddled with a group of Indian students in the shade of a brooder house. "He's teaching them how to take care of chickens back in their tribes. The Indian women to the right are learning how to graft fruit trees. We have orange, grapefruit, lemon, tangerine, mango, and some that Joe Hocking hasn't named yet. You know Joe?"

"Is he one of your people?" Marti asked.

"He isn't a member. He's kind of an institution here in the jungle— a Brethren missionary who's been around over 40 years. Raises chickens. Supplies eggs for the base. Quite an agriculturist. Joe really knows fruit trees. He's responsible for practically all the fruit trees around the base and in many parts of the jungle."

"He sounds like an interesting character. We'll have to look him up," I said.

"But what does farming have to do with Bible translation?" Marti asked.

Herb looked thoughtful as he framed his reply. "You see, we started here with just translators. Then we had to have planes to move the translators around. But what good was a New Testament without readers? So we got into schools and adult literacy. Follow me? Then the schools brought these Indian nomads into villages which created both health and food problems. So what good was Scripture if the people died from disease or starved to death?"

"But isn't the jungle full of food resources?" I asked.

Herb shook his head. "Wild game has become so scarce that the gov-

Right: Wycliffe members train Indian tribesmen at the base. Here Walt del Aguila makes a point about house building. (Don Hesse photo)

Above: Students learn how to graft. (Don Hesse photo)

Above: Herb Fuqua's class in calf tying. *Left:* Jungle mechanics course. A Peace Corpsman gives pointers. (Don Hesse photos)

The wives of teacher trainees go to school too. (Omar Bondurant photo)

Indians staff their own library at Yarina. (Leo Lance photo)

Ticuna sawmill. Better than using stone axes. (Ralph Borthwick photo)

ernment has established refuges in some areas. How many wild monkeys have you seen around the base?"

We had seen none.

"Folks say they were all around twenty years ago. Other animals, too. Traders have sold guns to the Indians which makes killing game easier. There's a big market for hides. And every week a plane flies a load of birds, monkeys, and what-have-you from Iquitos to Miami. Now add a scarcity of game to the limitation of hunting territory when the Indians move closer together so their children can attend school."

"You have a food shortage," Marti said.

"Right. And that's where we come in. But we have more in mind than keeping Indians alive," Herb emphasized. "We want to promote their prosperity and health and sustain their dignity as civilization moves in around them. We've got to help them get out of debt and develop some marketable products."

By this time, Vic Halterman, nifty in jeans and checkered shirt, had joined us. He drew a triangle in the dirt with a scuffed black boot. "Our program is planned around a triangular foundation. Instruction here at the base. Extension work in the tribe and then supply."

I looked at Herb. "How are you organized to get this job done?"

"I'm head of the program which includes the farm here and the work

Happy students
examine their
diplomas.
(Don Hesse photo)

This Candoshi teacher
puts his learning into
action in his jungle
classroom. (Rister
Jenkins photo)

in the tribes. Vic is in charge of community development. Gary Satter-
thwaite is here from Colombia to learn the ropes. We have community
development couples in the three largest tribes: the Olsens with the
Aguarunas, the LeClairs with the Shipibos, the Riggles and the Schmidts
with the Campas."

"But what about the small tribes?" Marti asked.

Herb grinned. "We hope the linguists can handle them. Some are
doing a superb job. Take Lambert Anderson out with the Ticunas. He
and Doris went there when the main village, Cushillococha, was just a
bunch of primitive huts. Today Cushillococha is probably the most pro-
gressive Indian town in South America. Educators and government officials come from all over just to see it."

"Herb isn't stretching the story a bit," Vic said.

"Tell us about it," Marti requested.

The agriculturists needed no urging to tell the story of the model
village.

Lambert had arrived in 1953 just in time to save the chief who had
been bitten by a bushmaster snake. He found the Ticunas close to the
Stone Age—filing teeth to sharp points, worshiping objects, polygamous.
They had survived the rubber hunters and a smallpox epidemic and were
then living in scattered small clearings along the banks of the Amazon.
No real community existed.

The five-toned, six-voweled language was extremely difficult. It is
only one of three known languages in the world to have five significant
tones. For example, *Inangu* could mean "he arrives," "he falls," "he
weighs himself," or "he drowns himself," depending on the tone of voice
in which the vowels were spoken. It helped that Doris, who joined Lam
later, had had musical training.

As translation progressed and some of the Ticunas became believers,
Lam, a jack-of-all-trades, sparked comprehensive development programs.
Dr. Morote Best, a close friend of Uncle Cam's who was under assignment from the Ministry of Education, took a personal interest in the
Ticunas. They became the first Indian tribe in Peru to receive title to
their ancestral lands—3,885 acres on both sides of Lake Cushillococha
near the Amazon. With Lambert's help they planned their own village
on the lake, laying out roads, a plaza, a school site, a soccer field, and a
church. They elected community leaders. Their first mayor was Fernando, who, some years after having killed a relative in a drunken brawl,
became Lam's language helper, a believer, and the first pastor of the
Ticuna church.

The villagers planted a variety of crops, started a rubber plantation
with five hundred grafted trees given by the Agriculture Bank of Peru,
and voted to set aside each Monday as work day in lieu of community
taxes. In 1962 they received a new diesel light plant, wiring, and all
other necessary equipment for a fairly complete power system. A month
later Mayor Fernando switched on the first street lights ever seen in an
Amazonian Indian village.

"It's hard to believe what those Ticunas have done," Vic exulted. "They have a beautiful chapel, four one-room schools, a sawmill, a clinic, a grocery store, a bakery, and a barber shop. And they recently sent out their first missionary."

"You forgot the cattle, Vic," Herb reminded.

"Mustn't forget that. They're selling beef to outsiders who used to be their creditors."

"Haven't you placed cattle in other tribes, too?" I asked Herb.

"Our tally to date is 92 calves in 25 locations among 12 tribes. In addition 30 head have been purchased from other sources and added to the initial projects. In all but three locations, these were the first cattle in the villages. With new calves, there are now over 200 head in the tribes.

"We help the Indians with financing from the World Neighbors revolving fund. The purchasers pay all transportation costs. We like to send out four or five heifers and a bull to the same area. We give them a shot, hoist them into the Cat, and fly them out to the nearest landing spot. They are usually taken on by boat."

Herb looked at us soberly. "Two hundred head of cattle for an area larger than Texas may not sound like much. But bear in mind that nothing like this ever happened in the jungle before."

MARTI: Jim and I were turning into our front yard when we noticed Arlene Agnew trudging past loaded down with bundles. "Aunt Arlene," as our girls called her, was our next-door neighbor, a translator assigned to the Culinas. We had become friends during a shopping trip in Pucallpa.

"Let's help," suggested Jim, walking down the road toward her.

We helped her get all the stuff in her house. "How about a cold glass of lemonade as reward?" she asked. "I could certainly use one myself," she commented, wiping her wet brow with a Kleenex.

I voted yes, but Jim declined, explaining he wanted to get over to publicity and finish going through the "customs" file.

Arlene and I sipped lazy-lemonade and talked. "Arlene," I asked, "I've noticed you marching back and forth carrying bundles all week. What is all this stuff?" I motioned to the stacks and piles of boxes all over the dining area.

"I'm getting ready to go out to the tribe, and these are things I've requisitioned to take with me. I'm hoping for tons more."

"Tons? Literally?"

"Yes. We've had terrible flooding in our village this past year. The floods began three months earlier than usual, and took the fields of many of our people. So I'm asking the base to request government assistance. If something doesn't happen, we're going to have people starving to death before the next crop comes in."

"But isn't there someone to help you?"

"When translators are in the tribe, we just radio in for needed sup-

plies and the shipper here on the base gets our things together and down
to the hangar for shipment. But as long as we're here, we have to get all
this stuff for ourselves, box and tie and bag it in plastic and get it down
to the plane. There just isn't anyone with time to do it for us.

"That's all I've done this past week," she explained, refilling our
glasses. "Might as well drink this up, you see . . ."

"Mommy, Mommy, Mother!" called an insistent voice next door.

"Oh my," I said, embarrassed, "I didn't realize how well you could
hear us over here."

She laughed good-naturedly, "Oh, that's all right. They aren't too
noisy. Why don't you invite them over? They can finish this lemonade
for me."

I stepped out the front door and called the gals.

They arrived all chattering at once. Doyle Nystrom had given Celia
a new bug for her collection. "It's called a Mr. Peanut bug, because his
nose looks like a peanut," she gurgled, thrilled with her newest specimen.
"And look how big he is!"

"Yes, that's a good one, Celia. I'd say he's 3½ or 4 inches long,"
Arlene said. "Did you know they glow in the dark?"

"Like a firefly?" asked our "dimple girl," all curious.

"Yes, except instead of a greenish glow, they have a bluish one. I like
collecting jungle oddities myself. Would you like to see some of them?"

Cyndi and Celia were enthralled with the collections of butterflies
and things, but Cheri wasn't too interested.

"And over here I have a box of toys, if someone would rather play
with them." The "someone" immediately began pulling out blocks and
things.

"You certainly are good with kids," I remarked, as she served them
lemonade.

"I enjoy children," she smiled, "and I keep some things around for
their amusement. When teachers training school is in session, our men
bring their wives and children with them. So I have seven of them in
and out during that time."

"Doesn't that cut down on your translation time?"

"Yes. During the summer course this past year days started at 6 a.m.
and would go to 10 p.m. Besides helping the teachers with their homework at night, I'd have to go over all their lessons with them, because
their grasp of Spanish is quite poor; they misunderstand many things.

"Then all the children got sick, and naturally I had to take them to
the clinic, because the mothers couldn't explain to the doctor what the
problem was; they speak no Spanish. I spent three or four hours a day
sometimes at the clinic getting children x-rays, medicine, and other attention they needed, but I tried to keep the afternoons open for translation work."

"What percentage of your time do you get to devote to actual translation?"

Her discouragement showed in her face. "Before we had any students in the bilingual school system, I spent about 30 percent of my time, but this past year it's been way less than that."

"These other things do have to be done, though. Who else could do them?" I said, trying to reassure her.

Celia came over then and asked, "Where do you find all your bugs, Aunt Arlene?"

"Oh," she laughed, "if you like bugs, you should come visit my tribe. If there is one thing we have in abundance, it's bugs. The gnats and mosquitoes are so bad that most everyone wears long sleeves, despite the heat."

"Yuueeeeh, I don't want to visit your tribe," Cheri voiced her opinion with the undiplomatic frankness of childhood.

"It really isn't that bad!" Arlene protested. "I'll bet you'd like my tribe. They are the best musicians in the jungle. They are called the Singing Culinas."

"Really?" asked Cyndi, joining the discussion.

"Yes. They sing about everything. When the women think it's time for the men to go hunt some food, they sing this to their husbands. Then the men sing back, 'Okay, we're going hunting now.' They sing when they come back, and the women welcome them with song. It's like an operetta. And they sing well, too. They even use four-part harmony, though it isn't the same as ours. Besides that they have fiestas with lots of singing and dancing and story-telling."

My three girls were all round-eyed and attentive.

"Please tell us some more about them," Cyndi pleaded.

"Well, it's nearly time for supper. Why don't we walk toward the dining hall while I tell you?" she replied.

They gathered around her as we walked along. "You look like a pied-piper," I teased.

"This is nothing. Indians always walk in single file, so whenever I go anyplace on the base with them I have thirteen Indians lined up following me down the road. That is a little embarrassing," she admitted.

The girls giggled at the thought of it. "Why don't you march your Indians around so we can see them?" asked Cheri.

"They've all gone back to their homes now."

"Tell us some more about them," insisted Celia. "Tell us about their fiestas." Celia likes parties.

"Well, their fiestas are rather unusual. They make a special kind of drink in canoes. Whole canoes full. And they all try to drink the most."

"You mean they have drinking contests?" asked Cyndi.

"Not exactly. They try to drink lots so that they can win the contests. You see, the way to win the contest is to vomit the furthest."

"Oh, that's gross," exclaimed Cyndi. We agreed.

Arlene laughed. "Maybe I'd better not tell you any more about that just before we eat."

As we filed into the dining hall, I had to ask more about her tribe's singing.

"What did you mean when you told the kids that the Culina harmony was different from ours?"

"They use the five-note pentatonic scale. Patsy Adams, the nurse who is my partner, has written a booklet in Spanish about their music; it has some of their songs in it. I'll give you a copy if you'd like."

"Yes, I would. Do they like singing hymns, or have you written any for them?"

"Yes, our first term. The Culinas love music so much, it's half their lives; we figured this would be an excellent way to teach them the gospel. Then while we were on furlough the Culinas changed the patterns of the hymns to 'real music,' using their own arrangements. They are continually making up new ones. Their singing helped us a great deal in learning the language. The songs are repetitive, which gave our ears opportunity to adjust to the words."

"Do they play instruments too?" I wanted to know.

"Yes. They have flutes and musical bows."

Jim joined us just as the line began moving. "Daddy, wait 'til you hear what we've learned about Aunt Arlene's tribe," exclaimed Celia.

"Oh," he answered condescendingly. "I've been learning all about death customs. Some of them are really quite gruesome. One tribe grinds up the bones of dead relatives and makes a soup which they drink. Supposed to perpetuate the ancestral line."

"Not while we are eating," I pleaded.

After supper was over we began our leisurely stroll toward home. Halfway there we passed "Black Bart" and Buzz Sawyer, who were testing out walkie-talkies.

"What's up?" called Jim.

"The vigilantes have gone modern," Buzz called back.

"I really believe those two characters enjoy playing 'cops and robbers,' " Jim laughed.

"What's the matter, honey?" I teased. "Won't they let you play?"

The girls were walking just ahead of us, with Puppy following. We could still see Olive and Arlene further down the block.

"You know, I used to feel sorry for old maid missionaries," I mused.

"And now you don't?" asked Jim.

"No. For one thing, most of the single gals we've met are just not the stereotyped 'old maids.' But more than that I think it's that they all have so much purpose and meaning in their lives. They've devoted themselves to their tribes, as other women do to their families. And in return they have discovered true happiness through serving others and they have won love and respect. They are living such rich, full lives I just can't feel sorry for them."

"If you were an 'old maid' would you want to join them?"

"I really think I might." Then changing my mood, I teased, "Would you like me to be an old maid?"

"No," he responded. "I'm glad you're not." And he gave me a hug right there in the road.

9.

The New Medics

JIM: A few days later we talked with Beth Hinson, one of the first nurses to serve at the base. She told us about "Doc" Altig. "He ran the first water purification system," she said. "When rain threatened, he'd climb up and scrub off the dining room roof so we could catch pure water. And Doc was a stickler for disinfectants. It got so that Uncle Cam would see him and say, 'Doc, I just swallowed a bug. I'm afraid his feet weren't disinfected. What should I do?'

"After Dr. Eichenberger arrived and later Dr. Swanson, Doc Altig joined Uncle Cam and the new pioneers in Colombia. Dr. Eichenberger is now on extended leave, so we're down to one permanent doctor, Dr. Swanson, and an STA, Dr. Jerry Harrell."

I called for an appointment with Dr. Swanson. When I arrived he was with a patient.

While I waited, Phyllis Woodward, the clinic nurse, gave a rundown on the clinic's schedule. "Mornings we see Peruvian employees of the base, their families, and students from the Indian School. Afternoons we treat our members. Except for taking emergencies flown in from the tribe, we're strictly a base clinic. Dr. Swanson does make occasional trips to tribes for mass TB tests, vaccination campaigns, things like that."

Dr. Doug Swanson, stethoscope around his neck, strode into the room, introduced himself, and invited me into his office.

"Do you sometimes run into things down here that are unique?" I asked.

"Yes," he said. "Cases that we can't handle we send to Dr. Binder at Hospital Amazonico. This is a fine private hospital just a few miles from here that takes care of Indians in the area around Pucallpa.

"Our main purpose is to provide medical care for our members. But as we get involved with the Indians, we can't ignore their needs. We have a tribal medical training program for health promoters—*sanitarios* is the Spanish word."

"These *sanitarios*, are they Indians trained here at the base?"

"Yes. Joan Lemke does all the teaching. I help prepare teaching materials.

"Here's the health manual we use. It was originally written by Dr. Eichenberger and has been revised somewhat. The instructions are given in simple Spanish and illustrated by dosage. The *sanitario* can see how much is needed—one-fourth tablet, for example, in this illustration.

"Dr. Harrell and I also conduct occasional clinics out in the tribes to ward off epidemics. But we don't have the personnel to station medical workers in the jungle. Many of the linguist wives are also nurses, but they can't handle everything. So we train health promoters. Maybe you'd call this a compromise solution because their training is limited. It's better than nothing."

"Do the Indians have any good home-grown remedies?"

"Our linguists are doing some research in this area. The Shipibos have a tea made from a certain leaf that seems to help their arthritis, but doesn't cure it. They also make a medicine from the bark of a tree that is effective for worms, but it's also quite dangerous. Some of the tribes make a tea that is apparently an effective oral contraceptive."

"How about the witch doctors?"

"They prey on the superstitions of the people. Still, there may be value in some of their remedies; depending on what they use. I guess some of them look upon the health promoters as competitors."

I phrased my next question carefully. "What has been the greatest satisfaction in your work?"

He answered sooner than I anticipated. "Serving our personnel. Saving them valuable time and money by just being on the spot."

"The value of a linguist goes far beyond himself," I observed. "His knowledge of a language and a tribe goes with him."

"Very true. For that reason I also do a lot of consulting by radio. I can talk directly by phone through the tower to all of our tribal stations. The tower has a regular doctor's sked each day."

"Tell me about an emergency."

"The little Tuggy girl broke her arm last week. The accident happened at eight in the evening. Her parents put the arm in a splint and gave her a sedative. They got me on the radio the next morning and I felt she should be brought to the base. At 1:30 a plane was there, 350 miles away, and back here at 5:30."

Before leaving I asked Dr. Swanson for a biographical rundown. "I developed an interest in medical missions through my church, First Covenant of Minneapolis, and Asbury College. When a junior in med school, I attended the Inter-Varsity Christian Fellowship Missionary Conference at Urbana, Illinois, and met Wycliffe people there. I started corresponding with Ralph Eichenberger and knew pretty well what the situation was before I got here. My brother is a medical missionary in Ecuador. My wife, Janet, is a nurse and we have four kids," he added. "The children love it here. Peter, 13, the oldest, is the champion fisherman on the base. You should have seen the string he caught in the lake this morning."

MARTI: The following morning Jim still had his mind on fishing. He went every day as a boy in the Ozarks—correction, every other day, he says. I finally got his mind back on medicine and our appointment to see nurse Joan Lemke.

That afternoon the tall brunette welcomed us into her brand new home, all smiles and none the worse for having lost a night's sleep delivering a Piro baby.

"How long have you been with Wycliffe?" asked Jim, getting down to business.

"Six years, next month," was the reply.

"What was your first assignment in the medical work?"

"I went out as a temporary partner with Jeannie Grover among the Aguarunas; then I made several trips to the Cashibos with Olive Shell; and I spent a short time with Beth Hinson and the Shapras."

"You really moved around," I commented.

"I was only a temporary partner. It was just great to get background in the different tribes before I started what I'm doing here."

"Tell us about what you are doing now," Jim asked.

"I work in the health promoter program, training Indians to do simple medical work in the tribes. The time I spent with the tribes gave me an understanding of the way they will have to practice medicine; the kind of equipment and standards which can be maintained."

"What would be an example?"

"The way they maintain sterile techniques in preparing an injection. The way they have to boil water over an open fire. They aren't going to have a clean surface to work on. You see, the people aren't accustomed to boiling water, whether for drinking or other use. Many of their diseases are caused by contaminated water."

"What causes that problem way out in the jungle away from civilization?" I wondered aloud.

"Civilization doesn't cause the pollution," Joan informed me. "Man contaminates his environment wherever he is. If we can just teach the Indians to construct and use simple latrines and boil their drinking water, a lot of problems would be solved."

"How do you convince them?"

"We instruct all the students here—in teacher training, agriculture, whatever. Then we do tribal clinics. The doctors hold as many of these as possible. They'll let the people look through the microscope and see the things swimming around. Sometimes they take two samples of water from the river, boil one for five minutes, then let the Indians see that boiling water kills the little 'bugs' in it. This is quite convincing.

"Another thing we do is take a little dirt from under their fingernails and do a culture. They watch the bacteria on the cultures grow. It is quite impressive. I make a slide of it so they can see the individual microbes. After this, I notice them washing their hands more often."

"What do you try to cover in the training course here?"

"It's difficult to explain, because there's nothing in the States to compare. They learn to recognize the most common diseases and how they can combat them. We realize that we can't make professionals of them in a twelve-week course, but this is a lot better than nothing."

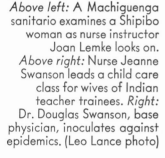

Above left: A Machiguenga sanitario examines a Shipibo woman as nurse instructor Joan Lemke looks on. *Above right:* Nurse Jeanne Swanson leads a child care class for wives of Indian teacher trainees. *Right:* Dr. Douglas Swanson, base physician, inoculates against epidemics. (Leo Lance photo)

"What are some of the most common problems?" I asked. "TB, parasites, that kind of thing?"

"Yes. There's a lot of TB. I did a study once among the Cashibos and found at least 70 percent of the skin tests to be positive. We are trying to slow down the rapid spread of this disease.

"Some other common disorders are intestinal parasites, diarrhea and vomiting. Linguists have found that the best way to get rid of worms is to treat the whole village at once. Then the general health of all the people is improved. But it has to be done over again every six months to a year," she explained.

"And of course, the linguists don't have time to do everything for these people, so it's better to teach some of them to do it," I commented.

"Yes, not only to give the linguists more time, but also because the people take pride in being able to help themselves."

"How many different tribes have these health promoters now?" Jim wanted to know.

"Let me think. We've had Shapra, Yagua, Shipibo, Machiguenga, Amuesha, and Aguaruna students. We also have some Piros this time."

"How many students at a time?"

"Usually four. This time we're trying six."

"Why so few?"

"Because this is a clinical-intern type course, not just lectures. Our

clinic is small, and we have just so many patients. It's quite a task
keeping track so each of the students gets adequate experience in everything." Her brown eyes became thoughtful. "I really believe that this
is the way I can best serve the people of the jungle. I'm only one and
can't be but one place at a time, but through my students, I can help
meet the needs of many people all over the jungle."

"Not to change the subject or anything," I said, "but we hope to visit
the Aguarunas. What can you tell us to prepare us?"

"Oh, I'm glad you're going," she smiled. "You'll like the Aguarunas.
They are very excitable and emotional—quite animated. You'll enjoy
meeting Jeannie Grover, too. She's something special.

"You'll need to watch out for that river up there. It is really treacherous. There are a lot of whirlpools, rocks and sharp turns. Get Jeannie
to tell you about the time we got caught in the middle of a revenge
killing and she stood up to a war party and made them leave their guns
on the riverbank before allowing them to enter the village where the
other faction was."

"She did what?" I exclaimed, flabbergasted. "Where were you?"

"I stood at the top of the bank and watched. They were completely
oblivious to me."

"I'm not sure I want to go to the Aguarunas after all," I said face-
tiously.

"The chances of running into a real adventure while you're there are
quite small. Day to day living is more likely to be repetitious and boring," she explained as she walked us to the door.

As Jim and I walked down the dirt road I mused, "That's some program she has responsibility for . . ."

"Certainly is," he agreed. "Did you know that Joan is a product of
Inter-Varsity, too? We keep finding people who have been influenced
by other groups."

"I like that. Christians working together and cooperating. I just realized that we haven't heard any gossip around here about other organizations."

"No, and if there were any, I think we'd have heard it by now. Why
are you stopping here?"

"This is Sheila Tuggy's. She has an iron she's going to lend me. She
said that she and Junie would be going back out to the tribe in a couple
of days and she wouldn't be needing it."

"Oh. Well, I'll see you later." He turned down the path that was a
shortcut to our house.

My knock on the door was answered by a curly-haired blond lady
with twinkling blue eyes.

"You came! Good. I was afraid you might be timid about using my
iron."

"I'm not very timid about anything," I confessed.

"Good. Then how about using my Honda too? We've had some robberies and I'd really feel safer having it at your house. As a matter
of fact, you could just move in here if you'd like."

"Oh, my. Thank you. But I really don't feel like moving again. It is a nice house. I love all your wood paneling."

"Thank you. Paneling is the cheapest and most practical thing to use in the jungle. My husband, John, built this house," she said with pride.

"These missionary kids are really versatile, aren't they? He *is* an M.K., isn't he?"

"Yes. He was brought up in the jungles of Venezuela, so he feels quite at home in Peru."

"You have a slight accent I can't place. Are you British?" I asked innocently.

"No, indeed!" She drew herself up as tall as possible in mock indignation. "I'm Schawtish!"

"That's it. You do look like a Scottish lass at that. How did you and John ever get together?"

"We met in jungle camp. It's a great place for meeting mates."

"What about raising children in the jungle? I heard about Junie breaking her arm. This type of thing doesn't happen often, I hope."

"No, thankfully. The children love the jungle. It's the only life they know. We have four by the way: Joy, Ruth, June, and Harold."

"And you live with the Shapras. They are long hairs, aren't they? And what's the significance of the long hair anyway? Or is that too many questions at once?"

She chuckled. "No. We're not sure if it's the Shapra branch of the Candoshi tribe, or the Candoshi branch of the Shapras. You'll find both terms used in the files. The so-called long-hairs are members of the Jivaro language group. These tribes sort of understand one another, but there are vast differences. There will be four translations for them.

"These tribes are headhunters," she continued. "They are very different in personality from the other jungle Indians. They're talkative, loud, animated, quite gregarious."

"Why are they so different?" I asked.

"Principally because they have never been subjugated by whites. No rubber hunter, lumberman, or missionary has ever dominated these people. They are quite proud and very winsome."

"How long has there been work in your tribe?"

"Lorrie Anderson and Doris Cox first went out in 1950. I presume you've heard what Chief Tariri said would have happened if a married couple had gone out."

"Didn't he say he would have killed two men, or if a couple had come he would have killed the man and taken the woman as another wife?"

"Yes."

"Aren't you glad you and John weren't sent there first?"

"Yes, indeed," she answered. "But the chief is a very good friend of ours now. He's our son's godfather. Our son's Indian name is Tariri."

"Why did you name him for the chief?"

"Well, we weren't exactly planning on a fourth child, but Tariri announced to us one day that he was praying that we would have a son. Girls bring no prestige among the Shapras, and I guess he figured we needed some prestige. We tried to explain that we weren't planning on another child, and to please stop praying. He just replied, 'Nothing can stop God from answering prayers.'

"We couldn't argue with him so we just decided to ignore it. Then surprise, surprise. We were expecting! When we had a son after three daughters the chief came to visit and said, 'See, I told you God answers prayers! You don't have enough faith!' "

"He sounds like quite a character."

"He is that, but he is very much a chief, and no one ever forgets it. He is very concerned about this situation that has arisen concerning Shikya's widow."

"Isn't that the teacher who died just recently?"

"Yes. You see, his widow is subject to the tribal custom that calls for turning the children over to Shikya's brother, or herself becoming the brother's wife. The brother is not sympathetic to Christianity, and he has two other wives who are real shrews. If they take the children, they'll make slaves of them. The chief is determined this isn't going to happen. But traditions die hard among these people and the situation could lead to bloodshed."

"Sounds pretty touchy, all right. What about the other teacher who's sick?"

"That's Shiniki. They aren't sure of the diagnosis. Lorrie wants to take him in to Lima, but he wants to stay in the tribe so he can die among his people. His pessimism is one of the things that makes me think he is suffering from cerebral malaria," she explained.

"Oh, that's your personal diagnosis?" I asked.

"Yes," she grinned. "I am a nurse, you know. I'm not relying purely on women's intuition."

"Seems as if half the translators' wives are nurses. Is this some kind of prerequisite?"

"Not really, but it helps in raising children in the jungle. For little things like broken arms. I think it's just one of those things that 'happen' among people who try to follow the Lord's leadership."

"How much longer are you going to be at the base?"

"I hope to leave as soon as Junie gets her x-ray the day after tomorrow. I know poor John isn't getting anything accomplished out there with the children. The big girls aren't much trouble, but our son is all boy."

"I wish I could meet the whole family. As a matter of fact, I wish I could visit your tribe, but the flight coordinator says there's no chance. It's too much out of the way."

"I wish you could visit us. We live in one of the most remote places. It's very hot there—lots of mosquitoes and malaria. All that makes it sound very undesirable. But if you could visit our beautiful jungle and meet our people, maybe in your book you could help people understand how human and lovable they are.

"The first time I heard about translating for primitive peoples I said,

'Lord, I hope you don't want me to do that!' I just didn't think I was the type. Now I can't imagine doing anything else."

"You sound as if you like your life."

"I don't mean to sound preachy, it's just that we have real contentment in serving these people. Please don't let your book make people feel sorry for the 'poor pitiful translators.' We feel very honored and privileged to have been chosen to bring his Word to these people who really need it."

"I'll try to remember that," I said, rising to go.

The next afternoon Jim and I were getting ready to visit the Kindbergs when Cyndi wailed, "Oh, Mother! I'm not going to get stuck with that kid again this afternoon, am I? Celia and I have to go to rehearse our play at the Snells. We can't do anything with her along."

"Then we'll just let Cheri come along with us. Would you like that, sweetie?" Cheri beamed and nodded her head.

"That's not fair," whined Celia. "Why should she get to go with you?"

"Look, neither of you wanted her. You have a very important engagement. So go to it. Cheri can play with the Kindberg kids."

So Cheri hopped down the street joyfully holding Mommy by one hand and Daddy by the other. She really enjoyed being the big cheese.

As we turned into the sloping front yard, Dougie and Virginia, the two youngest of the six Kindberg kids, called out to Cheri, "Come see our monkey." We'd been at the base long enough by this time that our girls knew nearly every child there. We were getting to know quite a few ourselves.

We walked over to the cage. There squatted the cutest little monkey ever. He was a light brown, tiny creature with a tail that was longer than the rest of him. He looked up at us with curious eyes, then jumped onto a perch and wrapped his long tail all the way around his body, once, almost twice around.

Cheri looked up at me, her face all aglow. "Oh, look, Mommy," she said sweetly, "He's hugging himself!"

"Don't get too near the cage," warned Dougie, importantly. "He bit me this morning. My grandmother, too."

That didn't sound encouraging, so I talked the children into playing on the front porch out of the sun.

Lee and Will escorted us into the coolness of their living room.

"I'd like you to meet my mother, Mrs. Duncan," said Lee, introducing us to a silver-haired lady.

"My, how unusual to have your mother with you on the field," Jim exclaimed.

"My husband died last year," she explained, "so I decided that instead of sitting around feeling sorry for myself I'd just start out on a missionary career. If you'll excuse me, I'll leave you young people to talk. I've got work to do." She bustled out of the room, and soon the pickety-peck-peck of a typewriter could be heard.

"She's typing for me," Will volunteered. "There are never enough typists around here. A lot of a translator's time can be saved by someone willing to do this unglamorous task."

"Will, if there is some place you and I can talk, then Marti can talk with Lee, and that way we'll get twice as many stories," Jim suggested.

"Divide and conquer, huh?" asked Will, grinning. "Sure, follow me." The men left and I turned to the dark-haired woman.

"You're with the Campas, right? Where are they located?"

"We're north of the Machiguengas. You visited the Machis, didn't you?"

I nodded.

"Well, they are very similar. Belong to the same language family, the Arawak. Their customs, manner of dress, traditions, even the folklore are similar."

"They wear the *cushmas?*" I asked.

"Yes."

"And the vertical stripes are for males and the horizontal for females?"

"Yes. That's true of all the jungle. All the tribes do that."

"You mean even the tribes that aren't related? That have never had contact with each other? How did they all decide which way was which?"

"No one knows. If you ask the Indians, they'll just tell you, 'That's the way it's done.' "

Then I continued, "How about some stories of the dangers of raising children in the jungle?"

"Oh, that!" she laughed. "We get that every time we go on furlough. One night in Chicago I was cornered by a lady who really thought we were tempting the Lord by raising our children apart from the modern conveniences that seem so indispensable in the States. I tried to tell her they were in no more danger here than in the U.S., but she wasn't convinced.

"A short time later I received a phone call. Our second son, Eric, had been hit by a car. He had a very badly broken leg, a concussion and facial cuts. He was in the intensive care unit a couple of days. His blood pressure wouldn't stabilize; we were afraid of brain damage.

"After that scare was over, it became noticeable that the leg in traction wasn't doing well, so a week later he was operated on, and put into a cast up to his chest. Months later he still couldn't straighten his leg or put weight on it. He will always have a limp. We're just thankful he still has his leg."

"Which goes to prove, it's safer to raise your children in the jungle," I said.

"Well, I doubt that it really proves anything. Except maybe that accidents can happen anywhere."

"How is the work with the Campas progressing?"

"There have been some very dramatic changes in the past thirteen years. Then you could go two hundred miles along the river without finding a Christian. There were no Campa schools. Now, anywhere you go along that river you will find people who know who Jesus is. There are eight hundred students in schools, and a couple of thousand professing believers. But there's still much to be done."

"And where does the translation work stand?"

"We're able to spend more time on it now, thanks to the Riggles and the Schmidts who are doing community development and Carol Whisler who's supervising adult literacy. We have nine books completed, printed, and in the hands of the people. Two more are approved, three are in process, and we are revising Mark."

Gail and Kathy, the middle Kindberg girls, came into the room, said hi, and then headed out the front door.

"Seems they already know you, Marti."

"Oh, yes. They're friends with my girls. I think I know all your children except the oldest."

"That's Bruce. He's working at the hangar this summer."

"Where is your home, Lee?"

"I'm from Boston and Will is from New Jersey."

"Let me guess. You met in jungle camp, right?"

"Not quite. We met before J.C., at one of our linguistic schools at the University of Oklahoma. It's a pretty familiar pattern around here."

"You wouldn't be a nurse, by any chance?"

"Yes, I am," she laughed. "Will says I'm the only doctor within seven hundred miles."

Gail stuck her head through the door. "Mother, come and see, quick!" she demanded, and disappeared.

We followed her into the yard, where some of the other kids were gathered around the monkey's cage. It was on the bottom of the cage writhing in pain, foaming at the mouth.

"What's wrong with it?" I asked.

Lee answered quietly, "Looks like rabies."

"Rabies! And he bit Dougie and your mother!"

She swallowed hard and answered, "Yes."

"But what will you do?"

"We'll have to cut off his head and send it into Lima for confirmation of diagnosis. If it is rabies they will have to start taking shots within ten days of the time they were bitten."

"Do they have the serum here?"

"No. I doubt that there's any available in Lima either."

"Then where will it come from?" I asked, while Cheri clung to me watching the monkey in its agony.

"I don't know."

10.

A Wing and a Prayer

JIM: At 7:30 A.M. the Jungle Aviation and Radio Service (JAARS) flight office was busier than bees in a swarm. Floyd Lyons was everywhere, answering the phone, weighing baggage, sorting mail, scribbling flight numbers on the schedule board, checking out pilots.

Sheila Tuggy came in behind us pulling stuff in her kids' little red wagon, and leading her daughter with the broken arm. "Looks like you won't get off until ten, Sheila," Floyd said apologetically. "The boys have to check out a problem with the plane."

Sheila shrugged and said to us, "We were supposed to go out yesterday. But there was an emergency. Poor John. I hope he isn't having too many problems with the children."

Doug Deming, a pilot, grinned at us. "If you've got time to spare, go by air. That's our motto."

While Marti talked with Sheila, I walked outside with Doug. "Haven't seen you around lately," I said.

"We just got back from a vacation in Lima. I had to renew my airline transport and instructor's licenses."

"Any difficulties?"

"No. Some of the fellows I instructed years ago are now high up in the Peruvian Air Force. They made me an honorary member of the Lima Air Club. We're old friends."

"How many JAARS pilots besides yourself?"

"Six. No, seven, with Leo Lance. Leo is assigned to photography temporarily and helps out on some flights. Besides me, there's Ralph Borthwick, Eddie Lind, Tom Brewington, Ted Long, George Woodward; and Ralph Schellenberger is on furlough. Two or three other guys could fly if they're pressed into service."

"I've met Leo, Ralph Borthwick, Woody, and Tom. Ted Long has been out with the Mayoruna girls."

"Ted's back. He's over there checking out his Cessna."

We walked over to Ted, a slim man with straight black hair and heavy eyebrows.

"How's the Mayoruna project?" I asked.

"No break. We flew over the village several times, the Indians waved, but none ever came to the river as Harriet asked them to. What the Mayoruna gals really need is a couple of men to come out and cut a trail. Rol has asked for some volunteers."

"Yes. We heard the announcement, but I don't know of any takers. Couldn't you land closer to the village?"

"No, because we'd need a land strip. The little river between the big river where the girls are camped and the village couldn't take a float plane."

"What have you got to do this morning, Ted?" Doug asked.

"An Army flight. Then I'm taking my family to Lima. We need to get away awhile."

"JAARS flies for the Peruvian Army?" I asked.

"Sure," Doug said. "We help them out whenever they need us. Train some of their people here at the base, too. It was Uncle Cam's policy from the beginning to serve the government and anyone else who needs help."

As we talked further I learned that Doug was the oldest of seven brothers and from a western suburb of Chicago. A veteran of the Korean War, his first jungle flying had been done in Mexico under the instruction of Missionary Aviation Fellowship's E. W. Hatcher.

Ted had grown up in Colombia, where his father was a chemical engineer for a sugar company for thirty years. "My brother-in-law is Larry Montgomery, the first JAARS pilot," Ted said. "He was a one-man airline. Sometimes he flew four and five days in a row."

Doug left to check on a plane that was being worked on under the hangar. I asked Ted about the JAARS safety record.

"We've flown twenty-two years without a fatality," he said. "I don't want to brag. It's just that the Lord must want these tribes to get the Bible."

"How about nonfatal accidents?"

He grinned slyly. "We've had a few close calls. About six weeks ago I flew Don Burns up to Ayacucho in the Cessna that's supercharged for high altitudes. When we got over the field, the town was having riots. So I had to backtrack about two hundred miles. I couldn't find the little airport on my map. Fortunately the tower located the place for me. We landed just as it was getting dark. The airport had no landing lights. Another fifteen minutes and we might not have made it."

"We plan on going to Ayacucho. Have the riots stopped?"

"I guess so. Burns has gone back. But several people were killed up there."

I left Ted and walked back across the grass to the flight office. Marti was talking to a young pilot with a crewcut, Eddy Lind.

"I've discovered that pilots do other things besides fly," Marti informed me.

"We don't go roaring off into the wild blue yonder every day," Eddie said. "Every pilot has a hangar responsibility. Right now I'm running an inventory on our fuel deposits. That chart shows where we have fuel cached and how much is at each place. We have 24 refueling points from 650 miles north in Arabela land to 550 miles south in Amarakeri territory.

"The pilots turn in their flight record which shows how much fuel they picked up at various points," Eddy continued, "so we can keep count of how much fuel is supposed to be at each place. And we can charge each plane for the gas it uses."

Floyd Lyons walked in and answered the jangling phone. "Yes, we've got the Amarakeri hides down here. They should have been picked up yesterday. I'll be glad to get rid of them."

The phone rang again. "Wednesday, I hope," we heard Floyd say. "We'll just have to play it by ear if the weather's marginal."

"Sorry I haven't been available," the slim Texan turned to us. "In the morning it's wild down here."

"How would you describe the job of a flight coordinator?" I asked.

"Nerve-wracking. Everybody wants to know when a plane will be leaving and arriving. And you should be here when there's an emergency. Seriously, though, it isn't that bad. The Lord helps us to stay calm and get the job done.

"Now what do I do? I plan each flight. We don't want a plane going out overloaded or underloaded if we can help it. We want to handle everything we can on each flight. You'll see when you go to the Aguarunas Monday."

"Oh, we'll be going then?" Marti asked.

"Let's say we've got the flight planned," Floyd replied.

The phone rang again. "That was Millie," he said. "Bishop Prevost will be at our house for dinner tomorrow night. This will give you a good chance to get a Catholic viewpoint of our work. You might want to stop by the radio shack to confirm that you'll be coming."

We left Floyd and wandered back through the hangar. "Black Bart" pulled his head from the motor of a Cessna and called to us. Marti asked how to tell the difference between a Helio and a Cessna.

"That's easy," Bart said. "The Helio has the little wheel in back and the Cessna has it in the front. Next question?"

A big mustached man with cap pushed rakishly back on his head came around from the other side of the plane. "Marti and Jim, meet Captain Midnight," Bart said with a perfectly straight face.

"Hi, George," I said and Bart's face fell. I had met George at church.

"We're working on 821, the plane that's supposed to take you out to Aguaruna country," George Tilt said. "Some specks of metal showed up in the oil. We changed the oil filter and gaskets, but are still checking. This engine only has 200 hours on it."

"How much before you change the engine?" I asked.

"The Cessna people say it will go 1400 hours, but we'll put in a new engine at 900 or a thousand. The high humidity and temperature down here make a difference."

We left Bart and George and climbed the stairs to the second floor. Reister Jenkins, the new JAARS superintendent, was supposed to be back from Lima.

Reister, a square-jawed engineering graduate from Texas Tech, gave us a warm greeting. "Sorry I haven't been around to help you."

"What's the secret of running a successful airline in the jungle?" Marti asked.

Reister smiled. "We keep the planes in good condition as long as we can. The Catalina has been flying for eighteen years. We try to keep a balanced budget, which is tough because our commercial flights must help subsidize our tribal flights. Our linguists pay from their support funds for trips to and from their tribes."

"How were the planes purchased?" Marti asked.

"One of the Helios was given by the people of Greensboro, North Carolina. Another came from Orange County, California. President Nixon—he was vice-president then—spoke at the dedication of that plane. The other single-engine planes we purchased. The Catalina was a gift from Mexico to Peru—in memory of Professor Moises Sáenz."

"I see the diplomatic hand of Uncle Cam behind all this," I said.

"He's the architect. I wasn't here then, but I've heard people talk about how they couldn't see the need for the Catalina in the early days. But it's been our workhorse and we could hardly do without it.

"Uncle Cam started JAARS down here. Well, at the start, Missionary Aviation Fellowship helped us. Betty Greene was the first pilot here for MAF. Also the first woman to fly solo over the Andes. But Uncle Cam felt we needed our own airline, so MAF withdrew. Of course, long before that he saw that aviation was essential in reaching the tribes of Amazonia. Now JAARS is also in Colombia, Ecuador, Bolivia, Nepal, and West Africa and New Guinea. Our international headquarters is now in North Carolina and new pilots are trained and evaluated there."

Marti looked puzzled. "I'm getting confused again," she said. "I see the relationship between Wycliffe Bible Translators and the Summer Institute of Linguistics. But where does JAARS fit into the picture?"

"I'll try to explain it. JAARS International is a subsidiary of WBT/SIL, and has its own board of directors. All JAARS personnel must take the linguistic support course and go through jungle camp. JAARS people are members of WBT/SIL and have equal voting rights. Maybe you could just say that JAARS is a department of WBT/SIL. JAARS is certainly not independent of Wycliffe."

"Okay, I get it," Marti said. "I just hope readers of the book can."

"Now I have a question," I said. "How much flying did JAARS do for whom last year?"

Reister shoved a paper across the desk. "Here's our full report. We flew a total of 2,427 hours and 40 minutes. This is broken down into types of service. Flights for our workers in the tribes amounted to 31.17 percent of the total. Next was Peruvian military flights with 18.08 percent, then oil companies with 16.05 percent. You can see also that we flew for Indians, the government, evangelical groups, other commercial flights, and so on. We flew a few Catholic priests who paid us like everybody else. When you go to the Aguarunas, we'll charge you."

Marti smiled. "I'm sure you will."

Reister looked at his watch. "How about joining us for coffee break?"

We followed Reister to a small eating area near the parts department.

Bart, Buzz Sawyer, Stu Shepherd, George Tilt, Floyd Lyons, Eddy Lind, and John Mishler, a little man whom Bart called "boss," were there. John was superintendent of maintenance.

Marti remarked about the unusual cargo which JAARS planes carried and Bart started on a story. "One time we took a load of cargo and people on the Cat to Bolivia. Coming back, we ran into bad weather and had to land at a border town. The customs official and the police came out to see who we were. One of the customs men was standing by a wheel well and heard a flopping noise. He looked and found six nice fish that had apparently jumped in the well while we were sitting on a lake in Bolivia. Bob Hettema gave him the fish and he cleared us for takeoff as soon as the weather cleared."

"Have you heard the one about Jack McGuckin and the tiger?" Buzz asked. "Jack used to fly with us. He's now in Brazil with Word of Life. Anyway, he was up in Iquitos for an exhibition and thought he would be flying the president around. But he got called out for an emergency flight. Coming back, he had some chickens and an ocelot as cargo. The ocelot—we call it a small tiger—got loose and grabbed a chicken, then started after Jack. He threw all the water he had on the tiger and packed luggage all around so it couldn't get to him. But the rascal jumped on another chicken and was trying to kill it right under Jack's seat. Jack called his wife who was the tower worker that day. She thought he had the president with him and acted very formal.

"While Jack was trying to explain the problem, the tiger got into the radio gear and the radio began cutting on and off. Gertrude thought the radio was acting up and called somebody at the radio shack for advice. When the guy said, 'Tighten the screws on your mike,' Jack snorted, 'That's not the problem. It's . . . . Oh, you wouldn't believe me anyway,' and hung up."

"I presume he got down," Marti said.

"Yeah, but the guy with the turtle almost didn't," George Tilt said. "It was one of our pilots. I forget who. Well, he had a big turtle to bring back to the base. He decided the best thing was to put it on its back under his seat. After he was airborne he felt a gnawing sensation under him. The turtle had eaten through the seat and was coming after him."

"That must have been an unsettling situation," was Marti's comment.

"Well, gotta get back to work and dream up some more stories for these people," Bart said.

Everybody left then except John Mishler, who offered to show us some training equipment.

"What's your title?" Marti asked John as he opened the door of a simulator.

"I followed Omer Bondurant as superintendent of aviation. Paul Wyse of the radio department, Art Jackson up at the power plant, and I are all under Reister Jenkins, the director of JAARS. Paul is on furlough.

"The Peruvian Air Force gave us this old C-3 Link trainer. It's built to handle the pilot proficiency tests on instruments. We can check out all the moves a pilot makes including landing."

"How about rough weather?"

"Yes. We can make it bouncy."

"How often do the pilots have to be tested?"

"At least once a year. We try to go a little beyond the U.S. Federal Aviation Agency requirements, which of course don't apply to Peru. Some FAA guys were here, incidentally, and said our standards were way above theirs.

"We figure three hours of maintenance for each hour of flight. It pays off. Bart recently found a bad fuel leak in the Cat that could have spelled a lot of trouble out over the jungle."

John continued showing us around. We saw hundreds of parts for the various planes and a "hot room" for items that would otherwise be damaged by humidity. "We keep an inventory check on every screw, nut, and bolt," he noted.

Marti felt she should be home when the girls returned from Children's Program. "Go ahead to the radio shack," she said. "We'll meet you at the dining hall."

I had Sheila Tuggy's Honda and scooted back to the long one-story frame building where "God's creative geniuses" (a translator's description) hung out. Millie Lyons gave me a howdy from behind her secretary's desk. "See you all tomorrow night," she said and waved me back to where the men were working.

I spotted Glenn Smith bending over a table, with his 12-year-old daughter beside him. "I'm trying to build a test harness for an automatic direction finder," he said. "Cindy is building a signal generator."

Glenn introduced me to two colleagues. Ron Borgers, an engineering grad from Michigan State, had specialized in computer instrumentation before joining Wycliffe. Loren Cook had been a radio announcer and engineer in Nebraska.

"We each have our areas of work," Glenn said. "I handle aircraft radio equipment. Ron takes care of tribal radios, batteries, and base telephone equipment. Loren looks after tape recorders, essential equipment for linguists, radio tower receivers, and the cultural radio station at the Indian School."

"The students broadcast news and programs in their own languages," Ron explained. "You'd be surprised how many tribesmen have transistor radios."

"I forgot something," Glenn said. "Loren is the chief engineer for the basket transmitters being used in the Mayoruna project. Ron and I have helped a little, though."

Loren then showed me the ham station in a back room. "We can make emergency calls home. Over here's a teletype for sending routine messages to our base in North Carolina, and on through to other JAARS bases."

I was really feeling grateful for the Honda when I overtook the owner of the cycle pulling her little red wagon back toward home. "Didn't your plane go?" I asked.

She sighed. "No. They've rescheduled it tomorrow. *Así es la vida.*"

"Would you like the Honda back until then?" I offered.

"You keep it. We'll be going tomorrow—I hope."

I kicked the starter and sped on for another block. Suddenly the engine coughed and died. Out of gas.

I pushed it into BEMO's (Base Electric and Maintenance Operation) station and asked the Peruvian attendant for a fillup. Art Jackson motioned for me to come inside.

Big and beefy, Art looked like the legendary muscled blacksmith. He had to shout above the generators as he showed me around. "This 200-kilowatt Waukesha generator and a smaller standby unit run the power plant and the water system," he said proudly. "We have our own purification system so the water doesn't have to be boiled."

"What happens when the generators go out?" I asked.

"People light candles and boil water. Everything run by power stops."

"Come over here and meet the newest member of our team, Lee Gray," Art said.

Lee, another big man, was working on a vehicle that resembled a fire truck. "This was an old watering truck that was used for building roads. We rebuilt it, painted it red, and it became our fire engine. Now I'm working on the pump. It'll hold two thousand gallons of water. Our old truck would only hold four hundred."

"Who's the fire chief?" I asked.

"Vic Halterman. He probably missed a meeting and was volunteered," the new man said. "We're looking forward to having you folks for dinner tonight."

Then I remembered Marti mentioning dinner with the Grays several days before. I was too ashamed to admit I had forgotten.

That evening we enjoyed a delicious beef roast with Lee and Shirley Gray and their six children. One, we discovered, was a Korean war orphan they had adopted.

Lee had been the project engineer on valves for attitude controls on the Apollo service module and LM landing vehicle. Before that he had helped build the attitude control engines for the old Luna orbiter that sent photographs back from the back side of the moon.

"How'd you happen to join this outfit?" I asked when we were seated in the living room.

"Shirley and I became Christians after our third child was born. We got very active in our little Baptist Church in Ogden, Utah. I was chairman of the deacons. We both taught Sunday school and did a little bit of everything. One Sunday when Kenny Gammon, the BEMO man you met in Lima, was visiting, he showed a film on Bible translation. What appealed to me was all the different vocations needed to get the job done. The Lord told me that night that I could do something."

Lee went on, "So with six kids, we sold our home and went through the process of becoming members, including jungle camp. And here we are, living in Kenny's house until the Lord provides the money for us to build."

Marti wondered how the family was adjusting. "We don't miss television, except for the football games," Lee admitted. "But our 16-year-old son wishes he could play football. Last year he played first string in a school of two thousand. Our school here is so isolated that the kids can only play intramural sports."

"I miss the mountains in Utah," Shirley said. "And the variety of foods we could get in the supermarket."

Lee grinned. "One thing I really like here is the siesta. And I don't have to commute twelve miles to work. Just walk across the street."

"How does the equipment here match up with what you were accustomed to in the space program?" I asked.

"There's no comparison. In aerospace I walked through an air shower and wore special clothes to work."

I looked at the big man who had turned his back upon a high-paying career to serve in the jungle. "Lee, could I ask—well, have there been times that you have doubted the wisdom of bringing your family here?"

"Yes, I've had second thoughts. The adjustment hasn't been easy, especially for our teenagers. It's easier on kids born here. One morning I was feeling really discouraged. I walked along praying, 'Lord, am I really needed here?'

"Suddenly the generator engine stopped. Everything went out. The radio tower, everything. As I ran toward the power plant, I realized that at that moment I was the most important man on the base. The Lord had answered my prayer."

The Catalina is the flying "truck" of the jungle. This bull is bound for a bilingual teacher's herd.

JAARS expert mechanics overhaul an engine. Safety is never left to chance. (Leo Lance photo)

Yarina radio tower: "Control Central" of the jungle.

Peruvian employee Americo Saavedra calling the roll of tribal workers.

Diesel engineer Art Jackson is an essential member of the Wycliffe team. (Leo Lance photo)

11.

Control Central

JIM: We had covered the flying end of JAARS, the radio shack, and BEMO. Now to the radio tower.

I called Grace Fuqua, wife of Cowboy Herb. "You're welcome to sit in," she said. "We've got two shifts. Kathy Pfeiffer, an STA, gives the news and takes the early roll calls. I take the late skeds and the unexpecteds. Maybe one of you should come at a time. The tower is a little small."

Naturally Marti preferred the late shift. I skipped breakfast and got there via Honda just as Kathy, a bouncy, freckle-faced redhead was flipping switches.

"I give news which we picked up yesterday, from the tribes, and add items from Lima House, the base, and a bit of world news," Kathy said. "Then I start the roll call of the Monday–Wednesday–Friday stations. The other half answers the roll on Tuesdays, Thursdays, and Saturdays. Sundays we handle only emergencies."

When the big clock touched seven, Kathy dialed 2004 to automatically toot the breakfast whistle.

"Good morning everyone. The time is now seven o'clock and 35 seconds. Here's the news for Friday, August the eighth.

"John Tuggy reports from Shapra land that Little Santiago has been selected as a teacher candidate. John hopes that Sheila will arrive today."

I laughed in the background.

"The Harts in Chayahuita land are busy tending to a compound fracture and several snake bite cases.

"Here at the base we've received word that the monkey that bit Mrs. Duncan and Dougie *did,* repeat *did* have rabies. They must start the series of shots in five more days. Pray that some serum can be located.

"Wes and Eva Thiesen, furloughing in the States, write that their daughter Nancy has announced her engagement to Bob Weber.

"That's all for today."

Kathy twisted a couple of dials. "Our tribal frequency is 5340. We'll be having skeds every five minutes now.

"Yarina, calling Yaquerana. Come in Yaquerana. Over."

I caught a woman's weak voice above the crackle. "Okay out here. We're trying to cut a trail toward the little river, but we're not making much progress."

113

"I read you, Harriet. Anything you need from here? Over."

"Yes. A pair of brown leotards and my green and white skirt. Over."

"Roger. Will send them at the first opportunity. Over and out."

"One of the Mayoruna gals?" I asked as Kathy made a notation in her log book.

Her eyebrows lifted. "How'd you know?"

"Just guessing."

"Yes. It was Harriet Fields. They're reporting in three times every day."

"Yarina, calling Ticuna. Come in Lam or Doris. Over."

A man's voice. "Okay, Kathy. I have a note for Leo Lance. Take the batteries out of our scooter and charge them so they won't sulfate. Got it? Over."

Kathy read the request back.

"Now, could you have Leo find out about the school books that were sent to Iquitos? We need to know where they are. And one item of news. We had a good field day in the village. The Tigers beat the Panthers. We gave out awards. Over."

The roll call continued. Dr. Gene Loos among the Capanhuas sent the solution to a linguistic problem for Joyce Oien in the technical library. Kathy explained that Gene, a Ph.D., was director of linguistics for the group.

Dick Montague with the Cashinawas asked for a kilo of salt and a large can of baking powder on the next flight. Bob Tripp with the Amarakeri wanted a box of .22 rifle shells and requested that some Indians from the occupational course be hired to cut his lawn for the next two Saturdays. Marge Levengood among the Ancash Quechuas asked for a connection with buyer Harold Beatty in Lima. Kathy made the relay. There was more interesting routine.

At 8:30 Kathy transferred medical calls to Dr. Swanson who spoke by phone from the clinic. All routine minor ailments.

"Sorry, nothing exciting seems to be happening," Kathy said during a breather. "Things may pick up when Grace gets here."

"I'll bet you've had some interesting mixups," I said while Dr. Swanson was finishing his consulting.

Kathy's eyes twinkled. "Not many, but the ones we have had were a riot. One time John Shanks thought he heard a pilot say, 'I have a pair of live Indians on board.' The pilot really said, 'I have a paralyzed Indian on board.'

"Let me think. Oh, yes. Patsy Adams in Culina land asked for 40 soles worth of coins. She got 40 kilos—about 100 pounds—of corn on the next plane.

"And Jeannie Grover called us for some baking powder. She got baby powder and the pilot brought back a note that said, 'The bread didn't rise very good or taste very good, but it sure smelled good.'"

From the window I saw Grace arrive on her scooter. Where was Marti? "I'm going to check and see if she's had a problem," I said.

Grace had just kicked the stand under her scooter and was starting upstairs. "Hi," I said, rushing by. "Either Marti or I will be back in a minute."

Marti was just leaving the house. "I've wasted 30 minutes trying to get this dumb recorder working," she said disgustedly.

"Let me run it down to Loren Cook in the radio shack," I said. "He'll fix it. Grace is expecting you in the tower. Sorry you can't have mine. I need it for an interview in the technical library."

"Okay," she agreed reluctantly. "But I'm not too great at taking notes. Talking is my forte. Anyway, when are you going to teach me to ride the Honda?"

MARTI: Jim roared off with the recorder and I walked to the tower to join Grace. As I entered, she looked around and grinned, then waved me to an extra chair and continued her conversation with a pilot. I gathered they were talking about an injured man.

She took two or three calls at once, then when she had a minute said to me, "I'm afraid you're not going to be able to ask me many questions. Things are getting pretty busy. I'll tell you what I can in between calls."

"I'll just observe and take notes."

"Squawk-squawk," went the radio. "This is Woody; I'm on the water now at Contamana."

"Roger," responded Grace. She flipped a key and turned to me, "You missed some excitement. A Peruvian man fell in a sawmill about thirty-five or forty air minutes from here at the Swiss Indian Mission base. Woody is up there on an emergency flight. The man's leg was nearly severed and he needs hospital care immediately."

"Will they bring him in to the clinic here?"

"No, we haven't the proper facilities. They'll take him to Binder's Hospital."

"Yarina, Yarina," called the radio clearly. "This is 492 over destination. Just dropped machete to our friends. They seem happy to see us again."

"Roger, Ralph. Keep in touch. Over and out."

"What was that all about?" I asked.

She smiled. "That was Ralph Borthwick flying over the Mayoruna village. We are being a little mysterious, I'm afraid. We have the army's permission for all that we are doing up there, but we don't want everyone in the jungle to know about it. Many Peruvians might get upset over our trying to contact this hostile tribe. They wouldn't understand just what we are trying to do, and that we have the government's blessings."

"Yarina, Yarina," called the box again. "This is George Hart. We have a food problem out here. Could we talk to Bart?"

"I'll set you right up," Grace replied.

She switched a button, dialed the phone, flipped some more dials, and then the person on the phone was talking to the radio.

"Could you explain that?"

"The Harts are out in the tribe with their three children. They're staying longer than they planned and are low on food so they're calling for assistance. Bart is getting food together and Dottie Jackson is baking some things for them."

"Oh," I said, a little perplexed. She was busy again, so I couldn't ask her why the Bartholomews and the Jacksons were in charge of feeding the Harts.

"Yarina. Yarina. This is Lima House calling Yarina." I recognized Mrs. Cudney's voice.

"Come in, Lima House. Read you loud and clear."

"Have you contacted the Burnses yet? We received another call from that government official. Says today is the last day. He *has* to talk to Don Burns."

"Negative, Lima House. They didn't keep their sked. Over."

"This is really important," said Mrs. Cudney. "Also we have confirmation on Ron Snell's flight back to the States on September fourth. Do you read me?"

"Affirmative Lima House," said Grace, and she repeated the message. "Over."

"Over and out," said Lima House.

"What do you do when people don't keep their skeds and you need to talk to them?" I asked.

"Pray," came the quick reply with a smile.

"Yarina. Yarina. This is 492. I'm short on gas. Would you check with Floyd and see where the nearest cache is?"

"Affirmative 492." Grace switched a key, talked with Floyd Lyons, the flight director. Relayed the message. Switched off.

"Now you asked me about the Burnses. They are way off in the sierras in Ayacucho. If Don or his partner Al Shannon aren't there to keep their skeds, their wives very often don't think of it. We don't worry about them. They are in civilization there. However, if any of our tribal people fail to keep a sked we send out a plane to see if an emergency has befallen them. Usually it's just something wrong with their radio. But we take no chances."

"Yarina. Yarina. Woody here. My man is in great pain. Don't think he could take an ambulance trip to Binder's. See if you can set it up for them to meet me at the swim ramp in Puerto Callao."

Grace did. They could. She reported back to Woody.

"He really isn't even supposed to be flying today. It's much too windy for the small planes to be out, and the forecast is bad. But if we don't handle emergencies like this there is no one else who can."

"What if the man were Catholic?" I asked.

"What's that got to do with it?"

"Well, we've heard criticism that you sometimes transport Catholics on your planes."

"I'm certain no one bothered to ask that man his denomination. He was too busy bleeding to death," she informed me coolly.

I felt properly rebuffed for having asked a dumb question.

"Squeeeeeeeeal. Squeeeeeeeeeeal," said the radio.

"This is Yarina. Come in, Fern," Grace answered.

"You understood that?" I asked, bug-eyed.

She put her finger to her lips to quiet me, while she concentrated on the sounds emitting from the radio.

"EEEEeeeeooooOOOOoooooeeeeEEEEEeeeeoooOOOOOooee."

"Affirmative, Fern," answered Grace. "The Indians are clearing the tree stumps from the strip and it should be ready in a couple of days. Did I read you correctly? Over."

"OOOooeeeEEeo," said the radio.

"Fine. I'll expect to hear from you tomorrow. Over and out."

"I don't believe it," I exclaimed. "I couldn't even distinguish a human voice."

Grace just laughed. "Your ear gets 'tuned in' to some of these noises after a while. I had a hard time at first, too."

"Guess I'll call our director and let him know his wife is all right," Grace said, while dialing the phone.

"Have you been praying for the Burnses to call?" she asked me.

I shook my head, embarrassed. I hadn't realized she was serious when she had said that. She took a couple more calls while I prayed silently. I sensed that she was praying between calls.

"Yarina. Yarina. This is 492 flying over the village. We're trying a basket drop now. One of our ingenious friends has taken the parachute from a previous drop and made himself a pair of shorts! Over and out."

"Yarina. Yarina," came a weak little voice. "Barbara Shannon calling."

"That's it!" Grace grinned, snapping her fingers.

"Good to hear from you. We have an important message for Don Burns . . ." She relayed the message that had come in from Lima.

"You mean that was Ayacucho?"

"Yeah," she interrupted.

"Do you always get such quick answers to your prayers?" I asked, impressed.

"We've seen some real miracles around here. Whenever there is some dire emergency we sound a 'general alarm' and give the prayer request to the whole base.

"Here in the tower we call prayer our 'sixth line.' We have five radio lines, but the sixth is direct to the Boss."

"Yarina. Yarina," crackled the radio. "Crackle—Lucy—crackle crackle—water," was all I got out of it.

"Negative, Lucy. I don't read you. Say again. Say again. Over."

It crackled some more. I could tell that Grace was concerned.

"I'll check. Call back in ten minutes. Maybe we'll get a better pick up. Over and out."

While dialing the phone, Grace explained to me, "That's Lucy Aiken and Norma Faust; they're out on their boat and the motor has conked out. They're taking on water and haven't enough power to use the radio much longer. I'm calling Buzz Sawyer. The Sawyers are their prayer partners.

"Buzz, this is Grace, . . ." she said to the phone.

When she hung up I asked her, "Are the girls safe? Are they near a village? They aren't going to sink, are they?"

"I'll ask them. I only know their location. Buzz thinks he knows what the problem is. He's going to get the part they need and fly out there and try to fix it."

"Yarina. Yarina," came the faint crackle. It had seemed like a long ten minutes.

"I can't read you. I can't read you. Buzz is coming. Buzz is coming. Do you read me. Over."

"Cr-a-ck-le," came the reply. "Cr-a-ck-le." Then silence.

"That meant affirmative. They understood me, but they've lost power and can't continue."

"How can you possibly know that?" I demanded. "It just said 'crackle.' "

"Because there were four definite syllables. Negative only has three. That's why we don't use yes or no."

"That sounds logical, but we still don't know if they are safe."

"Something else for your prayer list."

"Yarina. Yarina. This is Woody. Am I cleared to land?"

"Roger, Woody. There is a strong crosswind."

"I'll watch it. Over and out."

Grace turned to me. "If you look over to your left, you can watch the plane come down. With a wind like this, they have to land close to the shore. From here it looks as if they'll hit those trees, but they don't. At least I hope they don't. I never can bear to watch one of these approaches."

She turned her head away from the scene and closed her eyes. I morbidly watched. "It certainly does look scary," I agreed letting out my breath when I could see the plane in the clear.

"He's going to taxi down the lake now to the little town near the hospital. Have you gotten enough information? I'm afraid I haven't had time to tell you much."

"I've gotten about as much as I can take for one day. Doesn't this job make you a nervous wreck?"

"No, I've adjusted to it. The first few weeks were pretty bad. I've learned that when you leave the tower you have to leave the problems behind and trust the Lord to take care of the emergencies. It doesn't help the girls in their boat for me to stay awake all night worrying about them, nor will it get food to the Schmidts or the Harts."

"The Schmidts too? But they have a little baby, haven't they?"

"Yes. This was their first time out in the tribe, and they just didn't allow enough. If we get some good weather tomorrow, and there are no emergencies, we can send some food out to them."

"Please tell me it isn't this hectic up here all the time."

"Hectic? Why, I didn't think it was particularly hectic today. It's really rather quiet now, but in just a couple of weeks the tribal people will be sending their kids in to school, so there will be a lot of flights. I've seen the times when I've had someone on all five frequencies and both telephones all at once."

"Who gets top priority?" I asked.

"You just have to decide which is in the most dangerous position or what needs your immediate attention. You tell the others to stand by. We take care of the planes first. Then emergencies. You can't get rattled when people are depending on you," she said unemotionally.

I suddenly remembered something. "What is this prayer partner bit?"

She gave me the "Where have you been?" look, then said, "Everybody has a prayer partner or partners in the case of a couple. Buzz and Lolly are prayer partners with Lucy and Norma. That's why they were asking Buzz for help. Prayer partners not only pray for one another, but they also help one another in practical ways. And support people are always matched with tribal workers. That way we get to know and appreciate one another's work. Any other questions?"

"Yes. How do I find out if the girls survive the night, and if those two families get food, and if the Peru man lives, and all the other things I want to know?"

She smiled knowingly. "Guess you'll just have to stop by and see me tomorrow morning."

JIM: After dropping Marti's recorder off at the radio shack, I rode the Honda to the technical library. Joyce Nies was there preparing daily Bible studies for the Piro bilingual schools. "I haven't really been avoiding you," she said. "I've just been so busy."

She explained. "I've just finished the rich man and Lazarus from Luke 16:19-31. These are the questions the teachers will ask. You may have a copy if you wish."

I looked at what she handed me.

"What kind of life did the rich man live? Did the rich man love Lazarus as God loved him? How should a person who has more than his neighbors help them in their necessities?"

She passed along another set from John 3:1-18 and Matthew 19: 13-15.

"Who was Nicodemus? What did he think the new birth was? Why did Jesus say that to be born of the Spirit is like the wind? Why did God send his Son to this world?"

"You understand that we aren't the ones who teach the Bible to the children. Even if we could and wanted to, we couldn't possibly be in all the schools every day."

"Yes," I said. "And I'm wondering if there are many other countries in the world where the government allows the Bible to be taught daily in schools."

Joyce held up a finger. "Not allows, but *requires*."

"Do you have time to tell me about the Piro work?" I asked.

"It's a tremendous story. Esther hopes to write a book one day. But maybe I can help you a little."

The quiet woman began talking, slowly at first, then warming up, giving glowing descriptions.

"Esther Matteson—she has her Ph.D. now—was one of the first twenty-five of our group. She found the poor Piros ekeing out a living from slash-and-burn farming and watching the stars, discussing magic and demon activities, and laughing over immoral tribal stories at night.

"She learned everything she could about Piro culture. For example, they have a fantastic system of astrology. Names for various star constellations included the Anteater, the Turtle, the Jaguar's Paw, and the Crocodile's Chin.

"They have colorful titles for plants and animals. One vine is 'the turtle stairway.' A tiny white gourd is 'the mouse's gourd.' A blossom with pallid tendrils is 'the fish's beard.'

"Esther found a few searching for God. Two were chiefs, White Condor and Antlers. They were among the first believers. Antlers told us how his father had tried in vain to find God. When Esther translated the parable of the mustard seed, Antlers exclaimed, 'That's the way it was when God's Word was planted in my heart.'

"Esther had several short-term partners before me," Joyce continued. "I came about the time she finished Mark, in 1950. The whole Piro New Testament was published in 1960."

"That's amazing," I said. "How did she get it done so fast?"

Joyce measured her words for emphasis. "I know she wouldn't want me to say this. But she's a genius and completely dedicated to God. She's in Colombia now."

"I'm sure you helped."

"I did what I could," Joyce said softly, "but the translation was her work."

"How are the Piros doing now?"

"I can hardly keep up with all that's happening. We have schools, a school supervisor, several community development projects. Five young men are training to be pastors at the Swiss Indian Mission's Bible School. We have so many health promoters that we need a health supervisor. The Piros have their own newspaper—a first for all the jungle tribes. Chief Antlers and his son-in-law recently made a missionary trip to Brazil and preached to Piros there. It's just marvelous what the Lord is doing."

My head was spinning when I left the library. I stopped at the refreshment stand by the commissary and had a coke with a couple of teenage boys who were griping about school starting soon. Sherry Price was

50 Geso wane chinru, Nomole, ¿klu chinanu puna?
Giyagni rapyegitluna. Romyokyegimtatkaluna Geso.
Kashichatkaluna.

51 Ga wa getanu. Satu Geso-ymalutu gomyokamta.
Koshpaklu yoglolewapre. Rustaklu sasertotene gitsru-
kat-potu wayegreru. Yostak-jepitlu.

52 Giyagni Geso wane chinru, Psatkakanru pyoglole-
wapre. Rawya-waka putakanru. Gi rixanu pejnuruneko
yoglolewapi koschekachri, yoglolewapiko ruylatiko.

53 ¿Waka gkagwakluge gi numkata gagjiretlu Nuru;
walemka gitakyegitanutkano yokgipi mole waranka
pnute solalone gitowrene?

54 ¿Seyni gi rix-poko poyagkaakotanmaka tokanchi yo-
natkaluru wane chinachri rumkata wan-gixleta?

55 Waneklu Geso wane chinna wa gixolune yine,
¿Gishpakamta gixa yoglolewapi-yma gagaje-yma, ka-
chowguru pixka gixa kashretnoge? Pa gogne-mnu-na-
nuka gixa-yma ntuplanata. Nyimaklewata kpashi-wa-
ka-pjiya. Gi wa wane gkashichyano.

56 Seyni pejnuruko tyekaka wane gixkaluru poyagka-
kikolupa wa yonchi, Goyakalu tokanu geneklewatachine
yonga. Ruknokamtluna pejnuruneko yimaklene. Rasu-
katkana.

The reason for Wycliffe: tribal New Testaments. This passage from Matthew 26 is in the Piro language. (Eureka Newspapers Inc. photo)

behind the counter and informed me that Ron and his friends were back from a raft trip. "Ron says they had a blast," she said.

Suddenly I became aware of the *Time* magazine in my hip pocket and was reminded to return it.

Dick Hyde, a husky bachelor and new member who lived just behind us, accepted my apologies and said, "I'm packing to go to the Amara-keris. Bob Tripp will be glad to read it."

"Are you Bob's partner?" I asked.

"Sort of. Wayne and Vern Borthwick are with him now, but need to come in and return to college. Bob will have to put up with me until he gets a regular partner or until I get married."

"Engaged?"

Dick laughed. "Not yet, but I'm looking."

Dick gave me a capsule account of the Amarakeri work—quite a contrast to what Joyce Nies had related about the Piros.

"The Amarakeri are about as primitive as any group in the jungle," Dick said. "The first guys there found them wearing animal skins and using stone axes and bone knives. They had a terrible fear of black ghost spirits. One of the fellows left and later died in California. Bob Tripp took his place. Then the second of the original two left and I became Bob's partner. Doesn't sound like much of a success story, but Bob has Mark almost ready for publication. We have an adult literacy class." Dick stopped to laugh. "We make great dentists. Bob extracts the uppers and I take the lowers. The population is up to 140 now and a few people say they believe in Jesus and don't fear the spirits."

I thanked Dick and started toward the Yarina school. We hadn't seen the principal yet. As I crossed the soccer field, I saw a familiar figure carrying a load of books into a building. Ted James.

"So this is what teachers do all summer," I jibed.

He put the books down on a desk. "Not really. I have the Youth Service Corps. Fits in with my job as guidance counselor during the school year.

"The Summer Corps is summer jobs for our kids," he explained. "The kids work in the radio lab, BEMO, the hangar, the clinic, at the farm, all around. My oldest son, Dennis, delivers groceries. Quentin, my eighth grader, sweeps up in the carpenter shop. They are paid 20-25¢ an hour. A few work for nothing, just to be of service. They all get good experience."

"Marti and I had noticed kids working in various places," I said. "We should have realized this was organized too."

A young man entered with a stack of file folders under his arm.

"Here's Jim Smotherman," Ted said. "He's Uncle Jim to the kids until school starts. Then he becomes Mr. Smotherman."

I asked Jim and Ted about their backgrounds. Ted said he had taught for fourteen years in Hagerstown, Maryland, before being "recruited" by Will Kindberg. Jim, a former minor league baseball player for the Hollywood Stars, had also taught, and he held a master's degree. He would be starting his second year as principal.

They gave me some salient facts about the school: 172 students for the coming year with 45 high schoolers, a faculty of 20 (mostly STAs) and a 5-member advisory committee to the principal, elected by the adult members.

"We have some advantages and disadvantages," Jim said. "Our teachers come with wide ranges of experience from different states and with different philosophical backgrounds. But with such a large percentage of STAs we have a big turnover. We have small classes—our largest, 30, still has a good community spirit.

"We give the two standard scholastic aptitude tests which are given by schools and state universities back home," Ted said. "We find our kids are above average."

"A youngster here has the same problem that a pastor's son or daughter may have," Jim added thoughtfully. "Growing up, knowing the Christian language, the formula, the system—yet maybe never experiencing a true new birth conversion for himself. The fact that we're isolated and in somewhat of a closed community adds a deeper dimension. A youngster in the States can get away from his church role at school and in the community. Here, if he steps out of line at any time, he's in trouble."

"So there could be difficulty adjusting when he goes to college," I noted.

"Exactly," Jim said. "It's our job to try and prepare our kids for their adjustment to the larger society. Our prime goal is to help them have a good, realistic self-image. We want to help them know who they are and why they are here and why their parents are here."

MARTI: Finally I got the opportunity to talk with Olive Shell. I'd heard so much about her, and as she was one of the "originals" in Peru, I had a zillion questions to ask. She, however, had agreed to give me one hour—no more. But I wasn't really worried about that, because once you get people talking, they tend to forget about time.

She welcomed me into her neat, compact home, nestled among jungle trees and bushes. "I understand that you were the last one to get an aluminum roof," I said.

"Yes, they passed a rule that everyone had to have metal roofs, because the thatched roofs were a fire hazard. Personally, I preferred the thatch. These metal roofs are so noisy when it rains.

"What do you want to know?" She wasn't going to waste time talking about her house.

"You were in the first group that came down here, right?"

"Yes."

I gulped. I'd expected a more elaborate answer than that. "Well," I said, groping, "when did the group first meet each other?"

"Most of us were together in jungle camp."

"When was that?"

"1945."

"That must have been one of the first jungle camps."

"Yes, the jungle camp program was first set up because of the advance into Peru. We didn't want to bring a bunch of city people down here who didn't know how to survive in the jungle. That would have been a waste of time."

"Where did you stay when you first arrived?"

"In the annex of the Maury Hotel in Lima. After a few days, we got a house because it was cheaper. We couldn't afford to buy both beds and mattresses so we bought mattresses and put them on the floor."

"Can you think of any other hardships you had to endure?"

"We never had any real hardships. We didn't have everything we wanted, but everything we really needed. It was embarrassing at times, though."

"Embarrassing? How?"

"Uncle Cam always wanted the people in the government to know just what we were doing, so he kept inviting guests to the house, and we didn't have enough silverware and dishes to go around."

"How would you manage?"

"Take turns. I remember one government official picked up his spoon—it was just a cheap one, not literally silverware—and it was so bent he had to straighten it out before he could stir his coffee.

"Another time somebody got a fork with only two prongs. Those silly little things were embarrassing, but they didn't really matter. We always had enough."

"At least they must have realized you weren't a bunch of rich gringos."

"Right. We were down here to work. General Marin arranged for Gloria Gray and me to study Cashibo with a Cashibo fellow stationed at an army post in a suburb of Lima."

"So you had a little background in the language before you got to the jungle."

"Yes. Then we set up headquarters in Aguaytía. That was our first base, about a hundred miles west of here. It was on a river that flooded during the rainy season, and was low in dry season. It was just too unreliable for planes. Then, too, the planes had to take off under a suspension bridge."

"How far was it from your Cashibo tribe?"

"About a day's travel down river, and two and a half days back up."

"What kind of a boat did you use?"

"We traveled by canoe. The first thing I learned about traveling by canoe was to trust the Indians. They know what they are doing."

"Is it a large, dangerous river?"

"No. It's not a big river at all. A very simple river."

"Someone told me you have been traveling by canoe all these years and can't swim. Is that true?"

"I can swim enough to stay afloat, but I'm not a strong swimmer at all. I wouldn't stand much of a chance in a real current."

"How did you and the others first get established in the tribes?"

"We just went out and lived with them. Gloria and I lived in the home of a Cashibo chief for two-and-a-half months."

"Did you eat their food and everything?"

"We had taken along some 'civilized' food, but when it ran out, we used what was at hand—bananas, venison, wild hog, fish, lots of papaya and yucca, and for special occasions, monkey."

"So you survived. But you didn't have communications with each other. I should think the people back at the base must have been terribly concerned about you."

"We prayed. We used to have early morning prayer meetings. That was back when Ray Wakelin was trying to locate the Aguarunas by walking overland and visiting Indians, going up and down rivers. We were all quite concerned about him since they were known to be a fierce tribe."

"Is that how the 'prayer partners' started?"

"At first everyone knew each other, and all about how their work was progressing, but as we grew larger and more diversified, it was impossible to keep up with everything that was going on, so we started having special prayer partners."

"Who first thought of the idea?" I asked just as we heard a knock at the back door.

Olive answered as she went to the door, "I think Elaine Townsend did—but that's been a long time ago." At the door, she greeted an Indian in his language, admitted him, then returned to me.

"This is my informant, and it's time for me to return to work. I'm sorry, but your hour is up."

"But, but . . ." I sputtered, "I have so much more to ask you."

"Maybe another time," she answered, dismissing me politely.

I picked up my recorder, bid them both farewell and left.

When Jim returned home a while later he asked how my interview had gone.

"Not so great, I'm afraid. She isn't exactly the talkative type."

"Did you find out about her Ph.D.?"

"She didn't mention that."

"Did you get anything about the years she spent as head of the Indian School here at the base?"

"I didn't even know she had anything to do with the school. I'm a complete failure," I wailed in mock consternation.

"Oh, well, don't worry about it. We can get the information from other sources, and we have the files." Then, all puffed up because he had scooped me, he said, "Guess what I just found out. You know they asked for volunteers to go cut a trail for the girls in Mayoruna land, so they could set up camp further inland? Well, they've got 'em."

"Oh," I replied, unimpressed. "So who's going?"

"Ron Snell and a couple of Machiguengas."

"Ron Snell! But he's just a kid. Not even eighteen. Why on earth would they send him out there? I thought the Mayorunas considered males fair game."

"Calm down. In the first place, they are just going to cut a trail through the jungle, then help move the girls' gear. They are not going to try to make contact with the Indians.

"The most important consideration is that Ron was raised in the jungle. Things that most gringos still haven't learned after twenty years just come to him naturally. Even Rol Rich admits that Ron knows more about the jungle than he does."

"Yeah, I guess you're right," I admitted. "But he still seems awfully young for such an assignment. Just because he isn't *supposed* to have contact with any Mayorunas is no guarantee that he won't run into any. What do his folks think about this?"

"They had to give their approval, of course. Wayne insisted that Victorino and Eduardo, the two Machis who are here, go with him. Also they set up a committee to prepare some procedures that will insure their safety."

"I see why they would feel better about the Machis going with him. And Ron does have the time. And the brawn. But what worries me is that he hasn't enough sense to be afraid of anything in the jungle."

"Because it's home to him."

"I know, but I still say his folks must have a lot of faith to okay this adventure. It's one thing to be willing to take on a dangerous job yourself, and another to allow your son to do it."

12.

Dinner with the Bishop

JIM: Sunday evening the group held a dedication service for the three Mayoruna trail cutters. I sensed Rol was trying to allay any fears as he listed the precautions.

"Ron and the two Machis will have a pistol, but will use it only to signal for help and to scare Indians away in case of an attack. In no case will they try to wound an attacker. They will carry a small ET5 radio and talk to Ralph Borthwick as he flies over in the morning and afternoon. Ralph will give them needed correction and compass bearing and calculate their progress toward the small stream. The three men will cut 50 feet apart, with each finishing his section before the last man moves up. This will cut down the possibilities of a surprise attack."

Ron's dad, chairman of the planning committee, spoke. "Three years ago I offered to go to the Mayorunas," Wayne said. "But the executive committee wouldn't let me. Now my son and two Christian men from our tribe have a chance to help make the contact. I'm behind them all the way."

Victorino, Wayne's language helper, then spoke, with Wayne interpreting. "I came to Yarina to help my 'father' translate God's Word and straighten it out (everyone laughed at this). Pray for me and Eduardo and Ron as we go. Pray that someone will be able to give the Mayorunas God's Word soon."

Ron stood up, barefoot as usual. "I never thought Uncle Rol and the committee would let me go. Now I'm beginning to think it won't be a big adventure after all. Just cut and sweat, cut and sweat. Pray the Lord will keep us on the job."

Bob Nelson then led in prayer and everybody drifted outside to talk in the cool of the evening.

Bob Mickelson told us that two burglars had been caught and almost all the stolen goods were recovered. Both were still in jail in Pucallpa. And we learned something else. Betty Snell had not only baked a batch of sweet rolls for us, but also one which Wayne took to the jail and gave to the prisoners along with a Spanish Gospel of John. "Wayne wanted them to know we had no hard feelings," Bob said.

Early the next morning, I stopped at the radio shack and picked up Marti's tape recorder. Loren showed me a tiny transmitter built into a sardine can. "It was used in one of the basket drops," he said. "The parachute caught on the brace wire of the plane's float and didn't open. If the 'chute had opened, the plane would probably have been uncontrollable. When Ted Long touched down on the river later, he fished it out of the water. Shows how the Lord has been with us on the Mayoruna Advance."

I hurried back to the grassy lakeshore where Ralph Borthwick was preparing to take off with the trail-cutting team. Betty and Sandy Snell, the dentist Opies, and Marti were standing back beside Melody, who sat on the Snell's Honda. Ralph, Wayne Snell and his two sons, and the two Machis were loading the plane. Vera Borthwick was looking on.

Gladys Opie was wearing huge sunglasses with plaid frames. She suddenly realized that the curly-haired, barefooted boy standing on the plane's float was Ron Snell, leader of the trail cutters. "You mean he's going?" she gasped. "Why, he's only a boy."

Betty overheard and with a lump in her throat stammered, "He—he'll be eighteen next month."

Marti said, "Gladys, this is Ron's *mother*, Betty."

Gladys blushed scarlet. "If I didn't have such a big mouth, my foot wouldn't fit in it," she muttered.

Now the plane was loaded and ready for takeoff. Tall Ralph Borthwick kissed his wife goodbye. Ron came up and smacked his mother and sisters (Melody couldn't come down the little hill on the cycle) and shook hands with his father and brother. Both Sandy and Mel were sniffling. Feeling like the intruder I usually am on occasions like this, I continued taking pictures.

Ralph revved the engines, taxied out into the lake, turned and was off in a whirl of silver spray.

"Lord, don't let this be like the Auca incident," I prayed silently. "Please, Lord. Please."

"This," I told Marti when I reached her, "has gotten to be much more than a mere writing assignment."

That day at lunch we sat down beside a tall slim girl and two young Indians. "Hi! I'm Lorrie Anderson," she said. "Just got in from the tribe."

We introduced ourselves and explained what we were doing.

Lorrie spoke to the Indians in Shapra, then gave us their names. "The young man is my informant. The little girl is his wife."

Marti gasped. "His wife! She's a doll—a real beauty. But how old is she?"

"Eleven or twelve. They've been married about a year," Lorrie added casually. "They're quite devoted to each other."

While we ate, Lorrie recalled receiving the Shapra assignment eighteen years before. "Uncle Cam asked Doris Cox and me over for tea right after we arrived. We knew he was up to something. He told us that the Shapras were considered noble and ambitious, but dangerous, by a trader who had visited them. He asked us to pray about 'someone' going to them. We did and both felt we should be the someones. Chief Tariri took us into his village as his sisters and protected us. You've probably heard that story and how the chief became a Christian."

We had, but Marti wondered how Lorrie had fared. "Sheila Tuggy says that is great malaria country."

Lorrie smiled. "Doris and I both came down with malaria three days after we arrived. To make matters worse, we had left the radio transmitter in the plane and couldn't call the base. But the Lord helped us and we recovered. Since then, I've had malaria so many times I've stopped counting."

"Sheila also said you have lots of boas," I noted. "And someone else told us you were attacked by a boa."

"We have a good many. The unbelievers fear the boas, but pray to them. They think the boas can both cause and cure disease. And I did have a couple of encounters with boas that I wouldn't like to repeat.

"Once my partner and I walked to a river to wait for a plane. When darkness came we decided the plane must have been held up by the weather. We slept on the *playa*. When we awoke the next morning, we saw the biggest boa I had ever seen, more than twenty feet long. It was lying between us. We ran as fast as we could and the snake slithered back into the jungle.

"At Lake Capirona I wasn't so fortunate. This was also early one morning. I had the habit of having my devotions in a canoe—about the only place you can have any solitude among the Shapras. I was reading in 1 Kings 17 about the trials of Elijah. I wrote in the margin at verse 24: 'Often we need a time of trouble so we can more clearly see who God really is and what he can do.' I began asking the Lord to preserve the Shapras—so many revenge killings were occurring—until we could get more Scripture into their language. I heard a swishing thud from the left and an instant later this big boa was biting into my chest and arm. I was bleeding and screaming and hitting at the snake with my Bible while it was threshing around me trying to get a hold on my body. I knew what would happen next—it would pull me under the water. Then—I can't explain why—it had to be the Lord—the snake relaxed and let me go."

Marti had stopped eating and was staring wide-eyed at Lorrie. "I'd have nightmares the rest of my life after that."

Lorrie replied calmly, "It was a bit unsettling. But I don't want to frighten you. You don't see boas every day."

Later when we started to leave, Lorrie added a word of caution. "I hope you won't overdramatize things too much. Especially Chief Tariri. He never was a bloodthirsty killer."

Our girls had been spellbound—even Cheri. "Do you have a shrunken head?" Cyndi asked.

Lorrie smiled. "I've never even seen one. I mentioned it once to the Shapras and they asked if I wanted one. I said, 'No, I don't think so.' I was concerned about how they might get it!"

We were ready to say our goodbyes when Marti thought to ask, "Did Sheila ever get back to the tribe?"

"Oh, yes, finally, and her little girl's doing fine."

MARTI: "This jungle certainly does have everything," I complained one evening. "First we're told that this is the 'dry season,' so I didn't bring rain gear, then we arrive to discover that 'dry' is only a comparative term. It only rains every other day, instead of continuously. And now the equatorial jungle has a cold spell and we all freeze."

"I think we'll survive," commented Jim unsympathetically.

"I'm sure we will, but I haven't anything to wear to dinner at the Lyonses' tonight. I left all my warm clothes in Lima."

"Why not put on two or three dresses?" suggested my husband, who will never make anybody's best-dressed list.

I wore my warmest one, an aqua sleeveless shift, topped with the only sweater I'd brought, which was pink. "At least it matches my cold nose," I muttered, feeling very unglamorous.

We slipped and slid our way through a faint drizzle to the Lyonses' beautiful, spacious "summer cottage." The Texans gave us their usual warm greeting, but the screened-in home didn't match.

Cal Hibbard made his appearance. "I hope the bishop gets through all right," he worried. "That road is a mess after all this rain."

"You mean he might not get here? And Millie has gone to such trouble," I said, glancing at the beautifully set table in the dining room.

"Oh, it happens," Millie said good-naturedly. "With no telephone contact to Pucallpa there is no way of knowing for sure."

"If the road is impassable, he can't send a messenger to tell us," commented Floyd dryly.

I made a face and said, "Joy!" They all laughed.

"Tell us something about the bishop while we're waiting," Jim suggested.

"He's a Canadian," said Cal. "His order is the Quebec Foreign Mission Society. He's been a priest at least thirty years. Came to Peru in 1957, after spending years in China. You'll have to ask him about some of his experiences there.

"He was consecrated as a bishop, but his title is Monsignor Gustavo Prevost. He was a member of the Vatican II Council."

"Impressive," I said. "What do we call him?"

"Bishop will be fine," Cal reassured me. "Don't get too flustered; he's warm and friendly."

Not long after that the bishop's truck pulled up. The Lyonses welcomed him as an old friend. He was dressed very informally in a blue shirt and a dark grey cardigan. A Canadian Maurice Chevalier, only younger. He has the same charm, twinkling eyes, wit, and French accent.

Millie served orange juice cocktails, and he proposed a toast.

Good friends "Uncle Cam" and Bishop Prevost,
who distributes Scripture to Peruvian Catholics.

"The Hefleys are interested in some of your experiences in China,"
Cal said diplomatically.

"Well, I was a missionary in both Manchuria and China. I spent four
years in a concentration camp under the Japanese in Manchuria during
World War II, from 1941 to 1945. Then after being in China for three
years, I was imprisoned by the Communists in Shanghai and spent three
years in a Communist jail."

"Which prison was the worst?" I asked.

"Probably the physical conditions under the Japanese, but the brain-
washing attempted by the Communists made their prison the worst for
me. I must add that some things the Communists said were true."

"For example?" asked Jim.

"Exploitation in the Orient by the Western nations. They talked about
the churches in China, the Catholic and Protestant churches—how the
buildings look like the churches in Europe and the States. The word
'Christian' in Chinese literally means 'European religion.'

"One thing that was very evident during those trying times, I must
tell you. When the persecution came, then they responded as Christians.
I mean real Christians. The people stood up. Christianity mattered—it
really meant something. Being a Christian doesn't mean much when it
is easy," he said with conviction.

After the bishop told us a few anecdotes of his incarcerations, Millie
suggested we go to the dining room for our meal. I had been so intrigued
with the conversation that I had forgotten to drink my orange juice.

As we were served soup, the bishop commented, "Ahh, this is one of
my favorites. I'll bet you can't guess what it is," he said, looking directly
at me, his eyes twinkling.

It looked like vichyssoise and had the same consistency, but I couldn't
identify the flavor.

"It's good," I replied, "but you're right, I haven't the faintest notion what it is."

Millie's big brown eyes danced as she announced, "It's peanut soup. We're having a real jungle meal tonight. Palm heart salad is next on the menu."

As the soup bowls were removed and the salads served, the bishop told us about his first impressions of the Wycliffe group.

"When I first landed at Pucallpa, this skinny fellow here was there to meet me," he said, indicating Cal.

"Yes," Cal affirmed. "We had heard you might be on that plane. Uncle Cam wanted to meet you, but since we weren't certain about your arrival, he sent me, just in case. So I had the honor of meeting the bishop first, and of inviting him to Uncle Cam's for the next day," he explained.

"Yes," the bishop smiled, reminiscing. "The papal nuncio in Lima had warned me that relations between Protestants and Catholics weren't too good in Pucallpa. So when I came out here to meet these linguists I was a little leery, since I knew they were Protestants.

"I was introduced to Uncle Cam, and for a while we talked of little things, just getting to know one another. Then I perceived that Uncle Cam was truly an open person, so I also opened my doors wide. We became fast friends that very first day."

I noticed that the bishop used the expression "Uncle Cam" as freely as any Wycliffite.

"One time when I was visiting him, Uncle Cam told me, 'Here at my house there is a prophet's chamber. Anytime you want to visit, it's yours.' That impressed me very much."

"Have you made friends with any of the evangelical missionaries in this area?" Jim asked.

"I know only Joe Hocking, and I appreciate him. Though I don't know how much he appreciates me," he answered, raising his eyebrows in a very Chevalieresque gesture. "If you haven't met him, you should. He's quite a unique individual."

"We ran into him at the commissary the other day," Jim explained. "He invited us to bring the children over to see his chickens, and have dinner.

"What about the work of Catholic missionaries in the jungle?"

"The Franciscans first came to Pucallpa over two hundred years ago and plied their canoes up and down the Ucayali. I greatly admire these men. There is one area, for example, where they worked in Campa country. It took them six months to get there from Pucallpa. It's only two hours by plane.

"I have never been to a tribe, though I would like very much to visit one. There is such a shortage of priests, and so much work to do. But as a Catholic, I prefer to see the Indians evangelicals than to see them pagans.

"They say that the population of Latin America is over 90 percent

Catholic," the bishop continued, "but I say it is only 2 percent to 3 percent Christian. There is a difference between being a Catholic and being a Christian!"

"I've heard you've been distributing Scripture among the people in the Pucallpa area," Cal said. "How is it being received?"

"The majority accept it, but I don't know whether they read it. I asked the adults in evening school, 'How many of you have read the whole Bible?' None had. I asked about the New Testament, and only a few had read that."

"There have been a lot of changes in the Catholic church in the past few years," Jim commented, leading the bishop.

"Yes, indeed. There have been changes in attitudes on both sides of the fence." We laughed in agreement.

"You know," he continued, "Martin Luther was nearly hanged by Catholics, but if he were living today he would be a top member of the Vatican Council. He was just too far ahead of his time. Today we are trying to get away from the word *Catholic* and emphasize the word *Christian.*

"One of the first things that impressed me about Uncle Cam and these linguists was that they excel in the first proof of Christianity. Love. It is the first proof, the first witness of a Christian."

A couple of days later Joe Hocking, pioneer Brethren missionary, came by to take us in his dusty pickup truck to his home in Puerto Callao.

"When Jeannette and I came here, you couldn't just hop a jet and arrive in a few hours," he reminisced as we bumped along. "We came by boat to the mouth of the Amazon, then rode an Amazon river launch for five weeks to get to Iquitos.

"We stayed in Iquitos for the birth of our first son, Peter. We have six children," he digressed proudly. "First Peter, then Mary, Paul, Ruth, John, and Phil."

We pulled into a driveway which wound around a pastel green house sitting very close to the road. "Here's our place," he announced. "Come meet Jeannette. If dinner isn't ready I'll show you my chickens. I have over a thousand of them. Produce 250-300 eggs a day."

After he had introduced us to his tall, greying wife, I elected to stay with her and help with the finishing touches of dinner.

"Well, girls," I said, "would you rather set the table or see the chickens?"

They gave the obvious answer and trooped after the men.

Jeannette made me feel right at home as we worked together in the large homey kitchen.

"I'm sorry, but dinner will be a little late," she said. "We ran out of butane and Joe had to go into Pucallpa for more. What is this book you're working on?"

"We are doing research on two books—one to tell the story of Wycliffe's work in Peru and the other a biography of Uncle Cam."

"We can certainly give you a lot of information about both. Joe has a diary he's kept for the past forty years. The comings and goings of the linguistic group are all recorded in it."

"A diary going back forty years! What a find! Do you think he'll let us use it?"

"It's one of his prize possessions, but I'm sure he will."

As we were discussing the diary, the others returned. Joe insisted we inspect the books right then. He had a whole row of black notebooks filled with day-to-day accounts of little ordinary happenings, big important events, pictures of children's birthdays, and so many interesting things. I found the entry concerning Uncle Cam's first arrival in Pucallpa.

"Oh, Joe, this is priceless. I only wish we had the time to read through every one of these."

He beamed his approval.

During the scrumptious meal, which explained Joe's well-padded middle, we talked about Wycliffe.

"When did you meet Uncle Cam?" Jim asked.

"When he first got to Pucallpa the boys grabbed his bags and rushed him off to the mayor's house. I was acting mayor of the town at the time."

"You were the mayor?" I exclaimed, impressed.

"Well, I was really the Inspector of Public Works, but when the mayor would go away for two or three months at a time he left me to run the town."

"What was your first impression of Uncle Cam?" Jim tried again.

"He was a good diplomat. He didn't rush into anything, just moved into what was open. He accepted hospitality from the military, the Catholics, or the evangelicals. He met many people, and made friends of them all.

"His group was very small then. I really didn't know if they could make it. I remember one time they called a conference over whether to buy milk a case at a time instead of can by can."

"Why have they succeeded so well?" I asked.

"One reason," said Mrs. Hocking, managing to get in a word, "is Uncle Cam's ability to turn over responsibilities to other people. He doesn't try to do everything himself."

"Another thing," added Joe, "is this prayer-partner thing. It keeps them involved with and concerned about each other. They help one another in practical ways. Never underestimate the power of prayer," he advised.

"I agree," said Jim. "They started that system long ago, didn't they?"

"Yes. They had their base at Aguaytía then. I managed to have them 'discover' Yarina. Everyone saw the advantages of that location immediately. I helped clear the jungle to make the road, and planted many of the fruit trees. Most people who build houses let me do some of their landscaping.

Wycliffe's work is nonsectarian. Indian pastors taught from Scripture in their own tongue lead their congregations and perform church rites.

"Uncle Cam was always interested in my agricultural projects. I introduced grapefruit to the country. Also Florida lemons. I taught people how to make compost boxes and incubators."

"You were really the first member of the agricultural program then?" I asked.

"I wouldn't say that," he said modestly. "Agriculture is a hobby for me. I've always said that every missionary should have a sense of humor and a healthy hobby."

"Why is this?" Jim asked.

"It should be obvious why one needs a sense of humor. The hobby keeps you from getting lazy. The tropical climate gets to you if you let it."

All this time our kids had been stuffing themselves. Mrs. Hocking seemed complimented, but I was embarrassed.

"Quite a cook I picked for myself," Joe bragged, smiling at his wife, who lowered her eyes and looked very pleased with his approval.

"What we need now is some negative comment about Wycliffe's work here. We don't want to do a whitewash job," I said.

"Oh, I just might be able to help you out there," Joe replied, his bright blue eyes twinkling. "You know I appreciate those folks out there, but I'm not a member yet.

"My main criticism would be they just aren't evangelistic enough to suit me. They really aren't missionaries in the sense that most folks would use the term. They are doing the 'ground work' by getting the Word into the vernacular of the tribes, and of course whenever people start reading God's Word there are some conversions. Some good old-fashioned gospel-preaching missionaries need to come in behind them and reap the harvest they are sowing."

"But they are here as linguists. Their contract with the government states that very clearly, and they scrupulously adhere to the terms of that contract," Jim broke in defensively. "Why, it would be unethical to do anything else. And if they broke the contract, think of all the good . . ."

"Whooooah," laughed Joe. "I'm on their side, too. But you asked me for negative criticism, and that would have to be the thing most mentioned. I'll admit that most of the people who condemn them don't really know about all that is being done."

I just had to put my two cents' worth in. "It seems to me that as Christians we sometimes underestimate the power of the Word of God. When we visited with the Machiguengas, we saw Christian villages with a church, a native pastor, native believers, with their own songs and styles of service and everything. I really don't see that while we give people the Bible it is necessary to impose our brand of culture on them."

"Well," laughed Joe, "It's plain to see you two have been thoroughly convinced. I just wish I could get you as interested in my latest project. I've been trying for years to get Scripture down on tape for distribution to those who can't read. It's a natural tie-in with the translation work of Wycliffe. Some of them are interested already. And with the advent of cassettes, why, we could . . ."

I smiled to myself as Joe ran on enthusiastically about his latest brainchild. I could see why he and Uncle Cam were friends. They are so much alike, always busy, always planning two or three steps ahead of anyone else.

JIM: Lolly and Buzz Sawyer graciously gave a small dinner party so we could meet Jack Hough, the affable field director for the South American Indian Mission, the largest evangelical mission in the area.

"Wycliffe and SAIM complement one another," Jack said, "although we have no direct ties. We are gradually doing away with our Indian schools because the bilingual program is filling the need. We have our own radio network, but charter JAARS planes when we need them. The Catalina brings our people in for field conference during January. We often consult the Wycliffe doctors and in Lima stay at their group house."

"It isn't all one way," Buzz put in. "Our pilots and linguists stop at SAIM stations for overnights in the jungle. And they give us weather reports."

"We try to help each other," Jack continued, "which I think is what Christians should do."

I asked Jack to explain SAIM's objectives. He did so without hesitation.

"Our primary objective is to organize indigenous churches that will evangelize all the people. We work both with Peruvians and Indians. Actually some of the Peruvians aren't too happy about so much emphasis on helping the Indians. Dr. Binder's Hospital Amazonia serves Indians, and takes only emergency Peruvian cases. And, of course, the bilingual school program is just for them. The Peruvians say, 'Why aren't you helping us?' We do have pastors' conferences and supplement the salaries of some native pastors. And we have a bookstore in Pucallpa and a literature ministry. Things like that."

The SAIM director stopped and snapped his fingers. "I didn't mention our regular Bible school for training pastors. That's crucial to all our work. Our school is smaller than the Swiss Indian Mission's but they take only Indians."

"Do your missionaries work in the Indian languages?" Marti asked.

"We have a couple of single girls among the Campas who are studying the language with Will Kindberg. They have about twenty-five baptized believers up there. I wish we had more working in the Indian languages. But personnel and funds are our big problems."

Jack stared off into space. "I wonder. I just wonder," he said, "how many little lost tribes there are in these jungles. I know the big population centers are important, but Christ loves these people, too. I wonder how many there are who have never heard the Word."

A huge rhinoceros beetle suddenly fluttered against the inside of the screen. "What a monster!" Marti exclaimed. "Celia would love to have it for her collection."

Buzz treated it very respectfully. He finally scooped it into a jar, screwed on a lid, and handed the jar to Marti. "He's all yours," he said, as if it were nothing.

Jack said they had to be going, so we thanked them and our hosts, and left with the beetle.

The next afternoon, Sunday, the base bus stopped out front. "Anybody here for the Swiss Indian Mission?" Will Kindberg called.

We climbed on the bus. Mrs. Duncan and Lee were there too, along with two other couples—Ed and Eva Riggle and Virgil (the driver) and Leona Pease—and about a dozen Campa and Piro students. Mrs. Duncan looked pale and drawn.

"Has the serum arrived yet?" Marti asked immediately.

The white-haired grandmother shook her head. "No, and we're getting concerned. I used to worry about how the shots would hurt; now I'm afraid of not getting them. They're trying to locate some serum in the States and have it flown down."

As the bus jolted along the road that runs past the Pucallpa airport, Will talked about the Campas. "These seven Campas on the bus and their friends at SIM are typical of the Christian men now coming up. They'll be the salt of the earth in the new Campa society. We hope the Campas will build a group of strong churches and follow the Amueshas into the Peruvian Evangelical Union. Do you know about them?"

"Just what I've read in the files. Mary Ruth Wise and Martha Duff are the translators. The Amueshas set up their own Bible school for training believers and in 1967 their churches joined the national evangelical association."

"That's a first for any Indian church in Peru," Will said. "Maybe a first for any in all of South America. What's significant is that they were accepted on an even par with the Spanish churches. The Amueshas border the Campas on the northwest. Both groups have similar social and economic problems. White colonists are moving in and grabbing up land. We're trying to help the Indians get title to their own lands and build an economy that will make them self-sufficient. It's very important that they not be dependent economically or spiritually upon outsiders."

Will was off and running. "I know that some people say Bible translation is not worth the effort when the majority group is moving in on the minority. They say that the minority languages will soon be abandoned. Many years from now that may happen to the Campas, but they need the Scriptures now in their own language."

The bus slowed and turned through a gate which bore only the sign: SIM—Kilometer 15. We rode a couple of miles over a dirt road that ran through a cattle pasture and stopped before a row of frame dormitories. The Campas and Piros eagerly piled out and ran to greet their friends. Will and Ed followed.

A tall, balding man, wearing khakis and a checkered red shirt and speaking with a thick accent, introduced himself as Ernesto Hauser, director of the school. At our request, he ticked off salient facts about the Swiss Indian Mission. "We operate this Bible school and an orphanage for Quechua Indian children in the mountains. We are 23 couples, all European—Swiss, German, and French. Uncle Cam and a Peruvian evangelical senator helped us secure 2500 acres that border on the lake. We have 43 Indian students from 11 tribes.

"We believe that to understand the Indians, we must live with them and learn their language and customs. So most of our faculty spend six months in tribes and six months here. We have a few couples who are full time tribal workers.

"During the six months of school the students meet twice weekly for services in their respective languages. They study Scripture both in their language and in Spanish. We use the Wycliffe-SIL translations. Many of them preach when they're home for six months.

"Let's take a walk around," the director suggested. "We began here in little thatched buildings in 1959. We now have twenty-nine of these frame buildings. On the left are the students' dormitories with quarters for both married and single students. On this side are our missionaries' homes and the classroom buildings. Up ahead is our power plant, sawmill, and shop. We make all our own furniture. The trees are cut from the property which we're gradually clearing to expand grazing for our cattle herd. Did I tell you that the students do almost all the farm and shop work for their tuition and room and board? They study four days and work two days each week. When they go back to their tribes to be pastors, they'll be better able to support their families."

We stopped beside an enormous cooking pot set over a 6x4-foot grate. "Students from different tribes gather around and cook yucca," the director said. "Some may even have fought each other in years past. Here they're together in Christian fellowship. But we respect their differences. The Campas, for example, will not drink cow's milk because they say milk is made for babies. However, powdered milk is quite all right, so we give them that."

The sun was setting over the lovely campus as we drove away. "Did you notice that every building was spic and span?" I commented. "And they didn't know guests were coming."

13.

The "Watermen"

JIM: "C'mon, let's weigh in, folks. We've already got the cargo in the plane."

Marti frowned at Floyd Lyons who was impatiently standing over the scale. "There are just no secrets around this place," she grumbled.

"Wrong, lady," the wiry Texan drawled. "I'm the only one who knows."

"Say, have you heard if they've located any serum?" It wasn't necessary to explain *what* serum.

"No, they haven't," he answered seriously. "And they only have until the day after tomorrow!"

Floyd handed Marti a mysterious package. "Deliver this to Martha Jakway."

"What is it?" she wanted to know.

"Just about 80,000 soles for the Aguaruna teachers. It's cash—so don't lose it."

"Just, huh?" Marti said. "Do I get a commission?"

Floyd scowled at her and said, "Let's go, folks."

Our girls were staying at the Nelsons and had seemed unconcerned that we were flying four hundred miles across the jungle. They felt completely at home on the base.

We followed Floyd's little motorized baggage cart to the lake and climbed into the black and yellow Cessna that floated near shore. Tom Brewington, the newest JAARS pilot, climbed in after us. I sat in the copilot's seat and Martin behind in the jump seat.

At 4,000 feet Tom leveled off above the *café con leche* Ucayali that curled and crooked below us as if it were uncertain of its destination.

"This little bird will fly faster and haul more than a Helio," Tom said. "But the Helio has a shorter takeoff and stronger cabin. A crash could turn this cabin into tinfoil."

He eased back on the stick. "We'll get on top of those clouds up ahead. The Cessna can climb at 800 feet per minute. The Helio is only half as fast.

"These clouds are harmless," he assured us. "But you have to be careful about a line of thunderstorms. They might spit you out."

Tom passed across a sheaf of flight maps. "We'll zip along the Ucayali

for about an hour then cut across to the Marañón. I guess you know
they're the two main headwater streams of the Amazon. See where they
come together northwest of us to form the big river."

We passed the first radio checkpoint and Tom checked in with the
tower. "Just talked to Millie Larson," Grace said. "The weather's two-
eighths out there."

"That means it's almost clear," Tom interpreted. "At eight-eighths
the sky is completely overcast."

The plane slipped smoothly over the river that coiled through the
green carpet below us. "One air mile must equal three on the river," I
said to Tom. "I can see why river travel takes so long."

I fished out a thick file on the Aguarunas and handed a sheaf of old
letters to Marti. "Homework," I said cheerily.

I had scanned the information gathered from the Nazarene Foreign
Mission Board and the history files back at the base. The Aguarunas
were long-haired headhunters by tradition and hostile to encroaching
whites. Early Jesuit missionaries had made little headway in the valleys
along the tributary streams to the swift Marañón. About 1900 the
"watermen" had massacred an entire settlement of whites who had
moved into the area.

Roger Winans, a determined, dedicated Nazarene, had been the first
evangelical missionary to contact the Aguarunas. After burying his first
wife and son on the coast, he married a single missionary and started
over the mountains in 1926. After more than three weeks of painfully
slow travel, they met a small band of Aguaruna men who were wearing
loincloths and carrying blowguns and spears. They took Roger and his
wife to the house of the chief, Samarin. The chief was impressed with
the missionaries' miracle medicine and invited them to stay. After Esther
Winans constructed an alphabet and prepared a "talking paper," Samarin removed a crown from his head and placed it in her hands—giving
her symbolic authority to teach his people.

Three years later, the second wife of Roger Winans died in childbirth. The missionary returned to the coast and brought back another
wife. When Chief Samarin became a believer, other Aguarunas followed.
The Nazarenes established a string of mission schools but made slow
progress because they lacked understanding of the language.

In 1947 Titus and Florence Nickel, two of Wycliffe's original Peru
twenty-five, came to begin a scientific analysis of the language. Unfor-
tunately, circumstances prevented any systematic continuation of their
project. Their supplies ran out, and their trip to the Pacific coast to
replenish them took a tortuous 21 days. Though Larry Montgomery of
JAARS flew them back—in one hour and 55 minutes—they were soon
called back by Uncle Cam, who felt Titus was needed for building
houses at the new base. Ray and Alice Wakelin returned in their place,
but Ray came down with severe malaria and had to return to the States.

A faded letter dated 1950 caught my attention. "Hey, listen to this,"
I called back to Marti above the roar of the engine.

Left: A "dramatic" moment in the life of a jungle pilot.
Right: "The weather is eight-eight, but I saw
grandma going to her garden. It's going to be a
nice day."

"Elvin M. Douglass, the director of the Nazarene mission to the Aguarunas, is asking for help from Wycliffe. He regrets that the Nickels had left, and, oh, get this quote: 'We've had work among the Aguarunas for nearly thirty years, and we cannot see any results of a permanently desirable nature. . . .Our greatest handicap is our inadequacy as trained linguists. Without the aid of competent translators we cannot see how the work is going to be done. . . .We request translators be sent as quickly as possible to complete the work. Whatever our mission has in resources is at their disposal. We want them. We need them.'

"Isn't that terrific?" I asked Marti.

"After all those years," she said, "it took a lot of gumption to admit that they couldn't do the job themselves."

"Well, we're starting that crossover between rivers," Tom was saying. "But don't worry. We'll be over water again pretty soon." He flipped the radio switch. "Eight two one starting the crossover to the Huallga. Will report back in fifteen minutes. Over."

"Okay, Tom," Grace squawked back. "Be listening for you."

I watched the Ucayali slowly vanish from behind. Now there was nothing but the green jungle below. "If we went down and weren't killed," I said to Tom, "how long would it take to find us?"

"Who knows?" he said thinly. "Maybe never. But there's very little chance of our going down, and if we do I've got a survival kit and a reflecting mirror. The problem might be finding an open space to catch the sun."

Tom looked at his watch. "Nine more minutes to the Huallga. Then we've got one more little crossover before we hit the Marañón. We'll stop at a little spot called Puerto America and pick up some gas."

The fast-flowing Marañón looked mighty good. "She's high," Tom said as we dipped below the treetops. "Gotta watch for logs and brush." He banked slightly to the right over a huge treetop, then straightened up and dropped onto the water.

A dozen or so ragged children waited expectantly on the north bank. Behind them four or five fading houses faced the river. We taxied toward them.

The pilot cut the engine, stepped out onto a float, and tossed a rope to one of the boys. Then he stepped into the mud and waded ashore to pull the plane closer. "All that's good about this place," he said dryly, "is gas and Inca Cola."

While Marti talked with the young Peruvian woman who kept the store, Tom and I rolled a drum of gasoline from under a shed down to the river bank. Sweating in the sun, he wrenched open the barrel and wrestled it over to fill his five-gallon gas can. Then he climbed onto a wing, opened a fuel tank, and began to pour the gasoline inside. "Nothing to it," he said, wiping the perspiration from his eyes.

I climbed onto the wing and took over the pouring. After putting forty gallons in both sides, we rolled back the barrel and doused our thirst with supersweet Inca Colas. When Marti and I were back in the plane, Tom took the rope and began jumping up and down on a float. "Gotta get 'er out of the mud," he shouted.

When the floats came free, he used a paddle—standard equipment for jungle flying—to maneuver us away from the bank. With the current moving us downstream, he climbed in the pilot's seat and started the engine.

"What if it didn't start?" Marti asked.

"We'd break out our fishing gear," Tom said laconically. "It usually takes hold, though."

From Puerto America Tom flew straight west toward the ascending foothills of the Andes. We slipped through two mountain passes, rounded a bend, and dipped down for a landing. The water was faster and clearer up here.

Tom made another beautiful landing against the current and swung toward a sandbar where a small crowd waited. Marti and I jumped out and waded ashore to greet Millie Larson and her temporary partner Allene Heitzman. Marti passed a mail pouch and a box of foodstuffs to Millie. "I hope the dentist sent my temporary filling," Millie said.

The pilot squinted at the mid-afternoon sun. "Marti and I'd better move on if we're going to see the people upstream. See you tomorrow if the good Lord's willing and the creeks don't rise."

So Marti flew off with the pilot and I stayed to spend the night with the single girls. All Marti said upon leaving was, "How romantic!"

MARTI: With Jim back at Nueva Vida I got to sit in the copilot's seat, which is a lot more fun because you can *see.* "A small plane certainly is different from a big jet," I shouted. "You really feel as if you're flying."

"Now you know why people get hooked on it," Tom yelled back while he wove the plane around the clouds instead of flying over them as a jet would have.

It was too frustrating to call back and forth over the noise of the engine, so I contented myself with sightseeing. The terrain was quite mountainous now, and very beautiful, not at all what one expects of the jungle. I'd always thought all jungles were flat and swampy.

The further north we got the clearer and swifter the river looked. Where we finally landed the current was really rapid.

I looked over to the shore and saw a bunch of Indians, mostly kids, and a tall blond gringo with a baby perched on his shoulders.

Tom positioned the plane, cut the motor, scrambled out with the agility of a monkey and threw the rope. We were soon secured.

"You take care of the mail pouch and the money, and I'll drag out the supplies," he ordered.

I climbed out and introduced myself to the gringo, since he was the only one who spoke my language.

"I'm Dennis Olsen, and this is my son, Curtis. We understood a couple was coming."

"My husband stopped off at Millie's. We figured if we split up we could get twice as much information. What's the name of this place?"

"Temashmum."

"Does that translate?"

"Not that I know of. We call it 'Little Rome,' since it's built on seven hills. Come on with me to our house and meet my wife. You're to spend the night with us, so we'll take your gear along," he said, picking up my duffel bag and a small box of food.

"Fine. What's your function?" I asked, flipping on my mike as we climbed one of the seven hills."

"Community development. Right now we're experimenting with rice to see what kind will grow around here. This would give them a money crop and also improve their diet."

"What kinds of rice are there?"

"Two kinds—paddy rice and dry rice. You get a much higher yield with paddy rice, and I like paddy rice better, but it isn't easy to grow here, so they are trying dry rice. The four-month variety."

"How big a project is this?"

"We cleared two hectares. That's five acres. I've kept records of how many hours they have invested in the project."

"Do you pay them for this work?"

"Oh no. This is their project. They're all for it. The only thing I give is know-how."

"Are you teaching them crop rotation?"

"Not yet. We've only been out here since April, so we haven't had our first crop yet. We'll plant two crops and then put it in cudzu."

"Cudzu? That's the leafy, viny stuff they have on the farm at the base?"

"Yeah, same stuff. It revitalizes the soil and at the same time keeps the jungle from reclaiming your field. The next time you want to use it, you don't have all that clearing to do."

"But is it good for anything itself?"

"Yes. It's good for animals, almost any kind—cattle, chickens."

"Do they have cattle out here?"

"Some of them do."

All this time I was huffing and puffing along behind the long-legged Scandinavian, watching his beautiful, blue-eyed, cotton-topped son.

We came to a hut. "This is our new home," Dennis said proudly. "Come on in."

I followed him into the hut. A smiling freckle-faced redhead greeted me. "Hi. I'm Suzy. Welcome to the Olsens!"

Dennis put my duffel bag and box of food on the floor. I held onto the money.

"How about mail call?" he said, looking at the pouch I was carrying.

"Oh, sorry about that," I replied and handed him the pouch. The two of them excused themselves and greedily dug through the contents to see what was theirs. While they read I inspected their new home.

The main room was a combination kitchen–living room–dining room all in one. It had the usual *pona* walls, shelves, furniture, and dirt floor.

Three steps led up to the rest of the house, two rooms with *pona* floors. Dennis had put the baby in the first of those rooms and he was contentedly crawling around on the bouncy floor, playing with his toys.

"I'll take the rest of the mail over to Martha and Jeannie," said Dennis. "They'll be anxious to get it."

"Oh, take these things with you, will you, Dennis," Suzy suggested. "We're all going to eat together over there tonight and they don't have enough dishes for everyone, and I have some things for our potluck dinner."

"Maybe I ought to go with Dennis," I said. "I have to talk to Jeannie."

"Fine," Dennis concurred. "Bye, Suzy. Come on," he said to me as we walked out the door. "We'll go see if Jeannie has dismissed her class yet."

"Jeannie has a class? I thought she was a nurse."

"She is. But she is running her own *sanitario* class in Aguaruna since the fellows she is training don't speak enough Spanish to qualify for the classes at the base."

"Is she teaching the same things as Joan?"

"I believe so. Yesterday Suzy set up a frog exhibit to show the circulatory system. That really went over big."

"Is Suzy a nurse too?"

"Nope. Medical technologist."

We were down in a little valley by this time and could see Jeannie giving instructions to some departing Indians. After introductions, Jeannie took the boxes that Dennis had been carrying and we started toward her house.

"Sure you can manage that all right?" Dennis asked Jeannie.

"Of course," she replied independently.

"I dismissed class a little early today," she explained to me as we walked along. "The boys have gone after some roofing—well, glorified tar paper is what it really is. Anyway, they are going to use it to build a community john.

"We had an interesting lesson yesterday, about the circulatory system."

"Dennis mentioned something about it. How did you do it?"

"Suzy tacked down the frog's foot on a slide and then lowered the microscope so that you could see the blood moving through the veins. They were really impressed by this, so while we had it set up, we let the school children come over and see it. Then the adults got curious and all the long-hairs had to come see also."

"Who are the long-hairs?"

"The older generation."

"You mean in this culture the older generation has long hair, and younger cuts its hair? Boy, that's a switch!"

Jeannie and Martha's hut was at the top of a hill. When we finished our climb, Jeannie introduced me to her partner, then began opening the package we'd brought in on the plane while Martha went through the mail and I asked questions. "I'm glad to turn this money over to you, Martha. It's too much responsibility for me," I sighed in relief. "By the way, where did you go to school?"

"The University of California at Santa Barbara."

"And your specialty is education?"

"Yes."

"Tell me about your work."

"I teach the teachers, train the supervisors."

I wasn't having much success getting Martha to talk about herself, so I turned to Jeannie.

"Jeannie, how about bragging about your partner a little? She's too modest."

"Glad to," Jeannie said, as she finished cutting open her package. "Martha is doing the biggest job of anybody in the tribe. I don't know exactly how to define her job, but she has 114 teachers under her and four besides that who are supervisors. She trains the supervisors. The supervisors train the teachers. Each supervisor has 20 some teachers under him, and handles about 10 schools. She has to see that they all get all their supplies to all their schools which are spread over 100 miles. She keeps track of how many students there are and at what level.

"She also interviews people who want to be teachers. She trains teachers to teach adults, which is a different thing entirely. And she has to see all teachers get their pay when it comes."

Jeannie stopped in her oration long enough to pull something from the box.

"Oh, no!" she wailed. "I ordered salt for the cows here and they sent me Epsom salts! Good grief, this is enough to give the whole tribe diarrhea. You wouldn't believe some of the misunderstandings that come through ordering by radio." She sighed, then packed it back into the box.

"Oh, well, back to Martha. She has been giving the teachers a refresher course. She takes them down to the classroom and has them observe some really good teachers. For about two or three years now she has been shaping up our teachers. The people have been pushing to get more teachers, so it has been a tremendous pressure on us."

"When was the first bilingual school started?"

"Fifteen years ago."

"If you could have a couple of helpers, what would you have them do?"

"One for adult education and one for the supervisors," Jeannie answered without hesitation. "Then all Martha would have left to do would be to teach the teachers."

"That's all, huh?"

They looked at each other and smiled. "Yeah, that's all," they said almost in unison.

While we were talking, Martha was cooking and Jeannie was setting the table. Martha looked tired.

"Is there something I can do to be useful?" I asked.

"Yeah. Keep out of our way," teased Jeannie.

I looked her over a while—a very warm, vivacious female, I decided. Certainly not the old maid type. Very trim and full of energy. She had spent over fifteen years living with these Indians in the most primitive of circumstances but looked much better than many of her contemporaries in the States who spend untold time and money on creams, lotions, steam baths, and beauty parlors.

Supper preparations were interrupted by some Indians who came to see Martha about something. "Iyu, iyu," they kept repeating. Jeannie instructed me to say it back to them, so they would not think I was very unfriendly. So I said, "Iyu," and they smiled. Probably at my pronunciation.

They discussed something with Martha. Then we all said "Iyu" again and they left.

"It's hard to believe these people are headhunters," I said. "They all seem so friendly."

Jeannie grinned. "I guess you could just call them 'friendly headhunters.' "

"Joy! Are they really still fierce?"

"Oh, we haven't had a revenge killing in six or seven months," she replied in a reassuring tone. I didn't feel very reassured.

"Tell me something about your medical work," I asked.

"Well, even though medicine is my specialty, I've had to be involved in many phases of the work. This is true with everyone. There is so much to do and not enough people to do it.

"I guess the most frustrating thing about the medical work is so often the Indians don't bring their sick to us until it's too late.

"The work is tough. Like the time we vaccinated six thousand Indians against measles. But I don't mind that. What gets to me is when they bring in someone like the man who came today." She shook her head. "He has a lump right in the middle of his midriff. I'm not sure what it is—a big hard mass—must be a tumor of some sort. He says his liver has come down. But he has been sick for eight months. If they had brought him to me then, we could have flown him to the base for an operation. There's nothing we could now do except prolong the agony, so an operation is out of the question.

"It's hard to make this kind of decision, but it has to be done. We can't spend time and money working on someone that is terminal. There are so many other people who could be helped." She shook her head sadly.

"Aren't some of their homemade remedies helpful?" I asked, trying to get away from an obviously painful subject.

"That's a well-told fairytale. Witchcraft kills many more than it cures. Don't believe those Indian paradise stories."

"Could you give an example?"

"Well, one time they brought in a young woman, in her twenties I would guess, who was paralyzed. Probably from polio. Anyway their method of treatment was to put her feet into the fire. Since she had no feeling in her lower extremities, her feet stayed in the fire until they were burned off. Then they just pushed her a little closer and a little closer to the flames."

I shuddered despite the heat. "How nauseating," I commented. "Could you help her any?"

"By the time they brought her to me her feet had been burned off half-way up her calves. She was so full of gangrene we had to let her die."

Dinner was nearly prepared, and I was ready for a more appetizing topic. The Olsens came in, bringing the baby and his high chair. They were followed by the pilot.

As we sat around the table eating, they started swapping stories. I kept the recorder on my lap with the mike on the table so I could pick up their voices.

"You're not really going to use all these way-out experiences in your book, are you?" Tom asked.

"Probably not. But we have a file called 'Tall Tales Missionaries Tell,' and you never can tell what might become of them.

"Jeannie, Joan Lemke told us about an experience you had. You made a bunch of Indians lay down their guns before you would allow them to cross over a creek to the village. The way Joan tells it, you were absolutely fearless. Were you afraid?"

"Not right then. This group was coming after a widow and her children, because of a revenge killing," she explained to the others. "They were all dressed up with feathers and everything. Really quite exciting.

"The teacher with us was so scared he was absolutely white! He said, 'Oh, sister, they have come here to kill!' But I really couldn't believe it. So I told them to leave their guns on the other side of the creek. They all looked kinda sheepish, put their guns down, took their clothes off, came across the creek, put their clothes back on and marched toward us.

"The widow they were after was away working in her *chacra* (garden), but they found two of her children and were going to take them. The poor little kids were screaming and hollering like anything.

"I told them, 'Their mother isn't here. Wait until she comes back and you can talk to her.' So we grabbed the kids—I poked one woman, who was really drunk, in the nose—and Joan put the children in her bedroom and sat in front of the door.

"The men were furious, but they finally left the village, shaking their fists and saying, 'You better have that woman and her kids here by next week or we are really going to shoot this place up.' "

"Did they come back after her?"

"Yes, and she went with them. She knew that sooner or later she would have to. At least by going willingly she could keep all her kids with her.

"You know," she continued, "I really wasn't afraid until afterward when the teacher said, 'Sister, they are really mad. They are not fooling!' "

"Were there any times when you really were afraid they were after you?"

"No, not really. They have always been very friendly, although we have had a few difficulties with witch doctors from time to time."

The baby started fussing and rubbing his eyes, and we conceded that it was time for bed.

"We'll have to leave right after breakfast in the morning," Tom said to me.

"But there's so much more I want to learn about," I moaned. "It's really frustrating. There should be a whole book about the Aguarunas, and we'll have to try and tell it all in one chapter."

The moon hadn't risen yet, so the night was velvety black as Tom and I followed the Olsens back to their hut for the night.

When daylight came, it seemed as though I had just lain down. Everything was quiet, so I just stretched and looked around a bit.

I was fascinated by the thatched roof. It was oval-shaped, and the weaving was beautiful. The two seams reaching up to the center of the roof matched perfectly. A real work of art.

Then the delicious aroma of fresh brewed coffee came to me, and I realized the reason it was so quiet was that everyone else was up already and in the other room. I quickly dressed and stuffed my gear back into the duffel bag.

As I entered the "all-purpose" room, I was greeted with a cheery good morning from Suzy.

"You should have called me so I could help," I said, embarrassed to be the last one up.

"Oh, that's all right. I'm glad you slept well. We were afraid the night noises might keep you awake."

"Night noises! I didn't hear a thing."

"Good. Our neighbors have a habit of laughing and talking at odd hours during the night."

Dennis and Tom were talking on the radio to the base, trying to get instructions clear. Finally Tom said, "I'll call back from Nueva Vida; maybe we can get a clearer signal from there. Over and out."

We listened in on the other calls to and from the base.

"This is like a glorified party line," I remarked. "You get to hear all the news from the other tribes each morning."

We sat down to eat. Scrambled eggs, bacon, freshly made home baked rolls and coffee.

"Suzy, you give me a complex. You made all this over that open fire?"

They laughed at my incredulity. "Well, we don't have this fancy a breakfast every day," she admitted. "But then, we don't have company very often either."

"You guys are really impressing me with what a tough life you lead," I teased.

After breakfast Jeannie came over to make a call to the doctor and to tell us goodbye.

"Martha couldn't come. She already has visitors," she explained.

"I understand. I wish I could have stayed longer so I could have made friends, and had time to get her to talk."

"I'll bet you're glad everyone isn't as shy as I am," Jeannie kidded.

"Oh, you make my job easy," I admitted. "I really do wish I could stay longer though."

"Maybe next time—when you write that book about the Aguarunas."

Jeannie made her call while Tom and I got our things together. Then we all started toward the plane.

"Don't forget to return the Epsom salts," Jeannie reminded Tom. "And please explain exactly what I want and why. We really need that salt."

Tom and I were soon flying over the seven hills of "Little Rome." I wondered if Jim had had as interesting an experience in Nueva Vida.

JIM: After Marti and Tom flew away in a dash of spray, I climbed the hill with Millie, Allene and a sharp-looking Aguaruna named Nelson to the two rows of thatch huts that are Nueva Vida ("New Life") village. Naked little boys chattered behind us.

We stopped briefly at the most unusual clinic I have ever seen. With bamboo walls, balsa doors and thatched roof, it was a quaint replica of the clinic at Yarina. The waiting room was just inside the front entrance with a bamboo bench facing a bamboo counter window that opened into the receptionist's (Nelson's uncle's) office. Behind this office was the "doctor's" (Nelson's) office. Three examining rooms, all with bamboo beds, were situated off a wide hallway that ran the length of the building.

Millie pointed to two portable typewriters at the front end of the wide hall. "Nelson and I work here. We just finished Galatians and are now into Romans." She saw the look on my face and added, "He's brilliant, a genius." She explained. "Besides being my translation helper, he's the pastor here at this village which, incidentally, he named Nueva Vida. The children go to school at another village a few minutes down the river where Nelson's brother is the teacher."

We started toward Millie's house. From the outside I wouldn't have known it from the rest. Inside, there was a three-log fire. Over the fire hung a large blackened basket holding a chunky object. "The Indians got this rock salt from a mountain," she said. "I'm drying it out for them."

Across from the fire were shelves holding canned goods, cookware, the all-important radio, and other supplies. Behind the shelves on a raised platform were their beds. A utility table completed the furnishings.

Millie smiled. "The people take good care of us. They built our house. They bring us water and food. We're obviously dependent upon them. They guard our things from outsiders when we're away. In fifteen years I've never had anything stolen by an Aguaruna."

Millie, an attractive tall blue-eyed Scandinavian, wearing a fading beige shirtwaist dress, walked gracefully across the dirt floor. The pioneer type, she looked as if she had just stepped off a covered wagon. "Please excuse us while we read our mail," she said.

Allene finished first and I had a chance to ask about her work. "Virginia Hart and I work with the Pajonal dialect of the Campas. They're close to the Kindbergs' dialect, but different enough to merit a separate translation. I'm working on some of my data here while I keep Millie company. We'll be going to the base in a few weeks. She's head of translation checking and is on the executive committee."

Allene said she was from Kansas City; Millie came from northern Minnesota at the headwaters of the Mississippi. I thought it interesting that Millie was now at the headwaters of the Amazon.

"I didn't plan it this way," Millie said, "although at Wheaton, where I majored in English lit, I became interested in the tribes. I came to jungle camp with Brazil in mind, then I heard teachers were desperately needed in Peru. I was at Yarina when the Wakelins were here with the language. They asked me to come out and help with some linguistic problems. Jeannie Grover, then a nurse at the clinic, came along with me on this 'temporary' assignment. But then Ray got sick and had to leave. We decided to continue the work while he was gone. He was never able to return, so we stayed."

Allene prepared supper while Millie sat on an old drum beside the fire and talked. Two small naked boys slipped in and sat discreetly against a wall.

"Did anyone ever tell you that the Aguarunas should be left as they are?" I asked.

Millie pushed a log closer into the fire. "A few people in the States have dropped the hint. What they don't realize is that no people, no matter how remote, can escape change. The question is what kind of change: the change that demoralizes and corrupts as outsiders move in or the change that comes with education, economic independence, dignity, pride in heritage, and most important, transformed lives through the gospel in the people's own language. The Peruvian government prefers the latter and is behind our efforts to effect this type of change."

"But do the Aguarunas want this kind of change? Or would they prefer to just remain as they are and be swept up in the tide of whatever comes?"

"They do want planned change. For themselves and their children. They want it enough to move out of their little valleys and into villages where their children can attend school. I think they've got a good chance now to build a strong society."

Millie rocked gently back and forth on the old drum. "The Aguarunas have been exploited and abused by outsiders but they haven't been broken. They're proud, aggressive, independent, hard-working, and just plain smart when they're given a chance. They're clean, too. You should hear them fussing about whites who come down the river and dirty the beaches."

Allene called us to supper. Millie kept talking while we ate. "Please don't think we're responsible for all the progress out here. The pioneer Nazarene missionaries may have been lacking in linguistic training, but not in desire or example. Many of our best teachers attended their school. The Aguarunas still refer to Roger Winans as 'Father.' We built on their foundation."

"Are the Nazarenes still working among the Aguarunas?" I wondered.

"Yes. But they're way upriver. Dr. Larry Garmon, a chiropractor, is there now. They have some short-term Bible courses, but don't work in the language. Dr. Garmon has asked for some of our materials. A Swiss Indian Mission couple, Carlos and Doris Sachtler, have been here six years. They're helping organize churches and train pastors. They work in the language."

Could Millie estimate the number of Aguaruna believers?

"At least several thousand. I know some communities where all the adults are believers. About three thousand are now in the bilingual schools where Scripture is taught every day. More have graduated and would like to attend high school. But to do that they have to go to Pucallpa or out to the coast. One young man is studying at the University of Trujillo and wants to come back here and start a high school."

Allene began serving a banana spice cake.

"Is the Aguaruna church growing?" I asked, between bites of the delicious dessert.

"It reminds me of the book of Acts. Elias, an outstanding leader who has evangelized a lot of communities, translated the book with me. He worked the small river in back of us and now almost everyone there believes. Next January, he, Nelson and Tomás—a graduate of the SIM Bible School—are going into new areas to evangelize.

"I don't preach or teach, but I try to train some of the men by using the translated Scriptures," Millie continued. "Then I sit and listen and check the translation by what they say."

"When will you complete the New Testament?"

"Since Martha and the Olsens have joined us, I'm moving faster. Jeannie has always been a lifesaver. I have eleven books completed. Hope to finish four or five more of Paul's epistles this year. Could I give you some of my thoughts on goals for Bible translation?"

"Sure," I said. "The tape recorder is all ears."

"Okay, the first goal is to translate the New Testament with the highest faithfulness to the original meaning which the translator can achieve. This is primarily the responsibility of the translator and the translation consultants.

"The second goal is to translate the written Word into mature Christian life in the tribes. This involves other work such as literacy, community development, church development, and so on, with support from the entire team.

"These goals should be pursued simultaneously and carefully. What good is a New Testament that will not be read? The books can sit on the shelves at the base or lie around until the termites eat them in a few Indian homes. We want New Testaments that will become worn and dirty with much use, that will solve problems of individual Indians and families and communities, that will revolutionize the tribes.

"Do you know what we mean by idiomatic translation? A literal translation is much easier and faster to make. You don't need to know what the passage means; you just translate the words. Idiomatic translations, however, must communicate the message of the original. It retains the meaning of the original, but not necessarily the form. So to be idiomatic, the translator must first know what the original inspired text means. This requires digging into the commentaries and lexicons. Second, he must know well the language and culture into which he is translating. This he learns only by hard study and living close to the people.

"Let me give you part of a poem used by John Beekman, our head translation consultant. I don't know the author. But it makes a good point.

> If you wanted to shingle the ROOF of your mouth
>   Could you use the NAILS of your toes?
> Can you sit in the shade of the PALM of your hand?
>   Or beat the DRUM of your ear?
> Can you eat the CORN that grows on your toes?
>   Well, why not grow corn on your ear?
> Can the CROOK in your elbow be sent to jail?
>   If so, just what did it do?
> Where can I sharpen my shoulder BLADES?
>   I'll be hanged if I know, do you?"

"That's very good. Tell me, are Spanish and English closer languages than Spanish and Aguaruna?"

"Oh, yes. Aguaruna doesn't have the plural of nouns or masculine and feminine. Spanish will use one word for *carry*. Aguaruna has different ways to carry and every one a different word. Carry with your hands is one word; on your back is another. Aguaruna has different words for *put*. Put down a machete requires one verb; put down a basket, another. There are many, many other differences."

It was after ten when I stretched the mosquito net over the bamboo bed in Nelson's clinic and squirmed into the sleeping bag. I was almost asleep when a noisy chant and dance began in the hut just behind the clinic. Some tomfoolery, I felt, was going on. Maybe they were having a ceremony preparatory to taking my head. I felt ashamed at the thought and tried to sleep, but the noise continued until well after midnight.

Next morning at breakfast I asked the girls how they had slept and Millie remarked, "I didn't hear a thing."

Outside the fog was thicker than the proverbial pea soup. Tom radioed from upriver and asked about the weather. "Eight-eighths," Millie said, "but I saw 'grandma' going to her garden. That means it's going to be a nice day."

While we waited for the fog to clear, Carlos Sachtler, the SIM missionary, came by for some creation and Moses stories in Aguaruna which our plane had brought in the day before.

Millie gave them to him and said, "I expect there'll be some new names in your village shortly."

After Carlos left, I asked Millie what she meant.

"They like to use Bible names for their children. Right after I did John, a little boy was named Nathaniel. When we start on the next Old Testament story, I expect to see some Samsons. Maybe even a Delilah, though I hope not. The Aguarunas also name children after people they like. The year after Dr. Morote Best, the Peruvian educator came here, we found a boy in one school named Doctor and another named Morote."

Tom kept calling until Millie assured him the weather was two eighths. About half an hour later we heard the plane and hurried to the river. Tom didn't want to linger. "Floyd Lyons just gave me instructions to go pick up John Tuggy and Chief Tariri and take them down to a lake," he said. "Something about an argument among the Shapras over a widow."

I looked at Marti. "That must be the widow Lorrie and Sheila have been concerned about," she said.

"I don't think Floyd was too happy about you two going along, but since you're out here, there's no way to avoid it. Maybe you'll get something exciting to write about."

Chief Tariri in
tribal dress.

When we landed at
Lake Huambra the
population came to
greet us.

Author Hefley (center)
visits with Chief Tariri.
Behind Hefley pilot
Tom Brewington savors
the fish while Tariri's
nephew looks on.

14.

"Here Comes the War Party!"

JIM: We flew back to Puerto America for refueling. After pouring
the last five gallons into the right wing tank, I yelled down to Tom, "I
used to think being a jungle pilot was glamorous. I've changed my mind."

"Yes," he said, "there's lots more sweat than glamor. I lose five pounds
on every trip."

We left the Marañón and started over flat jungle. Tom radioed our
position to the base. "We're starting the crossover to the Pastaza. I'll get
back to you when we arrive."

I located our position on the flight map. We were just south of the
Huambisa tribe which lived along the border of Ecuador.

Tom glanced briefly at the map. "I've heard those Huambisas used
to be some headhunters," he said.

"What are they now?" Marti asked.

"I don't think they take heads the way they used to. Dave and Nancy
Beasley have done terrific work there. They're on furlough now."

The altimeter reading was easing downward. "The Huambisas and
Aguarunas are cousins in language," Tom continued. "But until the
gospel got to them, they were blood enemies."

The Pastaza River was coming close. Tom began a wide bank to get
in line for the landing. "Now these Shapras are really something else.
They used to out-headhunt the Huambisas."

Tom slipped over the treetops and turned up a straight stretch. A
floating treetop slid under us, and then we were on the water. We taxied
around a bend and into the mouth of a small river where two big log rafts
floated—a landing dock. John Tuggy was on the bank waving. He wore a
sidearm on his right hip and a hunting knife in a scabbard on the other.
Davy Crockett, I thought, without the coonskin cap!

We walked across the logs. I looked around for snakes. The big boas
are in Candoshi country, we had been told back at the base. I asked John
if he had seen any lately.

He patted the .38 on his hip. "Killed a little guy yesterday. About
fourteen feet long." His mouth curled into an impish grin. "But the
place where we'll stay tonight has some big ones."

We got into the plane and Tom shoved us away from the logs with
the paddle. "Pick the chief up a couple of miles down river," John told
him as he taxied the plane into the main current of the big river. As

Tom flew along just above the water, I kept an eye out for the feathered headdress familiar from pictures.

"There he is," John exclaimed, pointing to a short man in khakis and duck-billed cap standing on the north shore. Tom set the plane down, cut power, then swung around to the shore.

Chief Tariri climbed aboard and greeted us in Spanish. He carried himself so majestically he seemed much taller than his 5'6". He was not impressed by us outsiders.

Tom lifted the plane over the trees and we saw Tariri's new aluminum-roofed house glinting under the equatorial sun.

"The chief bought the first cattle ever seen in these parts," John shouted over the motor. "Some Indians once laughed at him for this— behind his back, of course. They don't now. He's got twenty-four head and has become a real cattle baron."

Tom passed a flight map across to John. The translator pointed to a tiny, wiggledy river. He squinted through the windshield. "That's it," he said.

Apparently Tom saw the river, for he banked slightly to the right. John directed Tom down to about two hundred feet over a cluster of thatched roof houses. "Circle until they see us," he said. "They'll know to meet us at Lake Huambra in the morning." John explained that the tiny lake was only seven minutes away by air, but that the Indians wouldn't start until the moon rose. "They have a few things on their minds that need clearing up," he added.

"The widow and her children?" I asked.

John nodded. "That's one thing."

I located the small lake on the flight map. Another small lake lay just northeast of Huambra, the place where Lorrie Anderson had been attacked by a boa.

Smooth water flashing in the sun signalled that we had reached our destination. Dense vegetation crept up to the shore and I didn't see any sign of life until we hit the water. Then John directed Tom toward the eastern shore and I saw an open-walled house in a small clearing.

"The chief's nephew lives here along with another family," John explained. "He has other relatives scattered around the lake. I haven't been out here in two, maybe three years."

Tom pulled up to shore and I jumped out to loop a rope around a big root that reached out of the water. The dark water looked as if it had been stained, but was astonishingly clear. "That's the way it is year 'round," John said. "There could be carbon or potassium deposits."

"Now, this really looks like Tarzan land," Marti declared.

The Indians from the house came running to greet Tariri and John. The translator introduced Tom, Marti, and me in the language that only he and four or five other whites in the world understand.

A splash behind us turned me around. A long-haired Shapra man had arrived in a dugout and was already striding toward Tariri and John. Eight or ten other canoes were coming toward us from across the lake where apparently there were other huts. The lake was hardly more than three-fourths of a mile wide. We stood aside as the new arrivals strode by us to welcome their chieftain relative and John.

Tariri greeted each one with booming voice and laugh. He downed one gourd full after another of *masato*, a drink which—John later told us—Shapras offer to visitors. John, I noticed, drank sparingly while Tariri must have gulped down a gallon of the yellow stuff. We didn't imbibe.

John, Tariri, and the men all talked at once, loudly. The women stoked fires and boiled something in a huge black pot covered with banana leaves. Children gathered in knots to whisper and giggle at us.

I finally edged close enough to see what they were cooking under the leaves—foot-wide slabs of fish, which John subsequently explained came from 200-pound armor fish, supposedly prehistoric, that bear live young and have no interior skeleton. "The lake is full of them," he told us. I wished immediately for a rod and reel, but he dampened my enthusiasm by reminding me that there were probably 25-foot boas in the lake also.

John and the Indians talked a while longer and took a few target shots with an old shotgun. Then he said, "The men and I are going to look around the lake a little. We'll be back soon."

Suddenly we realized they had left us with the women and children, and we couldn't speak even one word of their language.

MARTI: "Well, I can always play with the kids," I told Jim. He nodded as if to say, "Do your own thing," and walked down to the plane where Tom was running a safety check.

I sat down on a rough bench and switched on my tape recorder. Half a dozen curious, naked little boys gathered around to inspect me. I left the recorder running and the mike on the bench beside me while I did some finger tricks. I put my hands together with one finger sticking straight up and another straight down. When I started wiggling the two fingers I got the desired reaction. They laughed and giggled and chattered away like a bunch of magpies. None of them could figure out how I did it. Some of the girls came over to see what was going on, and then some of the mothers sauntered over. All chattering away.

A smile from me was all the women needed. They really became friendly then! Too friendly. They began to feel my skin, running their fingers along my arms. Then they felt the freckles on my face, trying to rub them off. I presume they thought they were painted on.

Then they started feeling my hair and inspecting my scalp. They looked kind of disappointed, and I realized then they had been searching for lice. I wondered how long I could stay there without acquiring a few.

This inspection bit got old in a hurry, so I stopped my recorder and turned it to REWIND. They giggled at the funny noise. I put it on PLAY.

Quiet descended. Then when they recognized their voices, pandemonium broke loose. Were they impressed with themselves! They were really excited. When the tape ended they wanted to hear it again. I replayed it, but when they wanted to hear it a third time, I showed them my mike, talked into it, then played that. Ahhh! They caught on.

I handed the mike to one of the boys. He said something, then passed it on. After a number of them had talked, they all started calling to one of the women, teasing her, trying to talk her into something. They obviously wanted her to perform.

She finally walked over, took the mike, looked all around to make sure everyone was listening, cleared her throat, then began singing in a high thin voice. The song had very little melody, using maybe three or four notes, but I could tell they all thought the performance was great.

They continued amusing themselves with the recorder while I scrutinized them. They had high cheekbones, black eyes and hair. Beautiful features. I wondered how they kept their hair so neat without combs, and how they managed to cut their bangs so straight without scissors. Everyone had bangs, both males and females.

It wasn't long before the men returned from their canoe trip. Then they got in on the recording session. What hams! They really enjoyed performing. Everyone, including the chief, had to get into the act.

Everyone was laughing and talking and enjoying himself. Some of the women served more *masato*. Despite the language barrier it reminded me of one of my family's reunions at home.

"What do you think of the Shapras?" John asked.

"I think they're great fun. And they talk! They certainly aren't quiet like most of the tribes we have visited."

"I can believe that. Jim, you and Marti will have to sleep here in this hut. I had planned on our staying in a hut across the lake, but after inspecting the place I discovered a dead Indian in it."

"A what?" I gasped.

"A dead Indian. He died a few weeks ago. It's their custom to put the dead person in his canoe and hang him up under the roof until the flesh drops off. I didn't think you'd like sleeping under him."

"You're right! That's one experience I can live without."

I wandered over to where the women were cooking and inspected the big black pots that were the only cooking utensils. The banana leaves were lids to cover the fish. The stove was the usual three logs arranged with one end of each pushed into the flames.

Aware that I had acquired a following, I went down the slope toward the water. Sure enough, the kids still followed me. I felt like the Pied Piper. Then they started chattering about something in the lake they wanted me to see. When I went over to them, they pointed out a whole school of—not minnows, but tiny seahorses. The cutest things!

The sun was a big ball of fire sinking into the treetops across the lake. With its gradual disappearance, things began to cool off some and the flies, or gnats, or whatever those pesky things were, stopped biting me.

I started to skip, to see if my followers knew how to play follow the leader, but they couldn't do it. They not only couldn't do it, but they thought it was the funniest sight ever. They couldn't seem to catch on to how to skip, but they tried. Some of the men even tried, much to the amusement of the women.

When time came for the meal, everyone gathered together. Some of the Indians started eating, but the chief called out and they became quiet instantaneously.

"He wants to know why they didn't pray," whispered John.

The men looked at the ground and shuffled their feet around.

The chief spoke again. "What are you? A bunch of savages? Can't you thank the Lord for the food he allows you?" John translated.

Everything was absolutely still. No one spoke or moved. John whispered to us, "The chief can talk to them that way, but believe me, I'd never try it. He just asked who it was that the Lord allowed to catch the fish."

One of the men muttered something.

The chief gave him an order. "Pray." And the man prayed.

Then everything returned to normal. "You can see that Tariri is still very much the chief," John commented. "Being a Christian has changed him in many ways, but when he gives an order he still expects it to be obeyed."

We were served some of the fish. "Is it safe to eat?" I asked.

"Sure," replied Tom. "I've got some amoeba pills we can take after while. They'll kill any bugs we might pick up. And we brought our own water, so enjoy."

The fish was delicious. The women were pleased that we liked it. A very gay mood prevailed.

"You know, Jim," I said, "of all the tribes we've ever visited, I think I like this one the best. The people are so open and gregarious."

"Oh, naturally!" he replied. "You would like the headhunters!"

By this time the sun was halfway behind the trees on the other shore, turning them into black silhouettes. It looked like a scene from *National Geographic.*

"Your host is rigging up poles for your mosquito net," John said. "You'll have to sleep there on the ground between two families of headhunters."

"We have to sleep on the ground? Where are you going to sleep?"

"I brought a hammock, and the pilot always stays with his plane. It's really quite safe though. The dogs will protect you from any snakes."

"Fine. And what's going to protect us from them? And how are we both going to fit under one net?"

"You'll manage," was the short, unsympathetic reply.

I "managed" as quickly as possible. With the setting of the sun had come the rising of the mosquitoes, and if there is anything those pests love, it's a big bite of *me*.

Jim crawled in a few minutes later. Soon everything started to quiet down. The dogs circled around our net a few times, sniffing us, but decided we were harmless and wandered off. Great protectors!

The sun rises suddenly in the flat swampy jungle land, chasing away the darkness, mosquitoes, and any chance of sleep.

Besides having welts all over from the bugs, I felt stiff and sore. The dirt floor will never replace the innerspring mattress, I concluded.

I went down to the plane to see if there was anything in the medical kit to stop the itching. Alcohol was the best thing available, so I rolled down my knee socks (which hadn't helped in the least) and started to dab some on with cotton.

My little friends were goggle-eyed. They had never seen such a sight. They called to their mothers and soon I had an audience that would have delighted any hypochondriac.

Everyone oooooed and awwwwwed and clucked over the welts, which were quite impressive, if I do say so myself. The Shapras chattered away, pointing to the lumps, asking what caused this. I said, "Zzzzzzzz," making the appropriate gestures. They nodded. They got the message.

They began discussing this fascinating piece of information among themselves and seemed to come to the conclusion that it was really pitiful that I had such pale, puny, good-for-nothing white skin.

When I looked into their eyes and saw the concern and sympathy written there, I wondered again, "These people are savage head-hunters?"

JIM: This was our third day out from the base and both Marti and I looked seedy. She was a pathetic sight, sitting on her gunny sack, her face red from the mosquito bites, but still smiling at the curious women.

Looking across the lake, I saw big ripples spreading out from a wake; then I made out what seemed to be the distended prow of a canoe moving straight ahead. We had watched it for perhaps a minute when it suddenly vanished under the water. From what John told us later, it was evidently the head of a huge anaconda boa.

Except for hamming it up on the tape recorder the afternoon before, Tariri had paid no attention to us. I asked Marti to tell him in Spanish that we were friends of Uncle Cam and would be writing a book about him.

"Ahh," he brightened. "Señor Townsend is a great man. Very important. I, Tariri, send him my greetings," she translated.

The morning sun was heating up. I wondered aloud if the upriver Indians would be coming. "They will," John said. "A Shapra always keeps a promise."

Then he added, "The chief still has enemies who haven't forgotten the old days. We might see one this morning."

"In the group that's coming to meet us here?"

"Yes. They're a little unhappy. It was their school teacher who died. He was a believer and we had a lot of hopes pinned on him. His widow is a believer, but his brother who by tribal tradition has the rights to his children isn't. Naturally, the mother doesn't want to give them over."

"Why doesn't she just stay?"

"Her brothers in another village are demanding that she return home.

They're threatening to start trouble with her dead husband's people."
"The poor woman is caught in the middle, then."
"That's the way it is. It's all very sad. We've got to try and work things out. These people take their traditions very seriously, but the chief is determined that these children won't be taken away from their mother."

Shortly, John reported, "The Indians hear a boat motor."
"An outboard motor out here?" My surprise was apparent.
"They sell skins and logs to the traders for motors, shotguns, and other items," John explained.

Marti and I had climbed into the plane to talk to Tom when finally I saw the boat come into the little lake. It had about an inch of freeboard. As it came nearer, I could see it was packed with standing Indians, twenty of them at least.

"If one hiccups, the boat will capsize," Marti quipped.

I didn't appreciate her attempt at humor, for now it was apparent that the newcomers were bedecked with feathers and paint. Each held a shotgun against his side like a spear.

"Here comes the war party," Tom said apprehensively.

The boat pulled up beside the plane. A wailing woman—the widow—and her children were helped out, with the armed men following.

I looked for Tariri and his men and saw them waiting in a line inside the open-walled house. Each held a gun.

"Where did they get all those guns?" Marti whispered.

"I'd better call the base and ask the folks to pray. Something could happen." Tom clicked on the plane radio.

We watched spellbound as the armed visitors moved toward Tariri and his men. Between them stood John Tuggy, neither smiling nor frowning.

Marti followed them about halfway up the slope to where the women were sitting huddled together. They were all very quiet. It was hard to believe these were the same noisy, friendly people we had become attached to.

I was watching Marti taking notes when Tom nudged me. "Better get your wife back here. She's right in the line of fire!"

I went part way toward her, and then she noticed me motioning her to come.

"What's the matter?" she asked innocently.

"Get in the plane with us," I ordered.

"What about pictures?" I whispered to Tom when we were safely inside. He put a restraining hand on my arm and slid into the pilot's seat. "Yarina! Yarina!" I heard him say. "The party from upriver has arrived. We'd like to be remembered."

"Roger!" Grace answered. "I'll make that a general."

"Ask about the serum for Mrs. Duncan and Dougie," Marti demanded. Tom did. "It came today from Miami," Grace said. "They're going to be all right."

Now we watched as the two groups, each man holding a gun, lined up facing each other. John Tuggy, still standing between them, was doing all the talking. Ten minutes later he was still talking.

"Things are bad," Tom said. "It just isn't like John to be taking over like this. He must be trying to calm them down."

The widow, her head covered, had joined the other women near a corner of the hut and was wailing softly. A little girl in a tattered green dress was patting her shoulder, trying to comfort her.

Tuggy, even in a dingy white sports shirt, creaseless brown trousers and brown loafers, was impressive enough to hold the two groups where they were. He talked on and on until finally the men stepped back and seemed to relax. Tariri spoke, then the leader of the upriver group. Back and forth the conversation went. One time John went over and talked briefly to the widow. An hour passed. Now they were all sitting on benches, with guns cradled between knees. The women began serving *masato* in gourd bowls.

When Tom said, "It might be safe to take pictures now," we did. I even got up enough courage to sit down by the painted leader of the upriver group and take notes. I couldn't understand the language, but I could observe.

The man beside me had long hair with bangs reaching to his eye-brows. His face was smeared with black and red paint. Two pony tails adorned with feathers hung down his back. A bright red necktie (where did he get it?) was an incongruous sight, looped around his neck. His 16-gauge shotgun didn't have a trigger guard and the barrel was rusty. Small comfort.

He grinned at me and I smiled back. Suddenly without warning, he reached for my arm. I instinctively pulled back, but not in time. He had my arm! To my relief, all he wanted was to hear my watch tick.

The men talked for another hour, then I saw heads bow as Chief Tariri led in prayer.

All smiles now, John and Tariri called Tom over. "We want you to pick up Shiniki, the sick school teacher, and take him to the base," Tuggy said. The translator drew a map with his finger in the sand. "He should be a couple of bends down the Marañón between two tin-roofed houses. About here." Tom said we would look for him.

Goodbyes were said all around. I was dying to learn what had been decided but figured it would be better to wait until we were aloft. Tariri threw two clusters of ant-ridden orchids into the plane, climbed in, and sat on a gunny sack. The rest of us got in and waved once more. The widow was still wailing as Tom taxied out for the takeoff.

When we were up, I leaned over to Tuggy and asked, "What went on back there?"

He shrugged. "Lots of Shapra talk and some business. We talked about the possible causes of the death of the teacher. Some of them said it was witchcraft. So we discussed how God's Spirit gives believers power against the evil eye. We talked about who would take the teacher's place and found they had chosen one of the advanced students to step in."

"What about the widow?" Marti asked impatiently.

"She'll stay in her husband's house until her expected child is born. Her husband is hung up in a canoe in an empty house nearby, so she can go there and mourn him. She'll get death benefits from the ministry of education. Her younger brother will come live with her and look after her. All this is contrary to the custom, of course. The monkey in the woodpile is that her own brothers might try to take her back to their village. Then there would be trouble.

"But if this arrangement works out, it will mark a tremendous social change brought about by Scripture. Not long before the teacher died, I had translated with him the passage from James about looking after widows and orphans. He taught this in the community, never knowing that his wife and children would be the first test."

We dropped Tuggy and the chief off too soon to get more details of the talkathon from John. Sheila and her children and three of Tariri's daughters were waiting along with three long-hairs from a faraway village. They had traveled three days and nights to find John and ask him about a school for their children.

We had to make the crossover back to the Marañón and refuel for the third time before we could start looking for Shiniki, the sick teacher. Tariri and Tuggy's directions were inadequate. It was only after landing and asking about him in three places that we found the vacant-eyed Shapra in a hut near the river bank. All the way back to the base he sat on a duffel bag staring blankly into space. He was so motionless I wondered if he were dead.

When we finally got back to the base, our children were glad to see us. "But you could have stayed another day," Cyndi said. "We've had fun."

Lorrie Anderson was anxious to hear about the confrontation at Huambra. We told her what we knew.

"I'm certainly glad that's over, but I'm still concerned about the widow. I'm afraid this is only going to be a temporary solution," Lorrie sighed.

"What about Shiniki? We're sure glad to turn him over to you," I said.

"Dr. Swanson will examine him," she replied. "But we may have to take him to Lima for an examination. I just hope he doesn't have cerebral malaria."

"I'm curious about the facial markings that upriver group had." At long last Marti had the chance to see what she could find out. "They had taken red achiote and smeared it all over their faces and then painted black lines over that. I remember they had three black lines on each side of their mouths."

Lorrie's eyes grew wide as she exclaimed, "That *was* war paint. They really meant business then. The lines are supposed to make them look like jaguars, to scare their enemies."

"And you know what?" Marti said. *"It works!"*

15.

Lost Gold of the Incas

MARTI: Jim made final arrangements for the two of us to fly from Lima to Ayacucho to visit the Burnses and Shannons with the mountain Quechuas. The "James Gang" had shown us slides of their trip to Machu Pichu, the Lost City of the Incas, so we were looking forward to spending some time in the Andes.

The hospitable people at the base really pulled out all the stops that last week. We ate at a different home every day, and sometimes twice a day. Such "royal" treatment nearly overwhelmed us.

And the big event—the production of *Heidi* by the combined talents of the Snell, del Aguila, Oien, and Hefley girls, was staged in the Snells' living room. One end of the room was sectioned off with curtains, and the furniture rearranged in rows. Johnnie Oien rigged up a "WBT-TV camera" to cover the event.

They showed the passage of time with cats. Yes, cats. In the opening scene, Mel (Clara) was holding a baby kitten, white. During subsequent scenes they switched animals, each larger than the other. At least it was different.

Refreshments were served to the audience and a speech made giving thanks to "Aunt Betty," who deserved special praise for having put up with all the giggling girls during their innumerable rehearsals.

After the play, the girls didn't have much to do except fuss about leaving Puppy. "But Mommy, he won't have anyone to scratch his fleas for him," Celia wailed.

"I'm afraid he's going to have to scratch his own fleas, honey. Any dog that's smart enough to train three girls to do his scratching for him is smart enough to survive. The maids will take good care of him."

"But why can't we take him home with us?" Cheri wanted to know.

"Sorry, but he isn't our dog. And even if we could buy him, he would never be happy at our home. He's a jungle dog and he'd freeze in Illinois. Besides, he's used to running free all over the base. He'd be unhappy tied up in the city."

My sweet gals loved the puppy enough to want him to be happy, even though they would have loved to bring him home with us.

I had enough problems getting everything packed and returning all the stuff we'd borrowed.

We had supper with the Nelsons that last night. We were already

164

feeling nostalgic about leaving the base and Brucie and Linda Nelson were close friends of our girls so they hated to say goodnight when the time came.

We walked down the dusty road to the Shankses' house for the last time. Puppy climbed in with Celia and the little girls went right to sleep.

We could hear Cyndi in the other room, sniffling into her pillow for at least another hour.

"Should we go try to make her feel better?" Jim finally asked.

"No. There's really nothing we can say. We have to leave. Let her cry it out tonight and she'll do better tomorrow when she has to tell everyone goodbye."

The next morning we had breakfast at the Snells.

"You mean to thay, we goin' to eat out for breakfath?" lisped Cheri. "Boy! We thertainly have nithe friendth in the jungle."

"Aunt Betty" had everything ready when we arrived. The table had been moved to the screened-in porch that overlooks the lake.

"You people really make it hard to leave this place," I said.

"Any news from Ron?" Betty shook her head no and motioned toward Sandy. I got the message: "Ron's sisters are upset about his being out in Mayoruna land, so please don't bring up the subject."

"Well, are you all ready to leave?" Wayne asked.

"Just one more thing to do. The girls are concerned about leaving Puppy with no one to scratch his fleas for him, so I promised we'd get him a flea collar before we leave. I'll have to make one last trip to the commissary."

Sandy, our "swim-sitter," volunteered to take Celia to make the purchase. That gave us a few more minutes to talk.

"I'm glad Ron will be in Chicago this year, so we can get the first-hand story of his adventure."

"I'm sure he'll be more than willing to tell it," laughed Betty. "And having friends nearby might help him to be not quite so lonesome as he was last year."

"Oh, we'll have him come to the house some weekends. After reading those pitiful letters he wrote you last year, we'll have to do something."

Inevitably, the time had to come. We walked out to the Bluebird bus where Jim helped load our things. All the neighbors were there to bid us farewell. We climbed aboard and started off.

As I looked back at what had been our home for the summer, the last thing I saw was Puppy in his new collar, sitting on the steps with his head cocked and one ear up. He seemed to be asking, "What's happening?"

JIM: Upon our arrival in Lima, we took the girls to Lima House, where Mrs. Cudney and Ginger Gammon promised to keep a watchful eye on them. Then it was back to the airport for the short hop—250 miles—to Ayacucho. Instead of jungle green, this time we saw the snow-capped peaks southeast of Lima, an occasional blue lake, and brown spots of villages tucked away in canyons. Our flight ended with a landing on a high wind-blown plateau.

The old DC-6 touched the hard strip at the top of a high cliff and braked to a stop in a cloud of dust. As it turned, we could see the city of Ayacucho in the valley beyond, the red-tiled roofs warm in the morning sun. A tall, ruddy American with piercing blue eyes met us at the ramp. "You must be Marti and Jim. Hi! I'm Don Burns," he said jovially. "We'll pick up your baggage and be on our way."

When we had retrieved it, we piled into the Burnses' Landrover jeep. Don pointed across the valley. "That red area just behind the cross is our Quechua educational center. Underneath the red dirt is volcanic ash. That's why it's called Chalk Flats.

"We thought you might want to visit one of our Quechua schools in a mountain village. That is, if you don't mind a little climbing."

"Sounds great," I told him. "I think we get a deeper insight into what is being done by visiting the tribes than any other way. Marti, will you want to come along?"

"Hummmmmph," she replied. "As if you had to ask!"

"That means she's coming," I explained to Don.

"Fine. We'll spend the rest of today filling you in on background," he said, as he shifted gears to round a precipitous corner.

"Shall we have the history lesson now?" Don asked rhetorically. "Ayacucho reeks with history. The name means Dead Man's Corner. It was founded by Pizarro, a year before the so-called 'men of Chile'— Spaniards—murdered him and took over Lima."

We started down the hill to the town nestled below us. It looked as if there were a colonial church on every corner. "Why so many?" Marti asked.

"There's a story behind that," Don replied. "Many years ago when the miners went out into the hills to work, each time they struck a rich vein, they came back and built another church in honor of the Virgin. There are 33 Catholic churches and the population of the town is only about 30,000. The cathedral was opened by the first archbishop of Peru and the University of Huamanga is named after it."

We were passing the University. "After I got my doctorate at the University of San Marcos in Lima, I taught here three years," Don said. "This is where we got our start in the Quechua bilingual program."

Soon we were driving around the plaza. Quechuas in colorful ponchos and wearing the customary felt hats thronged the streets. Some were bent under heavy loads.

"Country folks," Don answered my wondering look. "Many come from villages in the canyons you just flew over. They walk for hours to get here."

Marti popped a curiosity question. "Why do they all wear hats—even the women and children?"

"They think the hats will keep the wind spirits from getting into their heads and driving them crazy. They've been taught that nature is against them: the wind wants to make them sick; the earth is waiting to swallow them up; and certain rocks want to grab and kill them. Now they're learning that God created the natural world and that he wants them to have dominion over it."

"Very interesting, but why do some wear their hats upside down?" Don laughed. "Oh, that's to show that they're married."

"Look at that poor man!" I exclaimed. "He has patches on top of patches."

"These Indians are well dressed compared to some you see in the villages."

"I've heard the mountain Indians are poorer than the jungle people," Marti said.

"They are," Don replied. "The Spaniards drove them up into the high altitudes where it's hard for anything to grow. The jungle Indians have gardens and game—although I hear the game is getting scarce—and water. Water is terribly scarce up here. This is our dry season; we haven't had rain in five months."

We were jolting along a narrow cobblestone street now. The houses were smaller and the plaster crumbling in places. A man in a suit waved from a corner.

"One of our town doctors," Don explained. "We flew him out to a village. He spent the whole day treating the sick and vaccinating them against smallpox, whooping cough, and measles.

"When time came for us to leave, a lady came up with three eggs wrapped in a rag—all the pay she could scrounge up from the whole village. The doctor looked at those eggs, blinked, and said, 'We can't take these eggs. I won't charge them anything.'"

Another man was waving for us to stop. He was a professor of anthropology on a study grant from the University of Jerusalem. As we drove away, Don noted, "Good friend. Comes to our Saturday night Bible study."

"But I thought you aren't allowed to conduct religious services?" Marti said.

"We don't play a clerical role," Don replied. "But we can witness and study the Bible with individuals. I learned this from Uncle Cam. He always has his guests read the Bible—bishops, ambassadors, generals, or whoever. Then he'll ask them what they think of the passage. We're studying the Gospel of John now. The Shannons have a Thursday night Bible study for *campesinos*—working class people. Sometimes they can't get all the crowd in the house."

"Beautiful," Marti exclaimed.

"We attend evangelical churches on Sunday. But neither Al nor I preach or take a leading part. When I first came to Peru, I wanted to be on the platform of churches. Preach. Lead singing. Uncle Cam convinced me that I could do much more for the Lord by keeping a low profile.

We were climbing up the other side of the valley now. The houses were little more than cobblestone hovels here. "All Quechuas," Don said. "They're half the population of Peru, but with very few exceptions, they're the poor half. Some have been put into Spanish schools and, when they can't learn, have been called stupid animals. No child can learn if you start him off in a foreign language."

Don stopped and opened a gate, then drove past a small house and slowed beside an L-shaped one-story brick building. "Offices, print shop and a classroom for neighborhood children are here," he said. "The caretaker's home is there near the gate. Across the meadow is Al and Barbara Shannon's new home. Our place is up ahead."

He drove on to the rectangular one-story brick home on the high side of the sloping grounds. "Seems hard to believe," Don marveled as we piled out, "that only three years ago this was just twenty-eight acres of barren land with a few pepper trees."

"How did you build all this?" Marti asked.

"The Lord provided through friends. Lawrence Routh, an electrical contractor, is the motivating force behind the acquisition of this center for Quechua education. He helped us get the land and encouraged people to give. And a group in the Philadelphia area sort of took us on as their project. Dr. Irving Davis, a California Ph.D. in economics, spent his sabbatical year supervising the construction. Irving and his wife, Jean, gave a sum from their own savings. Lawrence also helped with the construction and did the wiring and telephone work. The Lima Electric Company gave a 35-kilowatt generator that furnishes power for both us and the Quechua settlement under the hill."

Nadine Burns, her face glowing in welcome, came to the door. Don introduced us and she said, "You're just in time. Dinner is almost on the table."

We walked down a long hall from which doors opened into bedrooms and Don and Nadine's office. "We believe in togetherness," Don said. "We share an office here and one in the administration building."

Their sunken terrazzo living room was really nice. A huge natural stone fireplace with wide hearth opened into one wall. An alpaca rug hanging above the fireplace caught Marti's admiring eye. I was mentally estimating what the fireplace would cost in Illinois, when Don remarked that their residence and the Shannons' together had cost $7,800. "Labor is a little cheaper down here," he admitted.

"Our son here has to leave for school at Yarina tomorrow," Nadine said. "He's had four years in the Peruvian school here. Speaks Spanish better than we do. But much as we hate to see him go, we think he should." She sighed. "I think it's going to be harder on us than him," she said. "Our three daughters have already grown up and left."

While eating, we learned that Don and Nadine, high school sweethearts, were both from First Presbyterian Church in Berkeley. After two years at the University of California, they came to Peru at Uncle Cam's urging. "Some in the group questioned our being here," Don admitted. "I was twenty-three and Nadine only twenty-two and we looked younger. But we had three children."

"Yes, and some wondered why Don began studying at the University of San Marcos," Nadine added. "He got both his bachelor's and doctorate there. He majored in Quechua literature, and we didn't even know then that the Lord would send us up here."

"Uncle Cam was behind me," Don said. "He saw how much this would mean to the work. And it has. Some of the top scholars in Peru were once my fellow students."

"Tell us how the Quechua program got started," Marti said.

"Okay, but let me start way back. The Quechuas are descendants of the Incas, who were conquered by Pizarro and his men. Actually the Quechua rulers were Incas. *Inca* is the Quechua word for ruler.

"Now the Quechuas aren't a small tribe that nobody cares about. There are maybe fourteen or fifteen million Quechua speakers in Ecuador, Peru, Colombia and Bolivia. Six or seven million in Peru. But with few exceptions, because of their poverty and ignorance they have traditionally been a servant class."

Things were beginning to add up. "And I suppose a lot of propertied people would just as soon they stay poor and ignorant," I said.

"That's the idea," Don said. "To the Peruvian the jungle Indians are peanuts compared with the Quechuas. They're geographically remote, speak different languages, and are an exotic curiosity.

"Almost all evangelical and Catholic missionaries have with few exceptions tried to reach the Quechuas through Spanish. And still do. Until a few years ago that was the policy of the Peruvian government in education. Until 1963 it was actually illegal to teach Quechuas in their own language. Imagine that! It was okay to study and teach Quechua literature and history—we have some great Quechua scholars in Peru— but not to teach Quechuas in their ancestral language."

"How many Quechuas now speak Spanish?" Marti asked.

"The estimates vary. Some say a Quechua is bilingual if he can give his name in Spanish. Get back in the villages and you'll find almost all are monolingual.

"After I got my doctorate, I was invited to teach linguistics here at the University of Huamanga. That was in 1962. In 1964 the Minister of Education visited the Indian graduation exercises at Yarina. What he saw there made him think that the bilingual program could be the bridge for the Quechuas to attain full citizenship. He didn't believe as some have said for decades that the Quechua language will disappear if it's ignored and downgraded. He gave me a three-hour audience after the graduation and later in the summer approved our plan for a pilot program of bilingual education in the *sierra*."

"Where did you get the first teachers?" I asked.

"Where would you think?" Don replied with exuberance. "Right at the university where I was teaching. Well, I should say that the first teacher was Zenobia, a Quechua trained at Yarina.

"We began the first school at a place called Chakiqpampa. We plod-
ded for five and a half hours, on muleback and by foot, down a huge
canyon on the narrowest, crookedest, steepest trail you ever saw. We
crossed a river that soaked our feet in the stirrups and climbed the
other side of the canyon. Twelve thousand feet up, we reached Zenobia's
village.

"All the parents came together, and Pablo, a Quechua-speaking student of mine, told them they could have a school for their children with
reading, writing, and Spanish taught in their own language. He promised the children would be on vacation during harvest and planting
seasons. Then we presented Zenobia as their prospective teacher and
within a month thirty-five students were in school.

"Today there are twenty-seven teachers in over twenty schools. We
operate just like Yarina. The teachers come here for two months of
intensive training, keeping at least one year ahead of their students.

"Don forgot something that you should know," Nadine said. "He's an
official of the Ministry of Education himself."

"Thanks, sweetheart. I'm trying to work myself out of this job. My
title is Director of Bilingual Education in the Sierras. I'm paid a salary
which I put back into the work. We live off our support as WBT/SIL
members.

"Something else I should say. We know of five Quechua dialects that
need New Testament translations. The Ayacucho dialect in which we
work has about a million speakers. We have workers in two other dialects but no bilingual schools there yet. We're looking for linguists to
enter the remaining two dialects."

"How far along are you in translation?" I asked.

"Now why did you have to ask me that? We've prepared some passages for the teachers with questions—the creation account, some para-
bles, and passages on the birth, life, and passion of Christ. We have
these in a little manual for the daily Bible study. The archbishop here,
a good friend, wrote the prologue at my request."

"Are all the teachers believers—real Christians?" I asked.

"Remember this is a government program and teachers cannot be
judged on their religion. I can tell you this: all those who weren't believers when they entered have since accepted Christ. A few were evangelicals when they started. Fernando, the supervisor, was and still is a
lay minister. We attend his church. Another lay preacher who came into
the program had been stoned when he tried to preach in a certain village. He went back to this same place as a bilingual teacher and won
thirty-five people to the Lord. The program is only three years old and
already we know of believers in over ten villages."

"I think the maid would like to clear the table," Marti said. Nadine
nodded.

"Let's walk outside and stretch our legs," Don suggested.

The 9,000-foot altitude felt invigorating after the jungle. "See those
inlaid stones," Don said, as we walked in back of the house. "That's part

of the old Inca highway. One of the most marvelous feats of engineering in the world."

We turned and began walking downhill across a variety of grasses. "What you see here are different types of pasture grasses planted by Swiss agriculturists, sent by their government to help Peru. They have pitched in with us to help develop better grazing for the flocks of the Indians. The regular grasses will hardly grow during the long dry season," Don explained.

A gleam came into his blue eyes. "Do you know where the potato came from?"

I shrugged and Marti just looked curious. "I suppose from Ireland," I said.

"The Irish got it from Peru . . . just a few miles from here."

Al Shannon, a tall, slim Irishman and his pretty dark-haired wife, Barbara, served a delicious Quechua soup and a mountain trout dinner topped off with birthday cake. It was Al's thirty-eighth.

"There's a story behind those trout," Al said. "A few days ago we took a doctor out to two villages where an epidemic had killed fifteen people. It was a raw windy day. Some of the little half-naked kids had chafed chests. I mean that—chafed chests. You'll see when you go out tomorrow. The doctor did all he could and the people wanted to pay us, but they had nothing besides the rags on their backs. Finally they took their nets and caught the trout we are eating tonight. The Quechuas are the givingest people I know and the most deprived. Want to hear a figure that will shock you out of your boots? Their infant mortality rate is 80 percent. Eight out of ten babies die before they're one year old. It's a little better here in Ayacucho—only 75 percent. The doctors told us that."

Neither Marti nor I could think of much to say for a few moments. Finally I got around to asking what they did.

"Barbara's the bookkeeper and my title is coordinator. That means being everything from plumber to purchasing agent. We're here so Don and Nadine can do their specialized work in translation and literacy."

"How did you get into Wycliffe?"

"I was a computer trouble-shooter for IBM in Philadelphia. Cecil Hawkins, a JAARS man, came and spoke at our church. I had heard people say before, 'We need missionaries.' But old Cece said, 'We need a radio technician in the jungle.' So some of us formed a radio committee and helped on various projects; for example, we built a transmitter for the Yarina tower. Then Bernie May came and we invited him to dinner. He talked the technical language I understood. He said, 'We need a guy like you.' That was it and here we are."

We talked on with the Shannons, getting more stories and just enjoying these friendly people. Barbara, quiet beside her gregarious husband, talked about their three children and the buckets of mud she swept up after Thursday night Bible study attended by local Quechuas. "We don't mind," she said. "Treat them like people and they will respond to Christ."

As we stood up to leave, Al became philosophic. "Men aren't meant to live like robots the way some do in the States. I like Peru. There are less social pressures here. People are easy going and informal. You feel as if you're accomplishing something."

We said goodnight to Barbara, and Al walked with us to the Burnses' house. A full moon hung in the cloud-spotted sky. A mountain to our right looked just like Hawaii's Diamond Head. Below us the lights of Ayacucho twinkled in the hazy moonlight. Suddenly Al stopped and swung a broad hand around in a half circle. "The Spaniards thought there was gold in these mountains. There is. Not the kind of gold they looked for, but the gold of wonderful people."

MARTI: We woke early the next morning. It was cold; the Burnses' house was beautiful, but lacked central heating. So I dressed as warmly as possible. At the breakfast table Nadine said, "You'll need something warmer than that. The village Don is taking you to is much higher than here so it will be colder."

"But this is the warmest outfit I have," I answered.

"Come on. We'll fix you up," she said.

I followed her into her bedroom and she pulled out a warm skirt and sweater which I wore over my own slacks and top. Then Don found a big old waterproof jacket and hat for me.

"Think she'll be warm enough?" Don asked his wife.

"I don't know," I interrupted, "but if you put any more clothes on me I won't be able to move."

Before we climbed into the Landrover, Don said goodbye to his son, who would be gone before we returned.

"We'll see you at conference time, boy," Don said, ruffling the boy's hair. "And we'll be talking to you over the radio."

Donnie gave his father a hug, but said nothing. Then he turned and ran quickly back into the house.

We crossed through Ayacucho and began climbing. The dirt road was literally carved into the mountainside. It wound its way up the mountain in a series of loops and turns.

"You see those lines along the mountain over there?" Don directed our attention. "Those are Inca walls, built to terrace the land for cultivation. What a tremendous population they must have had."

"Oh, look, honey—llamas," I exclaimed, as we rounded a corner and a whole herd of the aristocratic-looking animals appeared.

"The first you've seen?" asked Don, with a grin.

"Yeah! Stop! I want to take some pictures," Jim ordered.

Don pulled over to the side and let Jim do his camera thing.

As we continued to climb I asked Don about the altitude.

"Well, let's see. I have an altimeter hooked up in the car for curious people like you. A little better than 10,000 feet right now. And we're still climbing."

Soon we pulled off the main road onto a twisty, rutty trail which at times ran precariously close to the edge of a huge gorge. I guess it was huge. I never did see the bottom of it.

I really thought that trail was rugged until we left it to follow Don's imagination and not much more for another fifteen minutes.

Then we stopped. Right in the middle of nowhere. The dial was past the 11,000-foot mark.

We climbed out of the vehicle. I looked around—the scenery was fantastic. The winter colors were drab with blends of white, red, and greenish black, but beautiful. The air was clear but thin and a drizzle of rain was still falling.

"I'll lead the way," said Don. "The name of the village is Mawkallaqta, which means 'the ancient city.' It's probably the oldest community in these parts."

"Why did you select this village for us to visit?" I asked.

"Because it's the easiest to get to."

"The easiest! I'd hate to visit the hardest."

"This is nothing. The hardest one takes an eight-hour hike to reach it."

"When will you get a lift from JAARS?" Jim asked.

"Soon, we hope. Ralph Borthwick has checked out two or three strips with a super-charged Cessna. We're waiting for some more strips to be approved by Civil Aeronautics. Almost every one of the schools are within 10 minutes flying time from Ayacucho."

By this time I was too busy keeping up with my long-legged hillbilly husband and the long-legged Scot to talk much.

Soon I noticed that I wasn't the only one breathing hard; the climb at that altitude was getting to Jim too. After five minutes both of us were really huffing and puffing. By this time I was too busy just working my lungs to even be embarrassed at the noise I was making.

"Want to stop for a breather?" Don asked after about ten minutes. I stubbornly shook my head no. I was determined not to complain.

"Well, I do," he insisted, much to my relief.

I could see the car far below us. It looked like a miniature toy.

After catching my breath some, I said, "When you told us it was a half-hour hike, you didn't mention it was all vertical!"

After several more breathers, the land leveled out a bit and we just puffed and huffed instead of PUFFing and HUFFing. Then a group of men, all wearing long ponchos as protection against the cold and drizzle, came toward us.

"Here's the welcoming committee," Don said.

"How did they know we were coming?" Jim asked.

"They have their own party-line system," laughed Don. "They knew we were on our way the moment we stopped the Rover."

As the group reached us, the men all greeted Don with what must be the Quechua handshake. Each put one hand on the other's shoulder and hugged each other with the other arm. Don went through this ritual with most of the men. Jim was taking pictures, and the men totally ignored me, a mere female.

They walked on with us to the school building which was nestled in a little cove at the end of the plateau. We could hear the excited babbling of the children who obviously knew visitors were coming, even though there were no windows on our side of the adobe building.

We entered the building, one by one through the narrow door. It was very dark inside. My eyes took a while to adjust. All the adults of the village filed in after us. They stood around the walls with us and observed the lesson in progress.

The one-room school was about 30' x 20'. It had a thatched chaparral roof and a blackboard across the front. Peruvian flags hung from the ceiling (six of them!) and on the side wall near the door was a map of Peru.

Mountain Quechuas greet us at end of long climb. Our escort, Don Burns, is at right.

Once dismissed as "stupid," these Quechua students now take their rightful place in Peruvian society.

My eyes had gotten used to the dim light so I started observing the people, the children first since they're always interesting.

To say they were poorly dressed would be a gross understatement. Many of them had no shoes of any kind. Their clothes were pitifully ragged and worn. I suddenly felt uncomfortable beneath the layers of warm clothing I was wearing. But despite the tattered clothing, these were beautiful children. High cheek bones, and bright black eyes with thick black hair.

One little fellow near me was writing industriously with a stub of a pencil, no more than an inch long. His seatmate was a little girl bent way over, her eyes almost touching the paper.

"Are they hard up for pencils?" I whispered to Don.

"They don't believe in wasting things," he whispered back. "They get one pencil and use it until they reach the eraser. A church in California sent us a big box full of them. Hundreds. They'll last all our students all year."

"Then what will they use?"

He shrugged his broad shoulders, "Maybe someone will send us more."

"What's the age span here?"

"About six to sixteen. School is from 7:45 to 1:00 so the children can go home and take care of the animals."

The teacher had some of the pupils perform for us and the parents. He smiled encouragement to each one he called on. They were shy, but obviously proud of themselves as they showed what they had learned.

The teacher wore a black cardigan; beneath this was a white V-necked sweater and under it a blue sweater. He had both shoes and socks. His pants were pressed and he had a western-style haircut. Quite a contrast to the parents in the room!

I turned my attention to them. They were just beaming. The pride they had in their children was almost a visible force. They were thrilled that the opportunities they had never had were being made available for their youngsters. Knowing that none of them could read or write made the scene very touching.

"Don," I asked, "don't you have a program for educating the adults?"

"We've tried. We train our own teachers and give them a bonus if they will also teach adults. But what we need is light, kerosene lanterns, because the only time the parents can study is at night. But one lantern costs over $30.00. For these people it might as well be a thousand."

"You mean because of the lack of light these adults will never learn to read or write?" I exclaimed. The injustice of it overwhelmed me.

Don nodded.

When reading and writing demonstration was over, the teacher declared recess time. Everyone filed out. Someone produced a ball and the kids were soon playing volleyball.

Much to their delight Don and Jim joined them. I would have loved to get in the game, but just didn't feel I could spare the oxygen.

Instead I walked up the small hill behind the school, thinking about what we'd seen and learned. At the top of the hill a whole new series of hills and valleys unexpectedly spread out before me. The beauty took my breath away. I sighed and watched the peaceful sight of a shepherd in a valley far below.

Then, not wanting to miss anything, I climbed back down the hill. I found the teacher talking to an old man who was sitting on the ground, leaning against the wall of the building.

"What's the problem?" I asked Don when he came over.

"He's very sick. Probably has pneumonia—he's been coughing up blood. The teacher will give him penicillin."

"Oh, is the teacher a *sanitario* too? Like they have in the jungle?"

"No, we don't have a separate medical program. We sure could use one, though. Almost all the teachers do know how to give shots and recognize some of the basic illnesses. When we go to a community we always bring medicine with us.

"We have interested some of the local doctors in the needs of the Quechuas. We're planning a *sanitario*-type program in connection with the Public Health Hospital in Ayacucho."

The teacher called us back into the school, this time for a math demonstration.

"This is one advantage the Quechuas have over the jungle Indians. They have a highly developed mathematical system," Don pointed out. "It's all based on units of ten. The best language in the world to learn mathematics in is Quechua. By the time a student finishes the first school year he is able to add, subtract, multiply and divide every combination up to 100.

Soon the adults started to leave. We said goodbye to the students and the teacher. The teacher asked each of us to sign in a book.

"They have one of these books in each of their schools to record who visits them. By the way, we always say 'their' schools."

As we left, we noticed the adults had gathered together in a huddle to discuss something. Then one of the men came over and talked to Don. He smiled, said something in return, and shook his head.

"They got together to see how much food they could scrape up, and invited us to stay for dinner," Don explained.

"You mean it would take the combined resources of the entire village to feed three gringos?" I asked.

"Yes," he answered, "and they were more than willing to do it."

I swallowed hard.

We waved goodbye to the smiling faces, and began the hike back to the car. "I was really impressed with your teacher," I said as we walked across the plateau.

"What do you mean?"

"Just the concern he has for those kids. He so desperately wants them to learn. You'd just have to learn with a teacher like that. You can tell he really loves those kids."

"Yes, and he's had a hard time of it. We assigned him to this village because it was his wife's home. So he brought his bride back to her hometown to live. They seemed very happy. Then last year she died in childbirth. Their baby died, too.

"It would probably have been much easier for him to have gone elsewhere to teach, but by then he was too involved with the children here. So he wanted to stay on. He lives alone in a little house next to the church."

We cut across a little field of some kind. "What's this stuff?" I asked Don. "It reminds me of heather."

"*Nebrill.* Look, the lady who owns the field sees us admiring it."

I looked around to see a tiny little Quechua lady standing outside a pitiful mud hut. It looked much less desirable than anything I'd seen in the jungle.

"She could tell you liked it," Don said, "and wants to know if you would like to have some."

We were walking closer to her as he translated for me. "You mean this poor Quechua lady wants to give me some just because I admired it?"

"Yes."

The old woman had already picked a bouquet, which she handed me as we came to the front of the house. I took it, and she gave me a big smile. I impulsively gave her a Quechua hug as I had seen Don do to the men.

"Tell her thank you for me, will you?" I asked.

"You already have." He was pleased.

We waved and continued down the mountain, which was getting quite steep by this time. Besides the altitude I had a big hard lump in my throat that made breathing hard, but I just had to make a comment. "Boy, these Quechuas really get to you, don't they?"

Don held out his hand to help me down a gully-like place. He beamed. "Glad you came?"

"Wouldn't have missed it for the world!"

Jim and Don did most of the talking during the trip back to the base. I had a lot to think about.

We slept under heavy blankets that night. The next morning I looked out across the valley and saw snow on the mountains.

The sun was brilliant when we reached the airport. The snowcaps sparkled and shone—fantastically beautiful.

"I'm so glad you could see the snow," Don said.

"Yes," I replied. "But we saw something much more beautiful."

16.

"Arriba!"

MARTI: Back in cloud-shrouded Lima, we found our children had survived. To put it more correctly, Mrs. Cudney and Ginger Gammon had survived our kids, who wanted to take the next plane back to the jungle. If that wasn't possible, then when would we take them to the zoo?

Vic and Helena Halterman were there with their little girls. Vic was unabashedly showing off an x-ray. "The first picture of my son," he kept saying. Helena was due.

Everybody was trying to convince him that another daughter wouldn't be a catastrophe. But he wasn't about to be swayed.

The baby was delivered two days later: a boy!

We talked to Grace Fuqua at the Yarina radio tower. Nothing dramatic had happened with the Mayoruna expedition. Ron and the Machiguengas had about two more days of trail cutting, then would return to the base. She would keep us informed if anything exciting happened.

We hadn't expected to stay in Peru so long, but after visiting Ayacucho, we felt we should visit the Lost City of the Incas. Surely the experience would make up for what the girls would miss in the first week of school.

Monday morning we flew to Cuzco, the ancient capital of the legendary Inca civilization. Our girls were excited, not only because of the trip, but because we weren't going to be interviewing anyone or doing research, but just spending a couple of days with them.

I was surprised and impressed by the beautiful modern airport in Cuzco. There were taxi drivers all around hustling for business.

"Which one shall we take?" Jim asked me.

I looked around and caught the eye of one man who just smiled at us instead of yelling "taxi" the way the other drivers were.

"That one," I said, indicating the smiling man.

He obviously understood me for he came over and introduced himself.

"Welcome to Cuzco. My name is Fernando Pinares. I'm at your service. I'm a guide as well as a taxi driver. If you do not have reservations I will be glad to recommend a hotel and show you some of the nicer eating establishments. Let me have your ticket stubs and I'll get your bags for you."

Jim handed him the stubs. As he dashed off to get the baggage, Jim commented, "Well, you certainly picked an efficient driver."

We corralled the girls, who were running in all directions, and followed Fernando to his car.

"Is this your first visit to our city?" he asked.

"Yes. We're going to see the Lost City tomorrow," answered one of the girls.

"Oh, in that case, I recommend the first thing you do after we find you a hotel room is go to the train station and buy tickets. They may be all sold out."

Fernando found us rooms at a small hotel facing the main square of the town, directly across from the cathedral. We made arrangements for him to come back after siesta to take us to some of the old ruins near the city. Then we went looking for the railroad station.

The ticket agent had only three tickets left. I explained we needed five, but he only replied, *"No hay mas."*

"What'll we do?" Jim asked.

"We'll take the three tickets and each hold a kid, I guess. We've come all this way. We certainly don't want to miss seeing the Lost City."

So we bought the last three tickets, and Jim carefully tucked the precious pieces of pasteboard in his shirt pocket.

Directly across from the station we discovered an Indian market. They had many of the same things we had seen at the Quechua market in Lima, but at about half the price. We bought each of the girls an alpaca poncho.

"Now we look like Incas, huh, Mommy?" Cheri was proud of her new costume. I didn't have the heart to tell her that she would never pass for an Inca, but all the girls did look mighty cute.

During our trip to the outskirts of town to the sites of some of the oldest Inca ruins Fernando filled us in on some Incan history. "When Columbus discovered America, the great Inca empire extended 2,300 miles along the western coast of South America.

"They had a very advanced civilization. They made great terraces for farming. Everyone had work to do, and no one starved. They are most famous as builders. As we look over some of the ruins you will see why."

"The restaurant where we ate had an Inca wall," volunteered Cyndi.

"Yes, when anyone buys property that has an Inca wall on it, they leave it. They'd never think of tearing it down."

"Why not?" Celia wanted to know.

"Because the walls are so strong. They're much stronger than anything we know how to make now. Why, a few years ago we had a terrible earthquake and nearly 70 percent of the city was damaged, but not one Inca wall moved!"

We were duly impressed by this.

"And just think. Those walls were made hundreds of years ago by people who had no mortar or machines. They didn't even have the wheel, yet the stones all fit together so well that even today it is impossible to fit a knife blade between them!"

"Wow," Cheri said. "How did those Incas get so smart?"

We all laughed. Fernando answered, "We don't know. Many men have spent their lives studying and trying to figure out just how they did it. But no one has discovered their secret.

"Here is the fortress of Sacsahuamán. While you walk around, notice how large some of the stones are. One is 27 feet high, 14 feet broad and 12 feet thick. How did they lift such heavy stones? No one knows."

We stopped at a couple more of the unbelievable ruins. The girls had their pictures taken with some llamas, the first they'd seen.

We returned to the hotel, ate, and went to bed early so we could get up on time for our train ride to Machu Pichu. But we almost froze until the manager came around with hot water bottles.

The next morning we just barely made it to the train in time. There were a lot of college-age kids on board, but ours were the only children.

"Mom, look," said Celia. "The top of the train has windows!"

"Yeah. I wonder why?"

The four of us girls snuggled together on one bench while Jim sat ahead of us with a professor from California. We asked him how the Cubs were doing. "Eight games out in front!" he replied. That made our day. It was the first baseball news we'd had all summer.

The narrow-gauged train backed, then went forward, then backed up again working its way up the mountain. When we got out on the plains we could see some of the towering peaks that we had flown over.

As we got closer and closer the peaks loomed higher and higher. It then became quite apparent why there were windows in the top of the train. It was so we could see the tops of the mountains—they were that high!

The little train wound its way along the narrow gorge following the rushing headwaters of the Urubamba. Each mountain seemed so tall it couldn't possibly be surpassed, but then a taller one would come into view.

"The Alps have more snow because of the latitude, but they are few and spread apart," one of the French students said. "Not nearly as impressive as these."

Everyone grew silent, intent upon soaking in the magnificent view. Even my girls were quiet. Then Cheri turned to me and said, "Look, Mommy, I can hold my thumb up by my eyes and it's bigger than that whole mountain!" And I had thought she was impressed!

When the three-hour journey was completed, we left the train to board buses that were waiting to take us up the two thousand feet to the mountaintop hotel.

The bus driver gunned the motor and we started the ascent with a roar. Back and forth we went, winding around horseshoe curves that took us higher and higher. We could look out the windows straight down into the valley. The girls cheered. "This is just like a roller coaster!" I looked at Jim. He didn't seem to be enjoying the ride at all.

It took thirteen horseshoe turns to reach the entrance of the ancient

Above left: Jim and Marti Hefley
pause to compare notes on a hill
overlooking Machu Pichu, "Lost
City of the Incas." *Right:* Cyndi
and Cheri with Quechua friends
at Inca ruins. *Below:* Celia
wearing Quechua poncho before
Inca wall. Though the Incas built
without cement, a knife blade cannot
be inserted between the rocks.

city. We walked down the path to the opening in the wall, where the
whole valley spread out before us. The mighty Urubamba looked like a
tiny green ribbon winding along the base of the mountain, but its roar
could still be heard.

We had worried that Cheri might give us trouble about hiking
through the ruins. It turned out that she was a better mountain goat
than the rest of us. The altitude didn't seem to bother her one bit as she
scampered along ahead.

We found "the street of stairs" which marched straight up the mountain, and started climbing them. We discovered one place where ten
steps had been carved from one boulder. When we got to the top, we
just stood there, awestruck at the panorama of the whole city stretched
out below us.

"Mommy," Cheri said again, shaking her head, "I just don't see how
those Incas got so smart."

"That pretty well describes my feelings, too," I told her. "And I
thought this would be anticlimactic.

"How will we ever describe this, Jim? We read all about it, and saw
those slides and heard about it from others who had been here. I
thought I knew all about it, but I was totally unprepared for this! It's
absolutely breathtaking. I feel as if I'm in another world."

"We're just not going to be able to describe it. We'll recommend that
people get Hiram Bingham's book, *Lost City of the Incas,* and read it for
themselves."

We walked and walked through the walled streets of the ruins, wishing we had made arrangements to spend the night so we could climb to the very top of the needle-shaped mountain that towered another thousand feet above us.

We made our way back to the restaurant with just enough time to eat lunch before we had to start the long journey back to Cuzco in the train.

The next morning we had to return to Lima. Fernando was right on time to take us back to the airport.

"You know," Jim commented, "the jungle Indians have many advantages over the mountain Quechuas, but they certainly can't match the scenery."

"Oh," said Fernando, all ears, "have you visited the jungle Indians?"

"Yes," Jim said. "We're going to write a book about the work of the Summer Institute of Linguistics."

"Oh, really? I have read much about their work in the newspapers. They do very good things for those Indians."

"Did you know that they are now working with the mountain Quechuas also?"

"I had not heard that." Fernando was thoughtful for a moment, then said, "That is good. That is a very good thing. It will help our people much. I am part Quechua, and I know the problems my people face.

"I know some people from the Institute. I was their guide a year or so ago. They were here with their two children for a vacation. They gave me a Bible, and wrote to me. We exchanged Christmas cards. Their name was Nelson."

"Not Bob Nelson?"

"Yes. Bob Nelson. Do you . . ."

"We know them. We know them," shouted our girls. "We stayed with them. They are our good friends."

"They are fine people. Religion that takes money from poor people and builds fancy buildings, I cannot understand. These people have a religion of love and concern for those who are in need. This seems right to me."

We had reached the airport. "If ever you come again," he said, "you write me and I will be waiting for you when you arrive. Tell your friends about me too. I will be glad to meet more of the *linguisticos.*"

JIM: The airport taxi dropped us off at Lima House just before noon.

"What's new?" Marti asked Mrs. Cudney the moment we saw her.

"Got a couple of new girls coming in tomorrow you'll want to meet— Marge and Helen who work in the mountains with the Ancash Quechuas, north of here in a beautiful valley that's called the Switzerland of Peru. Oh, Ron and the Machis finished the trail for the Mayoruna linguists yesterday. Harriet and Hattie will be going into camp at a clearing at the trail's end. Ron will be coming in here Tuesday on his way back to Moody. Hurry now and get ready for lunch."

While we were eating, Mrs. Cudney rushed into the dining room. "I just got the latest on the Mayoruna party," she said excitedly. "This morning Ralph Borthwick flew Harriet Fields and Ron over the clearing at the end of the trail Ron and the Machis had cut. They saw Indians. Harriet wants Ron to go back with her, Hattie and one of the Machis, to meet them. Ron has already radioed his father and received his permission. Grace said they should be leaving any time now."

There were a few seconds of absolute quiet as the diners absorbed this news. Then Marti gasped, "I thought Ron wasn't to have contact with the Mayorunas—that it was too dangerous."

"I thought so too," Mrs. Cudney said.

Sylvia Young, a redheaded new English member, was sitting with us. "How long will it take them to walk back to the end of the trail where the Indians were seen?" she asked.

"Grace thinks they may get there by 5:30. There's to be another Mayoruna sked at five. And Grace is to call us if anything comes in before then."

"Who will be in the radio room?" Marti asked.

"I've got to take care of the kitchen help," Mrs. Cudney said, "then I'll go up."

"I'll go," Marti offered.

"Me too," Sylvia added.

"Good," Mrs. Cudney agreed. "You can let us know if anything big happens."

Marti left, taking along a new *Reader's Digest* she had been wanting to read, and Sylvia went with her. The girls headed for the game room and the library. I told Marti and Sylvia I would look in on them in an hour. If there's anything I hate to do, it's sit and wait.

About 1:30 I opened the door. "Any word?"

"No," Marti said. "The radio has been awfully quiet. We talked awhile and then I watched the maids through the little window. They were hanging out clothes. I can't concentrate enough to read."

About 3:00 I peeped in again. Sylvia was drumming her fingers on the table. Marti was staring at the map on the wall. "How's it going?" I asked.

"I'm memorizing this map."

I stayed a few minutes, then said, "You people make me nervous. Be back in a while."

The next time I entered, Marti was staring out the window. "Now I'm watching the maids take down the clothes," she said.

"Nothing on the radio, huh?"

"We've heard a few squawks—people jiggling receivers," Sylvia said. "Grace comes on and says, 'Who is it?' The whole jungle network is listening."

"When's that sked?"

Marti looked over at the wall clock. "Five o'clock."

"I'll be back about 4:55," I said.

Kenny Gammon was with the girls when I returned. We watched the clock pass five without hearing a beep. At 5:30 the supper bell rang. "I'm going to eat," I said.

Marti frowned. "That's my husband. Nothing gets in the way of food. Ron and the Mayoruna girls could be dying and he wouldn't miss a meal."

"Oh, hush," I told her. "Someone has to corral the kids. I'll be back."

"I'll come with you," Kenny said. "You gals holler if you hear anything."

The people in the dining hall were unusually quiet. The tension was thick enough to slice with a knife. Even our children were concerned about Ron. They hadn't met the Mayoruna linguists.

Beth Hinson, who worked with the Shapras, was at the table with us. "I'm not saying it isn't dangerous and that we shouldn't pray," she said. "But I keep thinking about the Shapras. They protected us. Why, I feel safer among them than I do back in South Carolina."

Mrs. Cudney came over. "I've seen a lot of crises and the Lord has taken care of our people every time. He'll be with Ronny and the girls."

What I thought about saying but didn't was, "The five men who first tried to reach the Aucas had faith, too."

After supper Kenny and I slipped back up to the radio room.

"Here comes our loyal supporter," Marti jibed. "When something happens, he'll be right on cue. Never fails."

"I sat with the children," I rationalized.

I smiled at her, then looked at Kenny. He shook his head as if to say, "Women!"

At least an hour passed. I was feeling edgy along with the others. I began questioning why Wayne had allowed Ron to go. If he had been my son . . .

Suddenly the radio became alive. "Lima House. Lima House." It was Grace and her voice was tight. "I just talked to Ralph on the Yaquerana. He has no word from the others yet. Repeat. No word yet. We'll continue to stand by all night if necessary."

Kenny slipped out and spread the message. Mrs. Cudney and Cal Hibbard came in along with the dentist Opies and I forget who else. Kenny kept the door slightly open to let air in.

Darkness fell. We said little to one another. We were all, certainly, thinking about Ron, the Machi, and the two women in the jungle. The second hand on the clock crawled.

I thought of the Auca five's wives waiting by the radio for news from their husbands who were dead. Wayne and Betty Snell were waiting at Yarina.

Eight o'clock. Still nothing else.

One minute, two, three. Then came Grace's excited voice. "Lima House! Lima House! Call everybody into the radio room. Call everybody in. Over."

Mrs. Cudney ran for two or three more people and we waited until they returned. Had the big break come after years of waiting? Were our friends safe. Or . . . ?

Mrs. Cudney and the absentees entered the room. She took the mike. "We're all here, Grace. Go ahead. Over."

"A door may be open!" Grace said, her voice building in excitement. "Contact has been made. Repeat. CONTACT has been made. Ron reports that the Indians have arrived in their skins." She chuckled, breaking the tenseness slightly. "Correction, the Indians have arrived with their skins. Well, according to Ron, they are almost in their skins."

Grace then told us how she had received the news. Ron and Harriet Fields had reached the clearing later than they had anticipated. Hattie Kneeland had experienced trouble keeping up and had stayed back on the trail with Victorino, the Machi, to keep her company. Ron had tried to call over the little radio to Ralph at the plane, but could not reach him. But Bob Tripp with the Amarakeris, hundreds of miles away, had copied and he had called Grace to give her the frequency of the little radio. Ralph then had received the news from Grace. For some freakish reason, the little radio had been picked up long distance.

Before signing off, Grace told the network that the next report would come in the morning. Meanwhile, we should "remember" Ron and Harriet who would be spending the night with their "friends" and Hattie and Vic who would be sleeping on the dark trail. "Now," she said, "we're off the air for a time of thanksgiving in the auditorium."

At Cal Hibbard's suggestion, we at Lima House gathered in the adult *sala* for a time of praise. We sang the doxology, prayed, then Cal led us in a chorus of Uncle Cam's favorite hymn:

> Faith, mighty faith, the promise sees
> And looks to God alone.
> Laughs at impossibilities
> And shouts, "It shall be done!"

Marti rushed away to check on our children and to see them all in bed. The rest of us stayed around and talked.

"After all these years, they've finally made contact," I said.

"We're all very happy," Cal said. "But we have to remember that they're still out there. And we haven't heard from Hattie and Vic on the trail."

We finally went to bed. Marti couldn't sleep. "Worrying won't help," I told her.

"I'm not worrying. At least, I don't think I am. I keep thinking of poor Hattie and the Machi. I wish we knew how they were."

"We'll know in the morning," I said, and fell asleep.

Next morning, Sunday, Grace reported that Ron and Harriet had spent a peaceful but interesting night with the "friends." So far as everybody knew, this was the first time a white man—Ron—had stayed a night with Mayorunas and lived. Grace said Ron and Harriet were returning to the plane with four "friends" and that Harriet had been able to converse with them.

That afternoon the streets were filled with honking cars and Limaites waving flags and screaming *"Arriba, Perú!"* Peru had just tied favored Argentina in soccer and would be going on to Mexico City to play in the world championships. We all felt like chanting *"arriba"* too—but for a different reason.

Shortly after four o'clock Grace called to say that the Mayoruna party had reached the plane and Ralph was giving the "friends" plane rides. Ron would be coming in tomorrow to the base to pack for school and would arrive in Lima on Tuesday.

We had already decided to extend our stay in order to get the full Mayoruna story and the first pictures ever taken of the tribe, which Ron would be bringing. The children didn't complain about being a week late for school.

Monday we went sightseeing with Marge Levengood and Helen Larsen, who had just arrived from their beautiful Quechua valley. To the delight of the children, we found a place that served American style hamburgers, fries, and milk shakes.

Vivacious Helen, a redheaded nurse, told us she was from Michigan and a graduate of Wheaton. Marge, a tall, stylish brunette, called herself a Pennsylvania hillbilly. "I was planning on the Peace Corps," she said, "when the doctors told me I had throat cancer. They gave me a 50-50 chance and operated. Then the Lord showed me I should join Wycliffe."

"There are about 50,000 speakers of the Ancash Quechua dialect living in our valley," Helen said. "We've just started Bible translation and are also working on materials for a bilingual school."

"Our valley is really the most beautiful in Peru and our people the most wonderful," Marge bragged. "We live right at the foot of a beautiful snow-capped mountain."

"When are we going there?" Cyndi piped.

"You are going to school next week—in Illinois," Marti said. To Marge she added, "We'd love to see your valley. But there just isn't time."

Tuesday morning we met the great adventurer at the Lima airport. Besides baggage, he carried an imposing bundle, six feet long at least, containing a wicked-looking bow and plenty of arrows. Ron was grinning literally from ear to ear and not just because of the Mayoruna success. "Melody walked yesterday!" he exulted. "Not much. But she took her first steps!"

He had the pictures and would tell us the exclusive story. "There was some guy from a national magazine running all over the base looking for Mayoruna pictures. He didn't get any."

Back at Lima House we cornered Ron with a tape recorder. He gave a quick résumé of what had happened.

"You know that Hattie and Vic stayed behind on the trail. When Harriet and I reached the clearing beside the little stream, she gave a

Harriet Fields and Ron Snell with Machiguenga trail cutters from Ron's tribe.

Ron snapped the first picture ever taken of a Mayoruna in tribal surroundings.

'hooo, hooo, hooo,' which is sort of a jungle knock. Nobody answered. We walked into the clearing and I shined the light around. That's when we saw that the supplies, including the little radio which we had left the day before, had been taken. Then Harriet said, 'They're gone. Let's go down to the river and wash up. We'll come back and fix places to sleep.'

"I was getting a drink when these yells came from the clearing. I looked up and saw two lights and shapes moving among the trees. We walked into the clearing with Harriet shouting in Mayoruna, 'Don't be afraid! We're friends!'

"Finally one fellow crept out of the jungle holding a lighted candle. Another followed with a burning stick. They kept jabbering in Spanish, 'Don't kill me! *No me mata!* Don't kill me!' It took a while for Harriet to calm them down. One wore my sweat shirt and the other Harriet's sweater which had been in the supplies. They had bands of palm bark around the tops of their heads and G-strings. Nothing else.

"Harriet kept talking to them in Mayoruna until they seemed to understand that we were the ones who had made the trail and had flown over in the plane and dropped gifts. The candle had come from one of the drops. Suddenly the oldest of the two yelled, and two young guys bounced out of the jungle, carrying animal skins and bows and arrows.

"Harriet told them to call her 'mother' and me 'brother.' I was glad when they took her suggestion. She asked them about our supplies and the silver box—the radio. They ran into the jungle and got the stuff.

That's when I tried to call Ralph at the plane and reached the base instead.

"We had a spooky night. One of the Mayorunas, whom we called 'Witch Doctor,' wrapped himself around me like a monkey and moaned, 'I'm afraid, brother.' I had a time getting him off. Then when it seemed they might want to sleep, the one we called 'Clown'—we had seen him jumping around when we made the last plane drop—began tugging at my duffel bag. I knew he wanted to see what was in it.

"I whispered to Harriet, 'He'll find the pistol. But it isn't loaded. I've got the bullets in my pocket.'

" 'Take it out and show them how it works,' she said.

"So I did. I pointed it up and clicked the trigger, to show it was empty. They moaned in fear. Then I wrapped it in a small cloth and handed it butt first to Witch Doctor. He put it on the ground.

"I took off my shoes and they laughed. They thought my socks were even funnier. They rubbed my feet, top and bottom. Ticklish, you bet. Then they had to show us their feet, covered with callouses.

"After I got the mosquito net over me, Clown crept up beside me and whined that he was cold. When I tucked him in he said to Harriet, 'Mother, my tooth hurts.'

"Harriet told him we had 'stuff' put in our teeth to stop such pain. Naturally he had to see. He wiggled from under the net, and by flashlight looked at her fillings. My turn came next. Then he had to show us the hole in his tooth."

Ron continued the gripping tale, not stopping until he had gotten himself and Harriet back to the plane with Hattie and Vic and the Mayorunas.

I had just clicked off the recorder, when his eyebrows went up. "I've gotta tell you this. When we got back to the plane, I showed them a picture of my girl friend, Sherry Price. 'Who's she?' Clown asked.

"Harriet didn't know what to say at first, because the Mayorunas know only a husband-wife relationship. Finally she said, 'This is the one your brother hopes to take someday.'

"At this, one of the younger Mayorunas squealed, 'Aieee! I'd take her, too.' "

Ron stood up and stretched. "Tonight I've got to tell this story all over again to the rest of the folks here. Maybe I'll remember some more by then."

After we let him go, Marti sat motionless, looking glum.

"What's the matter?" I asked. "You look like you just swallowed a lazy lemon."

"I was thinking that housework is going to seem awfully boring after what we've seen this summer."

Postscript

The thrilling story of Wycliffe in Peru has continued to unfold since we returned home.

Most dramatic has been the role JAARS and two young women translators, Helen Larsen and Marge Levengood, played in helping victims of the tragic earthquake that killed 70,000 people and left over half a million homeless.

The earthquake did its worst in the beautiful valley which we did not have time enough to visit. Marge and Helen's house was partially destroyed, but they were not injured. They quickly radioed news of the tragedy to the Yarina tower (this may have been the first distress call to the outside world) and Yarina notified Peruvian officials in Lima.

While Marge kept the only voice in their shattered town of Macará open to the outside world, Helen gave medical aid. The girls worked practically day and night for the next 13 days.

Doug Deming of JAARS was the first pilot to land in the stricken valley. For five days he shuttled food and relief supplies in and injured victims out. Once when preparing to take off, he heard a plaintive call for help. He looked through the cockpit window and saw a man holding an injured boy.

Doug looked at the boy's crushed bleeding face and shook his head. "I can't take any more weight," he said sadly.

A moment later he heard a door slam—a soldier, closing the door, he thought. But when trying to get airborne, he realized something was wrong. After clearing the treetops with only a few feet to spare, he looked back and saw that the desperate father had put his injured son on the plane.

JAARS continues its fatality-free record, although engine failure forced pilot Ted Long to make a forced landing in a banana patch. Ted and mechanic George Tilt were returning from a trip to Machiguenga land. Ted was only shaken up, but George suffered a badly dislocated foot.

Next to the earthquake, the most dramatic story continues to be the Mayoruna Advance. After the peaceful contact, the Mayorunas who came to the plane escorted Harriet Fields and Hattie Kneeland back to their village. Here they learned that another Mayoruna group had been planning to attack them on the river. They also heard that Joe, the

189

Mayoruna youth who had lived at Yarina and then returned to his people, had been killed by his uncle.

The linguists were welcomed as "mothers" into the Mayoruna family. Mayorunas have flocked to the community where they are living, with population increasing from 42 to 300 during the first nine months. The "mothers" have seen and heard of several "white" Mayoruna wives living among the Indians, presumably captured in past raids.

A new airstrip in the village is operational, hacked out of the jungle by machetes, axes, and picks, with ponchos serving as wheelbarrows. Several seriously ill Indians have been flown to Yarina for treatment and Dr. Jerry Harrell has held a clinic in the tribe. Language study has moved ahead rapidly; in fact, Harriet Fields reports half the people willing to come to the base and help her in analysis.

Work continues to move ahead in other tribes. Believers are now reported in thirty-three of the thirty-six tribes where translators have served (including three tribes where work has been terminated). Twenty-one tribes have at least one book of the New Testament, with Scripture portions in at least nine others. The Campa, Ticuna, and Machiguenga New Testaments are now in rough draft and should be ready for publication soon. A record number of bilingual teachers studied at Yarina during the last training term. Forty-four mountain teachers (another record) also studied at Ayacucho. Peru's Minister of Education recently pronounced the Ayacucho pilot program a success and said that bilingual education will be extended to the rest of the almost seven million Quechuas.

Some miscellaneous personalia:

*After three years as WBT/SIL director for Peru, Rol Rich has returned to the Arabelas with wife, Furne. Dr. Gene Loos, translator for the Capanahuas, is the new director.

*Vic and Helena Halterman's son, Jonathan, is doing fine.

*Publications manager John Oien is crowing over the new printing plant built from a gift from the West German government.

*Radio technician Loren Cook is taping translated Scriptures and hymns in various languages to be reproduced on cassette players. A new recording studio has been built for this purpose.

*The Shapra widow continues to live with her children in her husband's village. The Shapra workers are still worried about the breach of custom by the husband's older brother not taking the children. The sick teacher, Shiniki, was given thorough medical tests in Lima and was found not to have the dreaded cerebral malaria.

*Floyd Lyons is still coordinating flights but hoping for a replacement so he can go back to flying.

*Don Burns reports that one of his Quechua teachers was severely beaten by cattle rustlers who resented the enlightenment he had brought the community. Because the teacher defied the rustlers who threatened his life, the president of Peru has ordered an investigation of the injustices to the nearly forgotten community.

*Mrs. Duncan and little Dougie Kindberg took their shots and suffered no ill effects from being bitten by the rabid monkey.

*Jim Price and his crew arrived safely in Miami after a trip in the Price catamaran down the Amazon, up the Atlantic coast, and across the Caribbean.

*Dick Hyde departed the ranks of bachelorhood and has a new partner. Sylvia Young is now Mrs. Hyde.

*Terry Snell and Betsy Funk made it to the altar.

*The Snell family delighted us with a visit while home for three months to attend Terry's wedding. They brought along Machiguenga Epi Pereira, one of Wayne's language helpers (a translator never stops studying!).

*Ron Snell is a senior at nearby Moody Bible Institute. After we returned from Peru, "Jungle Boy" (as our girls call him) helped us build a backyard patio that includes a jungle oven "just like we had in the tribe." Ron, a regular weekend visitor, is sporting (hiding) two boa constrictors, gifts from his folks.

*For Christmas, after returning from Peru, our daughters received a special present: a cute puppy with black and white markings almost like "Puppy" in Peru.

*And they keep asking, "When are we going back to Yarina?"

Appreciations

. . . go to Word Books for flying us to and from Peru, for the encouragement of Dr. and Mrs. W. Cameron Townsend, for the cooperation and hospitality of all WBT/SIL personnel in Peru (including Ron Snell's help in checking for accuracy), for the transcription and typing assistance of Paula Kelly, Nancy Block, Joyce Wilson, Carol Adeney, and Sandi Kelly, and for all others who helped make this book possible.

Although the book is prepared as a diary, a few interviews and episodes were presented out of sequence to keep a free-flowing narrative.

Space limitations made it necessary to pick and choose. There are so many more interesting stories that need to be told from the history of WBT/SIL in Peru. Some of these will be included in the biography of William Cameron Townsend which will be ready in about a year.

Although a number of key people have read the book for accuracy, readers close to the action will undoubtedly find a few errors. For these we take all blame and beg an understanding of the difficulty of the task.

For Further Study . . .

Little has been published about Peru's Indians and even less about WBT/SIL's work with them. At the outset we discovered inaccuracies in old studies of the Indian cultures and decided that we would rely entirely upon the research and views of WBT/SIL people. Anthropological studies and published views of other short time visitors seemed also to be below the level of the research of WBT/SIL. We know of no secular scholar who has spent years of study and loving association with any of the jungle tribes.

However, a few books which might provide the interested reader a better understanding of Peru, Peru's Indians, and the service of WBT/SIL there are listed below.

Tariri: My Story, as told to Ethel Emily Wallis. New York: Harper and Row, 1965. Authentic telling of the great chief's conversion. Perhaps the best book for understanding the culture of the Shapra, Achual, Huambisa, and Aguaruna Indians of Peru.

Amazonia Reborn by Jerry Long. Privately published in 1970 and available from Wycliffe Bible Translators, P. O. Box 1960, Santa Ana, California 92702, $2.95. A small paperback with good photographs and interesting sketches of tribal miracles.

Farewell to Eden by Matthew Huxley and Cornell Capa. New York: Harper and Row, 1964. Principally a documentation in detail of the life and fears of the Amahuaca Indians and how they are facing the change which confronts them by advancing white civilization. Anthropologist Huxley concludes that only WBT/SIL, in comparison to various missionary groups, is adequately helping the Amahuacas and other Peruvian jungle Indians with the social and technical assistance they need to survive. Cornell Capa's photography (148 photographs, many in full color) is superb.

The Call of the Aguaruna by Ethel King Dickerman. Nazarene Publishing House, paperback, 1967. Story of the Nazarene missionaries among the Aguarunas with surprisingly little reference to WBT/SIL.

Gospel Over the Andes by Roger Winans. Nazarene Publishing House, paperback, 1955. Notes of the pioneer missionary to the Aguarunas.

The Conquest of Peru by William H. Prescott. New York: Mentor Books, paperback. Classic, scholarly story of the Inca Empire and its subjugation by the Spaniards. None better.

Realm of the Incas by Victor W. Von Hagen. New York: Mentor Books, 1957; paperback, 1961. Archaeological history of Peru's mountain Indians.

Translation. Bi-monthly journal of the Wycliffe Bible Translators. Mailed free to those who have a continuing interest in Bible translation. Write: Wycliffe Bible Translators, P. O. Box 1960, Santa Ana, California, 92702.

Two Thousand Tongues to Go by Ethel E. Wallis and Mary A. Bennett. New York: Harper and Row, 1959; paperback, 1964. Dramatic history of WBT/SIL with interesting information on beginnings in Peru.

Peril by Choice by James C. Hefley. Grand Rapids, Mich.: Zondervan Publishing House, 1968. Biography of John Beekman, chief translation consultant for WBT/SIL. Explains WBT/SIL philosophy and application of Bible translation.

Lost City of the Incas by Hiram Bingham. New York: Atheneum, paperback, 1968. $2.65. The authentic story of the finding of Machu Pichu, told by the discoverer.